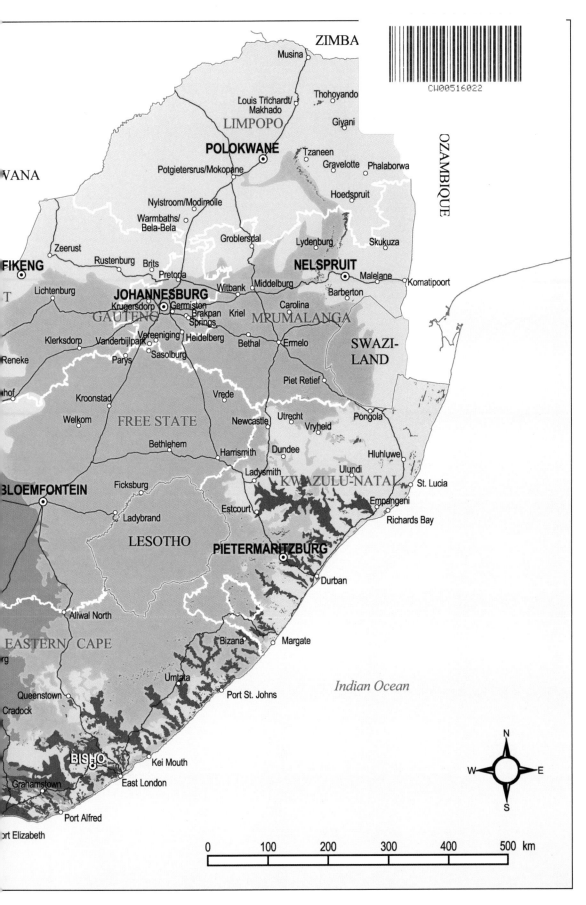

South African

Destinations

August Sycholt

BRIZA
www.briza.co.za

Published by **Briza Publications**

CK 1990/11690/23

P.O. Box 56569

Arcadia

0007

Pretoria

South Africa

BRIZA
www.briza.co.za

First edition 2009

English text edited and translated by Friedel Hermann

Cover design by Sally Whines

Design, typesetting and project management by Hendali Steynberg

Proofreading by Johan Steenkamp & Michel Cozien

Reproduction by Resolution, Cape Town

Printed and bound by Tien Wah Press (Pte.) Ltd, Singapore

ISBN 978-1-875093-60-1

Contents

Historical timeline

100 000 BC Skeletons found in caves in Eastern Cape and KwaZulu-Natal belong to groups of *Homo sapiens* hunters and gatherers in southern Africa.

26 000 BC Rock paintings dated by radiocarbon method are attributed to San (Bushmen).

20 000 BC Khoikhoi move across Namibia and Botswana and southwards along the west coast and some become pastoralists and settle in the Cape.

200-300 BC Bantu migrants cross the Limpopo and form rural communities. They are able to produce iron. The "Lydenburg Heads"are proof of their advanced culture of pottery. In the ensuing centuries they settle along the south eastern coast, the central highlands and in parts of Zululand and the Eastern Cape.

900-1400 This development peaks with the iron-age settlement of Mapungubwe in the Limpopo Valley.

1488 In search of the sea route to India the Portuguese explorer Bartholomew Diaz sails round the southern most tip of Africa and becomes the first European to set foot on South African soil near present day Mossel Bay.

1652 Jan van Riebeeck anchors in Table Bay in order to establish a halfway station for seafarers of the Dutch East India Company.

1658 The first slaves arrive from Dahomey (Benin), to be followed by others from West Africa, Mozambique, Madagascar and Asia.

1660 Horses – hitherto unknown in southern Africa – are brought in from Batavia (Jakarta). They enhance the military power and expedite expeditions to the interior.

1674 A fort built from stone blocks is inaugurated at the Cape. Today the Castle of Good Hope is a well-known tourist attraction.

1705-1713 For eight years Peter Kolbe studies the life of the Khoikhoi in the "Cape of Good Hope". His descriptions, published after his return to Europe *Among Hottentotts* are among the most widely read travelogues of the 18th and 19th centuries. The elementary school teacher from Marktredwitz was counted among the most well-known researchers of Africa in his time, but even then garnered much criticism, not all of it undeserved.

1760 Seminomadic pastoralist settlers move eastwards and meet up with the Xhosas, resulting in prolonged border wars in the south eastern Cape.

1772-1775 Karl Peter Thunberg (1743-1828) lived at the Cape from 1772 to 1775 as a doctor of the Dutch East India Company and also worked as botanist and zoologist. His books *Prodromus plantarum capensium* (1794-1800) and *Flora capensis* (1807-1813) were much acclaimed.

1778 Henrik Jacob Wikar deserted as soldier of the Dutch East India Company and became the first white man to cross the Gariep (Orange River) and bring back descriptions of the country on the other side of the river. After he had been pardoned he returned to the Cape and wrote a diary that was published in 1779. The name "Augrabies Falls" originated with him. It comes from the San word "Aukoerebis" – place of thundering noise.

1780-1783 Conflict between the Netherlands and Great Britain hasten the demise of the Dutch East India Company from the economical and political scene.

1781-1784 Francois LeVaillant (1753-1824), French discoverer and ornithologist, undertakes two extensive journeys across the whole Cape region and several small tours around the settlement. His ethnological works still fascinate by their stimulating and fast pace. None of the other early travel writers on South Africa received greater attention abroad. His contemporaries considered his travelogues to be "full of exaggeration and made-ups". However, he was an ornithologist of note.

1785 Shaka, future leader of the Zulus, born.

1795 First British occupation of the Cape during Napoleonic wars.

1797-1872 Sir Andrew Smith came to the Cape in 1820 as surgeon in the British army and he travelled in southern Africa as "discoverer" and botanist. He made his name as founder of the South African Museum in Cape Town.

1799-1800 Blue Antelope / Bloubok (*Hippotragus leucophaeus*) becomes extinct. This is the first mammal that is officially denoted as extinct in South Africa, the only proof of its existence in South Africa being a pair of horns at the Albany Museum in Grahamstown. Close relative: Sable Antelope.

1803 Cape reverts to the Netherlands.

1803-1806 W.H.C. Lichtenstein (1780-1857), famous German naturalist, doctor and zoologist, travels in South Africa and describes – among others – the Lichtenstein's Hartebeest that was named after him. He is founder of the Berlin Zoo and even in 1840 is concerned about keeping animals in zoos: "It is no longer satisfying to observe different species of animals confined to small cages, one wants to see them roam around freely." For Lichtenstein a zoo was a scientific institution.

1806 Second British occupation of the Cape.

1810-1815 William John Burchell (1782-1863), British naturalist and botanist, came to the Cape in 1810. He had a special horse carriage constructed and in July 1811 he travelled into the interior of the country together with six Khoi servants. This expedition was documented in two volumes: *Travels in the interior of Southern Africa* (1822-1824). In 1815 he returned to England with more than 50 000 plant species that he had collected. Most of these were handed over to the natural history department of the British Museum in London (today this department is known as the London Natural History Museum). Probably nobody else – either before or since – has collected so many species of interest to natural history in southern Africa and described so many new species. Burchell's Zebra is named after him.

1814 The Cape is formerly ceded to Britain and becomes a Crown Colony.

The first endeavours aimed at protecting wild animals in South Africa were undertaken by Governor Lord Charles Somerset (1814-1827). He decreed that certain animals were not to be hunted between July and November. This list was enlarged from time to time, but did not include predators, as these were considered vermin in those days. As of 1825 licences for hunting had to be obtained from government departments.

1820 About 5 000 British are settled along the Fish River to form a buffer against the Xhosa.

Shaka established around this time the first animal protection area in southern Africa at the confluence of the Black and White Umfolozi Rivers, approximately where today's Hluhluwe-iMfolozi Game Reserve is positioned. Hunting was only permitted every five years, but then his impis were allowed to hunt what they pleased. Poachers had their heads cracked with a "knobkerrie".

1820-28 Wars of conquest under Shaka Zulu lead to military might and rise of the Zulu kingdom.

1834 Boers protest against abolition of slavery and increase of British settlers. This leads to the Great Trek. 16 000 Boers leave the territory under British sovereignty. In search for land on which to settle they clash with Ndebele and Zulu.

1835-1837 William Cornwallis Harris (1807-1848), Victorian big game hunter, dwells for several years in South Africa and writes three books about his notorious hunting safaris on which he carries up to 18 000 bullets and enough lead to make some more.

1837 Voortrekker leader Piet Retief seeks to negotiate for land between Thukela and Mzimvubu Rivers. Dingane, chief of the AmaZulu has Retief and his companions killed.

1838 Battle of Blood River. From inside their wagon-barricade the Boers gain a victory over the multitude of charging Zulus of whom more than 3 000 are killed.

1845 After the annexation of Natalia by Britain, Natal becomes an autonomous district of the Cape Colony.

1854 Founding of the Republic of the Orange Free State. Griqua are dispersed into an area of no-man's-land with their leader Adam Kok. This later becomes known as Griqualand East.

1855-1932 Dr. Rudolf Marloth, a South African botanist, becomes world famous for his monumental works, like *The Flora of South Africa*.

1856 Natal becomes British Crown colony with representative self-government.

1857 2 400 soldiers from the German Legion in the Crimean War are settled with their families in the Eastern Cape.

1858-1869 Diamonds are found near Kimberley and the ensuing rush brings about great changes in this distant agricultural country.

1858 The Zuid-Afrikaansche Republiek (ZAR) starts to exercise control over the shooting of elephants in its territory

1858-1865 The last Cape Lions (*Panthera leo melanochaita*, possibly just a subspecies of *Panthera leo*) are killed in the Cape in 1858 and in Natal in 1865.

1860 Prince Alfred, second son of Queen Victoria, visits South Africa at the age of 16 and gets a bad reputation as result of his participation in a disgusting "hunt" near Bloemfontein, where game from the surrounding areas is driven on to a farm to be shot at close range by Prince Alfred and two others on horseback .

1866 Natal (today the province of KZN) introduces protection of game. The control of hunting concessions is greatly improved, and seasons when no hunting is permitted are introduced. Other provinces later follow suit and this prevents endangered species from becoming extinct, especially both species of Rhinoceros, Mountain Zebra and Bontebok antelope.

1871-1938 Frederick William Fitzsimons is a South African zoologist who came to Natal (KZN) as a young boy. At 20 he started to write documentaries on topics of nature and he soon progressed to become an expert on snakes and baboons. As the founder of the first snake parks in South Africa he became very well known. He also developed a serum that is still in use in South Africa.

1877 The first game rangers are appointed in Transvaal in order to reduce poaching with traps and slings and supervise the hunting season.

1877-1964 Harry Wolhuter, game ranger and author, is appointed by James Stevenson-Hamilton as assistant in the Sabie Game Park. At a later stage he also works in the Kruger National Park where he once killed a lion with his pocket knife. His interesting adventures can be followed in his book *Memories of a Game Ranger*.

1879 British troops triumph over Zulus, and Zulu kingdom comes under British rule.

1883 The last Quagga dies in the Antwerp Zoo.

Paul Kruger elected as president of the Transvaal Republic; applies strict Calvinistic principles. London Convention of 1884 grants ZAR (South African Republic) internal sovereignty.

1886 Discovery of rich deposits of gold on the Witwatersrand. Overnight it becomes the biggest gold-mining area in the world. Rise of Johannesburg which becomes the wealthiest city on the continent.

1892 First steam train from Cape Town reaches Johannesburg. J.R. Tolkien (author of *Lord of the Rings*) born in Bloemfontein.

1893 Paul Kruger elected as president for 3rd time. Under his government the first "locations" – residential areas for "Non-whites" – are established: Locations for black South Africans, for Indians and for Malays.

1894 President Paul Kruger founds the first official national game park, Pongola Game Reserve, east of Piet Retief. But pressure brought to bear by the farmers resulted in a deproclamation in 1921, and within five years the entire game population was extinct.

First steam train from Mozambique (Maputo) reaches Pretoria.

1895 An armed insurgence into the Transvaal (Jameson Raid) was meant to precipitate a revolt of the "Uitlanders" (foreign miners) and topple the government of Paul Kruger, but troops intercept insurgents.

1898 Efforts by Paul Kruger over a long time finally brought about the proclamation of the Sabie Game Reserve, forerunner of the Kruger National Park, in order to safeguard the already drastically reduced game population of the Lowveld. A further area along the Shingwezi River was added in 1903.

1899-1902 Lord Milner, governor of the Cape Colony, remains intransigent in talks with Paul Kruger that had been held to avoid a war. An ultimatum is sent to Great Britain resulting in the "Second War of Independence". Boer commandos gain some victories, but are crushed by the military might and resources of Britain. Anticipated German assistance does not materialise. The conflict ends with bitter humiliation of the Boers; their republics come under British rule.

1902 James Stevenson-Hamilton (1867-1957), lieutenant-colonel in the army and zoologist, is installed as warden of the Sabie Game Reserve. In the years 1926-1946 he is curator of the Kruger National Park. He writes important books such as *Animal Life in Africa*, *The Lowveld* and *African Eden*.

1906-1996 Laurens van der Post, South African author, officer in the army, adventurer, ethnologist and film producer, undertakes expeditions into areas in Africa that were still unknown and writes several books that become international bestsellers. Especially worth mentioning is *Venture to the Interior* and *The Lost World of the Kalahari*. He researches and documents the life, culture and myths of the San people and how they were confronted by Western culture.

1907-1975	Whaling commences in Durban in 1907 when the Norwegian consul, Jacob Egeland, and his countryman, Johan Bryde, found the South African Whaling Company. In the following year they catch 106 whales that are processed in the whaling station on the Bluff. By 1912 there are six whaling companies in Natal; whaling reaches its pinnacle in 1954 when 2200 whales are caught. By 1975 whaling from Durban has been completely discontinued.
1910	The Peace of Vereeniging (1902) paves the way for the proclamation of the Union of South Africa, consisting of the Transvaal, the Orange Free State, Natal and the Cape Colony. Franchise is restricted to European and some Coloured (people of mixed race) citizens.
1912	Founding of the South African Native Congress, changes to African National Congress (ANC) in 1923. The aim is to gain equal rights for Africans.
1916	Lichtenstein's Hartebeest (*Sigmoceros lichtensteinii*) is declared extinct in South Africa, after being sighted for the last time in what is known as Northern Transvaal. Around 1895 it had still been prevalent in the Pongola Game Reserve.
1918	Nelson Mandela is born on 18th June in a village near Umtata.
1926	Founding of the Kruger National Park in its present form.
1928-1931	Huberta the Hippo makes headlines all over the world after making its way from Zululand to King William's Town in the Eastern Cape, where she is killed by a farmer.
1930	The Black Rhino is extinct in the Kruger National Park. Later it is successfully reintroduced.
1931	The Kalahari Gemsbok National Park – today the Kgalagadi Transfrontier Park – is founded.
1931	South Africa gains full independence within the British Commonwealth.
1939-1945	South Africa enters Second World War as a member of Commonwealth.
1948	The National Party under D.F. Malan wins the election under the Apardheid banner. Numerous laws to cement the official segregation of races are introduced.
1949-1957	Apartheid laws take hold.
1955	ANC issues its Freedom Charter in Kliptown (SOWETO), a manifesto of the members against oppression by the whites.
1958-1966	H.F. Verwoerd becomes prime minister. The ideologist of separate development (Apartheid) creates basis for "Homelands" or pseudo-autonomous states.
1960	Ian Player, Nick Steele and their highly motivated team start to develop the technique of anaesthetising large animals which allows extensive reintroduction of both the Black and White Rhino.
	Police open fire on an anti-apartheid demonstration in Sharpeville and 69 people loose their lives. The world is outraged. African National Congress (ANC) and Pan African Congress (PAC) are banned and go underground. A leading activist in the ANC is Nelson Mandela.
1961	Verwoerd holds a referendum and South Africa leaves the Commonwealth and becomes a republic with Verwoerd as prime minister. ANC leader Albert Luthuli receives the Nobel Peace Prize. ANC's Umkhonto weSizwe (Spear of the Nation) prepares for insurrection by force.
1964	At the Rivonia Trial Nelson Mandela, Walter Sisulu and other ANC activists are sentenced to lifelong

	imprisonment for treason and brought to Robben Island.
1966	The first Red Data Book of the IUCN (International Union for the Conservation of Nature and Natural Resources) is published. It lists more than 8 300 endangered plant species and more than 7 000 endangered animal species, including in excess of 5 000 vertebrates. Listed for South Africa are Riverine Rabbit, Roan Antelope and Wild Dog as in danger of extinction and 14 species as highly endangered, as well as a further 25 species as rare.
1967	First heart transplant conducted by Christiaan Barnard at Groote Schuur Hospital in Cape Town.
1976	Pupils in Soweto demonstrate against forcible introduction of Afrikaans language as medium of instruction. Harsh reactions by police lead to 600 dead. International sanctions against apartheid regime gain momentum.
1979	Pilanesberg Game Park is founded, originally as National Park of Bophuthatswana which was then a "Homeland". The creation of this wildlife reserve was considered as a very ambitious undertaking at the time as it saw the re-location of thousands of species of wild life of all sorts.
1989-1990	President P.W. Botha resigns and his successor, F.W. de Klerk, declares the policy of apartheid to have failed. Nelson Mandela is released after 27 years in prison. Ban on ANC and 32 other opposition groups is lifted.
1992	A majority of the white electorate vote for dismantling of apartheid.
1993	Nelson Mandela and F.W. de Klerk jointly receive the Nobel Peace Prize.
1994	After the first free elections in the history of South Africa, won by the ANC with 62 %, the country gets one of the most modern constitutions in the world.
1995	Under the chairmanship of Archbishop Desmond Tutu the Truth and Reconciliation Committee is constituted in order to deal with the violence and crimes against human rights during the Apartheid era.
1997	The new constitution comes into force on 4th February 1997. South Africa is a parliamentary republic with an executive president.
1999	Nelson Mandela hands over to Thabo Mbeki.
2000	From 4 million at the turn of the 20th century the population has risen to 40 million.
2005	President Mbeki suspends his deputy, Jacob Zuma, due to a pending corruption trial.
2006	South Africa becomes the first country in Africa to officially recognise gay marriages.
2007	President Mbeki speaks out about determined legal actions against rape, drug trading and corrupt officials, but continues to remain silent about increasing general and serious crime that is getting out of control.
	The acting mayor of Cape Town, Helen Zille, is elected as leader of the main opposition party, the Democratic Alliance (DA).
	Hundreds of thousands of members of the public services trade union take part in the biggest strike since the end of apartheid, lasting four weeks. This leads to great disruptions in teaching, health services and public transport.
2009	Jacob Zuma becomes the 4th president of South Africa.

Introduction

Routes, travel and safaris

South African provinces	Size km²	Inhabitants in millions	% of total population	Capital
Gauteng	17 010	10.45	21,5	Johannesburg
KwaZulu-Natal (KZN)	92 100	10.11	20,8	Pietermaritzburg
Eastern Cape	169 580	6,58	13,5	Bisho
Limpopo	123 910	5,27	10,8	Polokwane
Western Cape	129 370	5,26	10,8	Cape Town
Mpumalanga	79 490	3.59	7,4	Nelspruit
North West	116 320	3,43	7	Mafikeng
Free State	129 480	2,88	5,9	Bloemfontein
Northern Cape	361 830	1,13	2,3	Kimberley
South Africa in total	1 219 090	48,7	100	

Source: *Statistics South Africa*

World Heritage Sites – South Africa is well represented

The impressive list of UNESCO is divided into Cultural Heritage Sites (C) and Natural Heritage Sites (N). South Africa even boasts a double pack in form of the Drakensberg Nature Reserve – uKhahlamba Drakensberg Park (C/N), proclaimed in 2000. Others are Robben Island (C) and the Cradle of Humankind World Heritage Site (C), the archaeological site of fossil Hominids in the caves of Sterkfontein, Swartkrans and Kromdraai, the wetlands of the iSimangaliso (previously the Greater St. Lucia) Wetland Park (N), proclaimed 1999. Further additions were the Cultural Site of Mapungubwe (C) in 2003, the Floral Kingdom of the Cape Fynbos (N) in 2004 and the Meteorite Crater of Vredefort-Dome (N) in 2005 and the latest addition being the IAi-IAis/ Richtersveld Transfrontier Park (N) in 2007.

South Africa is one of the most beautiful and impressive travel destinations on earth and is especially attractive to eco-tourists because of its mountains, deserts and grasslands, wide stretches of open country and a multitude of landscapes, resplendent in colour, atmosphere and contrasts, with a wealth of animal and plant species.

Although human habitation is increasingly leaving its marks of civilisation on the map of the world, almost half of our planet is still wilderness, scientists apply the term "wilderness" to any region of at least 10 000 square kilometres where the original vegetation is still present and human habitation is less than five people per square kilometre. Southern Africa boasts six huge game and nature reserves, comprising about 200 000 km², as well as 300 national and provincial nature reserves and thousands of private reserves.

They have plenty to offer to those who want to experience this fascinating world with a sense of wonder, experiencing something new all the time, relaxing and loosing themselves in the great wide open spaces. Whether on their own or in groups, they can savour the quiet of unspoiled nature or the exitement and adventure on safaris across the savannah and grasslands with magnificent bird life. Of course there are also the fabulous beaches along the 3 000 km stretch of coastline.

Western Province

The Cape of Good Hope beats the Kruger National Park by a slim margin as the most popular destination in South Africa. Table Mountain National Park takes up the largest part of the Cape Peninsula, right down to Cape Point. It includes Kirstenbosch Botanical Gardens, the area around the fishing harbour of Hout Bay, the penguin colony at Boulders near Simon's Town and the Silver Mine Nature Reserve. The West Coast and Karoo National Parks as well as Oudtshoorn in the Little Karoo with the spectacular Cango Caves also form part of this province.

Eastern Province

The incomparable marine reserve Tsitsikamma National Park is alone worth a trip, while the Addo Elephant National Park is not only the best place to observe elephants, but also the future refuge of the Big Seven. The long stretch of Wild Coast and various interesting places inland offer further attractions for exploration.

KwaZulu-Natal

The grandeur of the Drakensberg Mountains about halfway between Johannesburg and Durban offer hiking and trekking through remote wilderness; the golden beaches on the Indian Ocean, warm subtropical climate and colourful Zululand with its rich history beckon, as well as some of the oldest nature reserves of South Africa, where the two African species of rhinoceros were saved from extinction.

Free State

This is the region of the grassland savannah. The provincial capital, Bloemfontein, is the traditional stopover on the drive between the Cape and Gauteng and a pivotal point for the tourist attractions of the province.

Mpumalanga – Limpopo and Kruger National Park

The two provinces share South Africa's most well-known tourist attraction – the Kruger National Park. In addition there is the breathtaking mountain scenery that forms part of the Drakensberg Mountains where the Blyde River Canyon Nature Reserve lies at the heart of the world-famous Panorama Route.

Gauteng

By far the smallest of the provinces, it has the best infrastructure in the country and is the economic powerhouse of the whole continent. Interesting destinations can easily be reached from the two cities Johannesburg and Pretoria (Tshwane). Those who want to shun the relatively high crime rate of the inner cities can find a wide range of accommodation in the rural environment.

North West

The most important destinations, "Cradle of Humankind" and Maropeng, prehistoric extravaganza, lie close to the border with Gauteng Province, near Hartebeestpoort Dam. The area around the dam has undergone many tourist developments recently and is very versatile.

Northern Cape Province

The Kgalagadi Transfrontier Park in the vast, desert-like arid zone was previously known as Kalahari Gemsbok National Park, but today it is spans the border with Botswana and offers a fascinating contrast to the comparatively tame and green Kruger National Park with its perennial rivers.

Journeys and Destinations

Various options present themselves to the itinerant traveller. Good roads crisscross the nine provinces and bring the traveller safely to

Marvellous

Darwin's Journey around the world (1831-1836) in the *Beagle* somehow escaped the attention of the Iziko Museum in Cape Town, although it features a lot of interesting things. According to the report of Darwin's South African research team they observed during their hour-long hike in the vicinity of the 24° southern latitude 100 to 150 rhinoceroses, several large herds of giraffe and antelope as well as elephants, crocodiles, lions, leopards, hyenas and a multitude of smaller creatures, apart from swarms of birds and raptors. Darwin was amazed that the "sterile and arid region" was able to sustain such a variety of mammals in a country "that produced so little nourishment". The sojourn at the southern point of South Africa became the highlight of Darwin's five-year expedition that not only accelerated the development of his modern evolutionary theory, but lead to the publication of his book *On the origin of species* in 1859 – still a standard work on modern evolution biology.

Top: Maropeng, the Information Centre of the Cradle of Humankind World Heritage Site. (Maropeng means, "Returning to the place of origin")
Above: Kgalagadi lions at a waterhole

National- and important regional Nature Reserves

Name	Province	Size	Type	Features
Addo Elephant National Park	Eastern Cape	3 600 km²	Spekboom	Unique elephant population
Camdeboo National Park	Eastern Cape	145 km²	Karoo	Valley of desolation, Karoo fauna and flora
Mountain Zebra National Park	Eastern Cape	65 km²	Little Karoo	Cape Mountain Zebra
Tsitsikamma National Park	Eastern Cape	80 km²	Coastal	Rugged coast, Yellowwood trees
Golden Gate Highland National Park	Free State	116 km²	Mountains/Escarp.	Rock formations
Marakele National Park	Limpopo	440 km²	Northern savannah	Typical bushveld
Mapungubwe National Park	Limpopo	280 km²	Northern savannah	Archaeological sites, Limpopo River
Kruger National Park	Mpumalanga/Limpopo	20 000 km²	Lowveld	Variety of species
IAi-IAis/Richtersveld Transfrontier Park	Northern Cape	5 900 km²	Desert biome	Desert, rare plants and animals
Augrabies Falls National Park	Northern Cape	880 km²	Arid West	Largest waterfall
Kgalagadi Transfrontier Park	Northern Cape	40 000 km²	Kalahari, semiarid	Lion, Cheetah, Brown Hyena
Namaqua National Park	Northern Cape	680 km²	Arid West	Impressive wild flowers
Mokala National Park	Northern Cape	200 km²	Dry savannah	Varied rim of Kalahari
Agulhas National Park	Western Cape	180 km²	Coastal fynbos	Most southerly point of Africa
Bontebok National Park	Western Cape	32 km²	Fynbos biome	Bontebok, rich in birdlife
Karoo National Park	Western Cape	800 km²	Nama Karoo	Reclaimed Karoo vegetation
Garden Route National Park	Western Cape	+15 000km²	Indigenous forest	Forests, lakes and lagoons
Table Mountain National Park	Western Cape	220 km²	Fynbos	Cape floral kingdom
West Coast National Park	Western Cape	180 km²	Atlantic coastline	Unique marine birdlife
Wilderness National Park	Western Cape	2 600 ha	Indian Ocean coast	Varied and relaxing
Regional Nature Reserves				
Drakensberge	KZN	2 400 km²	Mountains/Escarp.	Pristine Mountain region
Hluhluwe-Umfolozi	KZN	960 km²	Southern savannah	Black and White Rhino
Pilanesberg National Park	North West	500 km²	Savannah	Mini-Kruger National Park near Johannesburg and Pretoria
Tswalu Kalahari Reserve	Northern Cape	1 000 km²	Kalahari, semiarid	Largest exclusive private reserve

pristine ecodestinations. Gravel roads lead even deeper into the wilderness.

Tourgroups in busses, some combined with short inland flights, make up the majority of visitors, followed by safaris and tours organised by small, individualised companies, usually with a personal touch. Individual touring is the ideal, because it leaves a strong impression of adventure and exploration. Camping enjoys undiminished popularity and a large number of sites (especially in the game parks and nature reserves) and private areas are available. Noticeable also is the trend to travel in comfortable caravans that have much to offer to the sociable and inquisitive traveller.

The people and culture – our rainbow nation

During the time of transformation in South Africa, from 1989 onwards, archbishop Desmond Tutu coined the phrase "Rainbow Nation". And indeed, of all nations in Africa it is the Republic of South Africa that has the greatest diversity of races and tribes. This not only led to problems in the past, but also created a kaleidoscope of cultures.

The ethnic mosaic of about 45 million people is made up of 78,5% Africans, 10% Europeans, 9% people of mixed races and 2,5% Asians. Average annual population increase is very high at 2,5%.

There are eleven official languages: English, Afrikaans, IsiNdebele, Sepedi, Sesotho, SiSwati, Xitsonga, Setswana, Tshivenda, IsiXhosa and IsiZulu (biggest language group). English occupies the prime position as official language of government. The majority of people of European descent and of mixed race still speak Afrikaans (a Germanic language that evolved from Cape Dutch) as home language.

Number and percentage of citizens speaking one of the eleven official languages as home language.				
Language	1996	%	2001	%
IsiZulu	9 200 144	22,9	10 677 305	23,8
IsiXhosa	7 196 118	17,9	7 907 153	17,6
Afrikaans	5 811 547	14,4	5 983 426	13,3
Sepedi	3 695 846	9,2	4 208 980	9,4
English	3 457 467	8,6	3 673 203	8,2
Setswana	3 301 774	8,2	3 677 016	8,2
Sepedi	3 104 197	7,7	3 555 186	7,9
Xitsonga	1 756 105	4,4	1 992 207	4,4
SiSwati	1 013 193	2,5	1 194 430	2,7
Tshivenda	876 409	2,2	1 021 757	2,3
IsiNdebele	586 961	1,5	711 821	1,6
Others	228 275	0,6	217 293	0,5
Not mentioned	355 538		n/a	
TOTAL	**40 583 574**		**44819 778**	

Source: Statistics South Africa, 2001 Census

Ndebele/IsiNdebele

The Ndebele originally came from KwaZulu-Natal. They are well known for their artwork and crafts, especially the decoration of their houses with striking geometric motifs and diverse beadwork that has symbolic significance.

Sotho/Sepedi/Sesotho

Sesotho is the language of the Basotho whose home country is the Kingdom of Lesotho and it is also spoken by various groups

Bantu Languages

In 1857 the German philologist Dr. W.H.I. Bleek started using the concept Bantu (Human being) in the language context to mark the family of Bantu languages that originated south of the Sahara. They are probably all based on a prototype of "Bantu language" since there are extensive linguistic overlaps that allow for a division into various language zones of the whole region south of the Sahara. In this way, languages like the Sotho group (North- and South Sotho, Tswana), the Nguni group (Ndebele, Swati, Xhosa, Zulu), as well as Venda and Tsonga belong to the southeastern subdivision.

During the Apartheid era the concept Bantu came to be used as general identification of African (black) citizens and used in official documents e.g. "Bantu Education Act" of 1952 (that prescribed an inferior education for Black South Africans) or the "Bantu Investment Corporation Act" of 1959 (regulation of capital transfer to Bantustans).

Matters of faith

With a nominal percentage of more than 80 %, most South Africans subscribe to Christianity. This not only includes the major denominations, but also the hundreds of smaller churches and sects. Ancestor worship is still very important in the rural population and often runs parallel to Christianity. In a desperate situation they often turn to the ancestors for assistance and comfort with the Sangoma as go-between who establishes the spiritual contact with the ancestors. The most important home-grown church is the Zionist Christian Church (ZCC). The majority of its 2-6 million followers live in townships and rural areas in the North Sotho region. Moria (Zion City) in Limpopo is the centre; here more than one million members meet annually at Easter. Zionists put their trust in healing by faith. This brings them into conflict with traditional healers, the Sangomas. Alcohol, smoking and pork are forbidden and promiscuity and violence abhorred. Members of the ZCC have a reputation of being honest and responsible.

of people in South Africa. The Sotho language group is subdivided into North Sotho/Sepedi, South Sotho and Tswana which are all very similar, but are regarded as separate languages. South Sotho is spoken in Lesotho and in the Free State, while Tswana is mainly spoken in the North West Province and in the neighbouring state of Botswana. North Sotho is also a common language in and around Gauteng, the most densely populated province, and to some degree in Mpumalanga and Limpopo. More than a hundred years ago the missionaries of the Berlin Mission Society established a basis for North Sotho as a written language. They had to make up symbols for those sounds that had no equivalent in the Roman alphabet. Furthermore, in the 1930's the Bible was translated into Sepedi/Pedi, one of the main dialects of North Sotho.

Basotho Cultural Village

The 'Basotho Cultural Village' inside South Africa lies in the area of the Golden Gate National Park and is dedicated to Sotho traditions. Among other things it shows traditional Basotho architecture, life in a chief's kraal, traditional healing, and there are presentations of music and dance.

Swazi/SiSwati

The Swazi come from the Pongola district in KZN from where they had been displaced by the Zulus in the 18th century. Around 1750 they settled in the region that today makes up the Kingdom of Swaziland. From 1903 it was a British colony and in 1968 it gained its independence as hereditary monarchy. Swazi (also called Swati or Siswati) is spoken in the regions between Machadodorp and Komatipoort and, of course, in Swaziland.

Tsonga/Xitsonga

The Tsonga came with the last wave of migrations that moved from the north into South Africa. They settled in the Limpopo Valley and are related to the Tsonga in Mozambique. About 750 000 live alongside the Kruger National Park. The Tsonga are keen fishermen, in contrast to the Zulus who regard fish as inferior food.

Tswana/Setswana

In South Africa Tswana is mainly spoken in the provinces of North West, Northern Cape and parts of the Free State. In neighbouring Botswana Setswana is the official language. The journalist and author Sol D.T. Plaatje was one of the first to made a contribution to spreading the written language. He lived in Kimberley for a long time and a museum there presents his history and influence. The Tswana still make traditional earthenware pottery and construct big, communal corn silos.

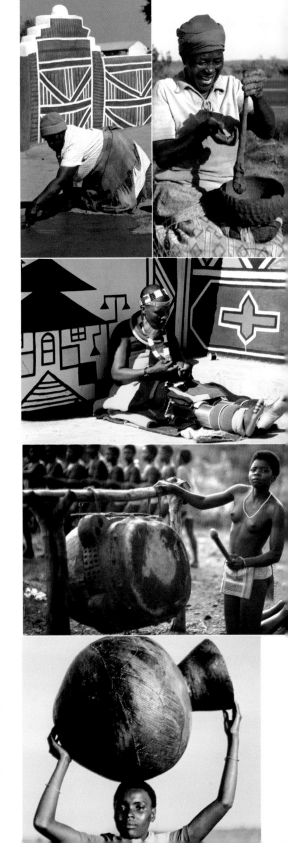

Venda/Tshivenda

Early migrants from the central parts of Africa settled in the relatively fertile north-eastern region of South Africa. Under the leadership of the legendary chief Thoho ya Ndou (elephant head) they crossed the Limpopo in the 17th century and occupied the area between the Soutpansberg Mountains in the west and what is today the northern part of the Kruger National Park in the east. Venda became an "independent" Homeland in 1979 with Thohoyandou as capital. Up to 70 % of the inhabitants were dependent on work in other parts of South Africa. Early on the Venda were renown as gifted iron and copper smiths and also as good weavers, potters, woodcarvers and especially drum makers. It is a great art to produce the different types of wooden drums. They are the only instruments allowed at the "Python dance" that maidens perform at a secret location during the Domba, the initiation ceremony. The custom originates from the time when the goddess of fertility – a giant python – was annually offered a virgin as sacrifice.

Xhosa/IsiXhosa

They form part of the South or Cape Nguni. The Xhosa are not really a coherent tribe, since they are split up into various groups that speak different dialects and live scattered over the region previously known as Transkei and Ciskei in the Eastern Cape Province. Apart from the numerous frontier wars that were fought against the white settlers encroaching from the west, the Xhosa had problems in the 19th century as a result of internecine strife and the spread of rinderpest. When they obeyed the appeals of the prophet Nongquawuse and killed their cattle and burnt their harvest great numbers died in the resulting famine. Others fled to the white settlers. Today the Xhosa are prominent in key positions in South Africa, including the first and second state presidents, Nelson Mandela and Thabo Mbeki. Circumcision is still widely practised in the rural areas, especially in the Eastern Cape, where death and maiming occur regularly through botched circumcisions and leads to passionate controversy.

Zulu/IsiZulu

Numerically the largest tribe, the Zulu evolved from a small and insignificant clan that became the supreme power under the "soldier king" Shaka Zulu by conquering the entire region and playing a major part in the historical development of southern Africa to beyond the Zambezi. Missionaries developed a written form of the Zulu language around 1830-1841. The central figure in their history is Shaka Zulu, an African Napoleon, a great reformer and commander of his fighting troops, but a cruel ruler and despot who – in the scope of ten years – created the Zulu empire that struck fear into the peoples of southern Africa in the 19th century.

Zulu cultural village
Visitors are shown everyday life and traditions of

the Zulu in epic and dramatic manner. Shakaland, the Ecabazini Zulu Cultural Homestead, Isithumba Village, Izintaba Cultural Zulu Village, Simunye and Kwabekitunga-Stewart´s Farm are lavish presentations for commercial purposes. The PheZulu Cultural Village that lies between Durban and the Valley of Thousand Hills endeavours to keep up with these presentations on a grand scale, and they are also emulated in other parts of the country.

Cape Malays

Muslims from Indonesia, whose ancestors had been brought to South Africa in the 17th and 18th century, either as slaves or as political exiles, retained their identity and culture in spite of the pressures brought upon them. The so-called Cape Malays are a very important group among today's population of South Africa. The tolerance and harmony that was the norm between Muslim, Jewish and Christian citizens at the Cape had always been exemplary. The foundation of Muslim tradition and culture at the Cape had been laid by the educated leaders that had been exiled to the Cape by the Dutch East India Company because of their resistance to the occupation of parts of Indonesia by the Netherlands.

Bo-Kaap Museum

This museum is housed in one of the oldest buildings in Cape Town (1768) that had been preserved. The layout and furniture reflect the lifestyle of a Muslim family in the 19th century and it contains many articles of Cape Malay culture. Today it forms part of the national Iziko Museums.

Coon Carnival – Second New Year

The parades through the streets of Cape Town that

take place annually on the 2nd of January are said to have their origin in the only day in the year that slaves used to get off and/or in the parades that celebrated the end of slavery. Today the Coons as they called themselves in imitation of the Black Bands in the American South, (abbreviation of the word *racoons* because of the face markings – who also painted their faces) or Kaapse Klopse, wind their way through the streets in colourful costumes to the sound of tambourine and banjo. There are prizes for the best bands and the hectic, fun-filled atmosphere

is very contagious, as anyone who has ever experienced the "Second New Year" will agree.

Coloureds

People of mixed racial background were (and are) called "Coloureds" in South Africa. Ever since Europeans started settling at the Cape this group started to emerge as the Dutch East India Company (VOC) imported slaves from the Far East, though they forbid the enslavement of the local population. As there was a great scarcity of white women, European men often had partners from other race groups. Farmers, soldiers and townsmen lived with Indonesian slaves and Khoi women in common law relationships. All people of mixed racial parentage were termed Coloured (Kleurling). Shortly after the National Party won the election in 1948 marriage and sexual relationship among different race groups was forbidden by law, but the Coloureds retained certain rights and privileges, compared to the Blacks. In a measure this was the result of their home language being Afrikaans.

Today about 85 % of approximately five million Coloureds live in the Western Cape Province and form the political majority there. Although Afrikaans is still the main home language, English is catching up and is certainly the most important second language.

Indians

When the farmers in Natal needed labour on the sugar cane plantations, Indians were brought into the country as indentured labourers from 1860 onwards. After serving their five-year contract the labourers were given the choice of returning to India or settling in South Africa. The majority

chose the latter option. In the course of time, Indian women were also permitted to immigrate. So-called "Free Indians" who had paid their own passage were mainly wholesale and retail traders that filled the growing gap in providing typical Indian foodstuff and spices and objects connected with worship. There were also teachers, doctors, journalists and lawyers – among them Mohandas Gandhi who lived in Natal from 1893 till 1914 and

Flotsam and Jetsam of War

San men from Namibia, Angola and Botswana, mainly from the Khwe and !Xun, were recruited by the South African Defence Force under the Apartheid government as trackers in their fight against Swapo in Namibia. When the war came to an end they did not dare to return with their families to their old homelands, fearing revenge actions. The South African Defence Force transported them to the Republic of South Africa and housed them in old army tents and left them to their fate. From 1991 onwards they survived for a decade on the perimeter of the military training field of Schmidtsdrift along the Vaal in the province of Northern Cape that borders on an area where even today some sporadic prospecting for alluvial diamonds is going on. The !Xu and Khwe hunter-gatherers became despondent, homeless refugees. Artists, human rights activists, ethnologists and lawyers took up their case in 1993 and tried to free them from isolation and help them to attain a dignified existence. With the project "Art against Forgetting" their natural talents in art were stimulated and as painters, potters and woodcarvers they derive their subject matter from their old traditions and the symbols that their forefathers had left behind.

Resettled San blacksmith from Schmidtsdrift operates historic bellows

organised the passive resistance and other political measures. But in spite of Gandhi's engagement for the rights of Indians, these were consistently reduced and ended in the Group Areas Act, which allocated separate residential areas according to race. Today more than 1,2 million citizens are of Indian extraction. Approximately half of them are Hindu, the others are Muslims, with a small percentage being Christian. 95 % speak English; Hindi, Gujarati and Tamil are spoken virtually only at home. The separation and isolation made for a closely knit community with strong links to the Indian culture, religion, music, dress code, etc. that is still prevalent.

San and Khoi

According to current perception the ancestors of San-hunters and Khoi were members of the human race who settled in Africa south of the Sahara and increased in numbers, due to successful animal husbandry and agriculture and they started to migrate. San (Bushmen) and Khoi (previously known as Hottentots or Nama) are grouped together as Khoisan today. They lived for about 40 000 years in genetic isolation from the rest of Black Africa and during this time developed physiological features that make them distinct from their cousins further north. Linguistic conformity suggests that the language of the Khoi evolved from the San languages. Therefore these two terms (San and Khoi) do not denote a racial classification, but rather a classification according to lifestyle. A San – nomadic hunter-gatherer – could easily advance to become a nomadic pastoralist and an impoverished Khoi could revert to being a hunter-gatherer. The San are considered the true original inhabitants of southern Africa and have been living in the Kalahari for more than 10 000 years. The lifestyle of these hunter-gatherers was only changed when pastoralist tribes from the north migrated south. Whilst the Khoi merged with other population groups, some of the scattered clans of San in the Kalahari region retained original affiliation and manage to uphold their meagre existence in some corners of South Africa, Namibia and Botswana. When the Kalahari Gemsbok National Park (9 600 km²) was proclaimed the remaining clans who lived there were given the entitlement to remain living there. Negotiations in this respect are ongoing.

DESCENDENTS OF THE IMMIGRANTS FROM EUROPE

The Afrikaner (Boers)

Free passage and generous land allocations attracted increasing numbers of settlers from the Netherlands in the 17th and 18th century. In time a creolised Dutch emerged which developed into Afrikaans – the youngest of the Germanic languages (and the only one that originated outside Europe) – whose vocabulary includes, apart from the Durch, words of Malaysian, English, French and various African indigenous languages. In 1925 Afrikaans replaced Dutch as second official language and it had a great influence on shaping nationalism and emphasising cultural identity, while literature made great strides, but the ever increasing pressure to enforce it eventually brought about resistance. When Afrikaans was introduced as medium in Black schools against the will of the pupils an uprising occurred in Soweto in 1976, and as this gained momentum general destabilisation in the country came about. With the new dispensation of 1994 Afrikaans was recognised as being one of the eleven officially acknowledged languages of the country.

British

Together with the First British Occupation of the Cape in 1795 came the English language and British culture. From 1820 onwards the British colonial government accelerated anglicisation by fostering immigration from Britain and declaring English the official language for government, education and business. As the immigrants from Britain tended to come from an urban background, they settled in towns and therefore separate identities evolved among the rural, predominantly Afrikaans-speaking population and the townspeople who were mainly English-speaking. To a certain degree this dualism is evident even today. In spite of the other ten officially recognised languages in South Africa, it is English that is the medium of communication for government and the lingua franca. Presently about half of the population is able to communicate in English, and numbers are increasing rapidly.

Germans

Next to the Dutch, the Germans made up the bulk of early settlers from Europe, but since they were mostly single males (often ex mercenaries) they were assimilated. In the 19th century there was a surge of German immigration, encouraged by the Missionary Societies, as was the case in Natal, and by the government, who were eager to settle areas in the Eastern Cape with the families of German mercenaries from the Crimean War. Towns with names like Hamburg, Frankfort, Berlin, Potsdam, Hermannsburg, Glücksburg, Lüneburg, Wuppertal and others bear witness to this era. But from about the middle of the 20th century the number of German schools began diminishing, especially in the smaller communities where these schools were taken over by the government and German was henceforth taught on foreign language level. Today only four large German schools remain, in Johannesburg, Cape Town, Pretoria

Huguenots

In 1687/88 the white settler population was increased by some 225 Huguenots who brought skills into the country. They were part of the more than 200 000 that left France for religious reasons when the Edict of Nantes was repealed which had guaranteed them religious freedom. some of the refugees came to the Cape by way of the Netherlands, and these industrious Calvinists proved a great asset to the blossoming agriculture and viticulture. They were quickly assimilated into the Dutch settler community.

Huguenot Monument at Franschhoek. The nearby Museum represents the life and culture of these early immigrants

The "Dundee Die Hards" are widely known as a war re-enactment team. They wear either khaki or red when mock battling against Boer Commandos or Zulu Impis

German Beer and "Alpine Kuhglocken" can be experienced at "Guenther's Wurstbude" in the Natal Midlands

and Hermannsburg. These are subsidised by the German government and are considered International Schools. The number of German businesses increased rapidly after the end of the Second World War. The Federal Republic of Germany is now one of the most important trading partners of South Africa.

Jews

Jewish immigrants always formed self-supporting communities. They came from countries in Central and Eastern Europe. After the British occupation there were also Jewish immigrants from the United Kingdom. In 1863 the Cape Town community built their first synagogue. After the discovery of gold and diamonds young entrepreneurs from England and Germany were soon playing leading roles in trade and industry; among these were prominent names like Oppenheimer, Marks, Barnato, Milner and others. Between 1881 and 1910 more than 40 000 Lithuanian Jews who had fled the pogroms came to South Africa. The Great Synagogue in Cape Town has about 1 000 members and is the largest in Africa. On the same premises lies the Jewish Museum and the only Holocaust Centre in Africa. In the 1930's many Jews fled Nazi Germany and their numbers rose before and during the Second World War to about 120 000, many of whom became politically active at all levels and also joined the liberation movements, or served in the opposition parties in parliament during the Apartheid era.

Portuguese

Without realising it, the Portuguese explorer Bartholomew Diaz sailed in his caravel as first European around the most southern point of the African continent. Due to a storm he was driven away from the coast and finally anchored near the bay that is today Mossel Bay (bay of mussels) and at Kwaaaihoek he erected a Padrão. These pillars with a crosses were made from wood or stone and considered Christian landmarks that served as navigation beacons. It was only on his return journey that Diaz sighted the Cape and called it "Cape of Storms". It was only in the 20th century that Portuguese immigrants came from Madeira to South- and South West Africa where they were mainly engaged in coastal fishing, but also moved into other spheres of the economy. When Portugal withdrew from its colonies, Angola and Mozambique, in 1976, many people from these regions moved into the Republic of South Africa. Today the approximately 300 000 South Africans of Portuguese origin form a prominent part of the population.

Greeks

The first Greeks to settle in South Africa became farmers in the Eastern Cape. They were eleven seamen who in 1880 had decided to stay here while on shore leave in Port Elizabeth. Other Greek immigrants who settled here later usually preferred cities like Johannesburg, Pretoria and Cape Town, but some of them also moved to smaller towns. Like the Portuguese, they often started out by running so-called Cafes – small general dealers that also served snacks and had extended opening times – while others went into the wholesale market. Greeks now make out the fourth largest section of citizens with a European background and have enriched the multifacetted culture with Hellenistic traditions and lifestyles and became prominent in many fields, including lecturers, doctors and lawyers. The most famous of the latter is George Bizos, who had fled as a thirteen-year-old with his father from the German occupation of his homeland and became internationally wellknown as a Human Rights lawyer. He was for a long time the judicial advisor of Nelson Mandela whom he defended in the Rivonia Trial, helping him to draft his impassioned defence speech that probably saved him from the death sentence.

French

Although France showed an early interest in the Cape, this did not materialise as a permanent presence – if one disregards for the moment the descendants of the French Huguenots – and it was only in the last century that a closer relationship came about. Meanwhile trade between France and the Republic of South Africa has increased markedly and today many French firms have a representation here. Not only the economic contacts are important, but also cultural and sport (rugby) relations. There are, however, few French-speaking citizens in South Africa.

Italians

Although Italians had sporadically immigrated to South Africa for a long time, it was as a result of the Italian prisoners of war being here during the Second World War that they came in greater numbers after the end of the war. They were notably prominent in the building and stone (marble) trade, as well as in tiles and ornaments. Like the other Europeans they integrated well and entered all business and professional fields, as well as the arts, and supported Catholic churches and schools.

Ecoregions in South Africa

Ecological biologists have divided up the South African countryside into eleven ecoregions or biomes, large ecosystems with various types of vegetation. These provide a glimpse into the diversity of symbiotic existence between plants and animals within a larger geographic area that sustains an adequate biological balance.

FYNBOS BIOME

The largest area of the Cape Floral Kingdom that stretches – with some interruptions – along the coastline of the Western Cape and up to 200 km inland is made up of fynbos in the sections with poor soil and Renosterveld in the more fertile parts. In the north this region ends approximately 250 km north of Cape Town at the Olifants River and in the east at Port Elizabeth. As the fynbos vegetation is so dominant this term is justifiably used as an equivalent to the Sixth Floral Kingdom.

Fynbos flowers flourish at the Cape of Good Hope

Cape Floral Kingdom

This region has the greatest variety of species: on approximately 70 000 km² (0,04 % of the earth's surface) grow more than 8 500 plant species, many of which are endemic. The three most important genera are the Protea family with more than 360 species, innumerable species of Erica and Heather (600 or more of which are endemic) and Sedges, the latter belonging to the genus Restios, tenacious plants that often have triangular stems. Furthermore there are quite a number of flowering plants that grow nowhere else in the world. Many of the flowering plants of this region have become popular garden plants around the world.

The Renosterveld (field of the rhinoceros) was home to large mammals, among them species that have been extinct a long time ago, such as the Cape Lion, Quagga, Bluebuck and Cape Warthog. Less than 3 % of the Renosterveld, that stretches in place almost to the coast, is still in its pristine form and 1 % at most is presently a nature conservation area. Human influence on the region has

IMPORTANT NATURE RESERVES

Cape floral kingdom:
Bontebok National Park
Cape Agulhas National Park
De-Hoop Nature Reserve
Elandsberg Private Nature Reserve
Table Mountain National Park
West Coast National Park
Cederberg Nature Conservation Area
(where three biospheres meet:
Fynbos, Great Karoo, Succulent
Karoo)
Kogelberg Nature Reserve
Van Staden Flower Reserve

Succulent Karoo:
IAi-IAis/Richtersveld Transfrontier
National Park (desert-like)
Namaqua National Park
Goegap Nature Reserve

Great Karoo or Nama Karoo:
Camdeboo National Park
Karoo National Park
Mountain Zebra National Park
(Intermediate zone between
arid Karoo and grasslands)
Gariep Dam Nature Reserve

Forest:
Tsitsikamma National Park
Knysna National Lake Area
Ukhahlamba-Drakensberg Park
Blyde River Nature Reserve
Wolkberg Wilderness Area

Thicket:
Addo Elephant National Park
Van Stadens Wildflower Reserve

Savannah and arid savannah:
Kgalagadi Transfrontier Park
Kruger National Park
Marakele National Park
Hluhluwe-IMfolozi Park
Borakalalo Game Reserve
Ithala Nature Reserve (grassland)
Loskopdam Nature Reserve
Madikwe Game Reserve
Mhkuze Game Reserve
Molopo Nature Reserve
Ndumo Game Reserve (wetland)
Pongolapoort Nature Reserve
Tswalu Kalahari Reserve

been going on for at least 2 000 years. Already the nomadic pastoralists of the Khoi were in the habit of burning down the grassy plains in order to obtain better pastures for their herds. Today the deep, fertile clay soils are agriculturally productive as vineyards and wheat fields.

SUCCULENT KAROO

This global "hotspot" lies in the winter rainfall area of the Northern Cape Province, between the Atlantic Ocean and the Great Karoo and has Namaqualand as its core. In the north the Succulent Karoo stretches up to the Orange River encompassing the |Ai-|Ais/ Richtersveld Transfrontier National Park. Southwards it reaches into the Western Cape Province. Further pockets string out along the Great Karoo right up to Oudtshoorn and the Swartberg Pass in the Little Karoo. This semidesert that finally goes over into true desert has a marvellous vegetation adapted to its location that consists of tough succulents and annuals with a short flowering season as well as tenacious bulbous plants (geophytes) that are able to withstand the periods of drought by virtue of their subterranean moisture conservation.

Carpets of Namaqualand spring flowers reach in some years far into the Karoo

This biome ranks among the few hugely important global "hotspots" in arid regions. More than 5 000 plant species have already been identified here, more than in any other comparable biome in the world. About 2 000 of these species are endemic. There are many rare plants among them and a large number of species are endangered.

Summers are extremely hot and dry. Winter rains bring some 200-290 mm of precipitation and in years with good rainfall this results in a gigantic explosion

of masses of flowers that stretches northwards as far as the Namib Desert and southwards right down to Cape Town. At such a time the sandy, dusty plains are covered with a carpet of flowers, from colourful daisies to other, less conspicuous species. During the remainder of the year fleshy-leaved, dwarf succulents predominate. The sparse trees and shrubs often have a light to almost white bark in order to reflect the heat, like the quiver trees that grow quite large numbers in the northern area.

The soil is quite arid and the lack of water further curtails any agricultural potential. For this reason the countryside usually lies fallow for years on end, sustaining, at most, some goats.

GREAT KAROO OR NAMA KAROO

The largest part of this biome is situated on the central high plateau of the Northern Cape Province with its typical table mountains. It also encompasses parts of the Western and Eastern Cape Province.

Due to the low rainfall the Karoo has semiarid vegetation that covers about 25 % of the country. Only about 5 % of the annual precipitation of between 100 and 520 mm reaches the river beds. The cold in winter and the heat in summer demand great adaptations of the plants. The vegetation is too sparse to evoke veld fires and consists predominantly of dwarf shrubs and grass. The few trees can only survive on the banks of the river beds.

In the click-sound language of the Khoi the Karoo was termed an "arid area", but since European farmers settled there it actually changed into a semidesert that is spreading to the north into the grasslands and reaches far beyond the Orange River into the Kalahari and eastwards it is creeping towards Bloemfontein.

Grass, succulents, annuals and hardy plants comprise the majority of the 2 180 plant species. They do not provide sufficient nourishment for herds of the larger African mammals. The days of mass migrations of Springbuck and other antelope are a thing of the past. The few remaining mammals mainly belong to the smaller species and are either nomadic or have adapted to specific locations. Birdlife is well represented with more than 270 species, as are reptiles with 64 species. Among the insects, termites are of special significance as a food source. Under favourable conditions locusts multiply into swarms of millions and cause great damage to the vegetation both in the Karoo and in other biomes bordering on it.

Most of the region is taken up by very large sheep farms of 4 000 - 15 000 hectares. They are partly responsible for the overgrazing on a large scale and increasing desertification. In some river valleys vines, olives, citrus and other fruit are planted. Only relatively small pockets are protected by nature conservation.

DESERT

Only a small part of the arid Succulent Karoo – inside the |Ai-|Ais/ Richtersveld Transfrontier National Park – can be termed true desert. Otherwise there is no real desert in South Africa with highly erratic rainfall of less than 100 mm and extremely hostile environment. Even the arid Karoo and the dry Kalahari still fall under semi-deserts. The enormous variety of succulents and other hardy desert plants is absolutely amazing. The Richtersveld boasts the most varied desert flora in the world with more then 360 plant species per square kilometre.

After a good rainfall season annual grasses and flowering plants make their appearance and carpet the otherwise bare surfaces. In the drainage channels, where water sometimes collects, hardy plants like the Welwitschia in the Namib Desert are able to survive and on the bigger dunes one finds sporadic tufts of the perennial grass *Stipagrostis subolica*. The insect world is numerous and varied; especially the black running beetle of the Tenebrionidae family is particularly prolific. Some of these make use of the moisture of the night fog, like the "Fog Beetle" in the Namib Desert that stands with its head lowered for this purpose so that the moisture drops run down into its mouth.

Goats thrive in the middle of the dry Orange River opposite Richtersveld National Park

FOREST

Only small pockets of indigenous evergreen and deciduous forests remain, covering less than 0,5 % of the land surface. In precolonial times the forest belt stretched along the coastal areas from Knysna right up to the Kruger National Park. It was up to 200 km wide in places. The remaining islands of woodland are only now – at the last minute – being protected from overexploitation.

IMPORTANT NATURE RESERVES

Grasslands:
Golden Gate National Park
Ukhahlamba-Drakensberg Park
Baviaanskloof Wilderness Reserve
Mkambati Nature Reserve
Oribi Gorge Nature Reserve
Songimvelo Wilderness Reserve
Suikerbosrand Nature Reserve
Blyde River Canyon Nature Reserve
Verlorenvallei Nature Reserve
  (grassland, important wetland)
Wolkberg Wilderness Reserve
  (remains of indigenous jungle)
Gustav Klingbiel Nature Reserve
Mount Sheba and Pilgrim's Rest
  Nature Reserve
Sterkfontein Dam Nature Reserve

Freshwater Environment:
Mapungubwe National Park
  (area feeding Limpopo and Shashe)
Nylsvley
Sterkfontein Dam Nature Reserve
  (grassland)
Rietvlei Nature Reserve (dam,
  grassland and marsh)
Ukhahlamba-Drakensberg Park

Coastal Areas and Coastal Waters:
Tsitsikamma National Park Coastal
  Reserve
Cape Recife Marine Reserve

Estuaries – River Mouths:
Berg River
Knysna National Lake Area
Kosi Bay
Mkambati Nature Reserve
Mzimvubu (Port St. Johns)
Olifant's River Mouth (West Coast)
IsiMangaliso Wetland Park (Greater
  St. Lucia Wetland Park)
Umtamvuna Nature Reserve

Sunset at St. Lucia Estuary

The last forests that are home to the "green giants" (ancient Yellowwood trees) are to be found in the Tsitsikamma and Knysna areas. A narrow stretch of coastal dune woodlands – at some points barely 1,5 km wide – runs from St. Lucia to the northern border of KZN. It is in this province that we find about one third of all the forests. Most of them are privately owned and the sustainability is questionable. It is for this reason that the remaining protected areas of cool, moist montane forests and scattered woodland areas along the escarpment in Mpumalanga and in the low-lying, misty valleys are of such significance. They still play a vital part in ensuring sufficient water supply. Exotic trees use up an average of 25 litres of water per day. Only small sections of the eight different types of forests are being protected.

A small forest of Mountain Cedars survives at Giant's Castle

As a rule indigenous mountain forests are older than wooded areas in subtropical environments, but they contain fewer species. They, too, are under threat by the ever encroaching tree plantations and the constantly growing need for fire wood. Forests are virtually frost free and can be found in winter as well as summer rainfall areas, often in gorges which the fires don't reach.

Displaced by the exotic species

Even the exotic tree plantations with almost 100 million eucalyptus and pine trees and acacias with dark wood cover only about 1,2 % of the land surface.

Another problem is the Australian Acacia known as Black Wattle (*Acacia mearnsii*), an especially noxious invader that – together with other problem plants – has been spreading over some 8 % of the country and is upsetting the ecological balance.

About 650 types of trees

In the indigenous forests of South Africa grow about 650 different types of trees, most of them evergreen. Among these are the "tree giants", like Yellowwood and Stinkwood that reach heights of 40 m and higher and form dense canopies where lianas like Monkey Rope (*Secamone alpinii*) wind through the branches. They provide protection for fruit eating and insectivorous birds and colourful butterflies. Thickets and herbaceous shrubs provide a habitat for Bushbuck and Duiker, as well as certain birds of the forest. The humic soil is enriched and aerated by ground organisms of plant origin, like algae and fungus, or animals like worms, mites, insects and moles.

THICKET

In scientific literature little is found on thicket biomes; it is considered typically South African. Local eco-biologists make use of the term to describe an area that consists of dense to sparse shrub land, interspersed with alternating, low trees and occupying a place approximately midway between forest and savannah. This type of thicket or shrub land only occurs on some stretches that are usually wedged between other biomes and is found near the coastal regions from the Western Cape to KZN.

About 42 000 km² belong to this extraordinary habitat that is constantly shrinking. In the region of the Addo Elephant National Park that contains about 5 000 km² of Spekboom succulents, thicket forms the core of this biome and boasts the greatest number of species of woody plants in the whole of South Africa. The tasty leaves of the Spekboom are eaten by most wild and domestic animals and in the Addo Elephant National Park they form the main nourishment of the elephants.

Destruction and fragmentation mainly occurs as a result of increasing agricultural use, industrial development and overgrazing; the latter having led to increasing aridisation in some places. However, this biome is of especial significance as it encompasses elements of the other six terrestrial habitats. Its genetic material could prove valuable in mitigating negative consequences of the possibly looming climate changes.

BUSHVELD/SAVANNAH

Savannah landscape with trees spaced apart and

pockets of grass make up the vegetation of the high plateau on the eastern side of the subcontinent and the low lying region in front of the escarpment, the so-called Lowveld. "Bushveld" is a South African term for this type of habitat that becomes more humid towards the north. Most of the characteristic tree types of the region can be found here, as well as the largest variety of mammals. South Africa's most fascinating trees grow in this landscape – not the green giants of the coastal areas, but trees growing in exceptional ways, bearing conspicuous flowers and an abundance of fruit. Acacias such as the Camel Thorn, Wild Fig, huge Baobabs and Euphorbia are typical.

The Bushveld evolved in areas with distinct rainy and dry seasons. Grasses dominate the symbiosis of plants. When the precipitation increases they compete with the woody plants, and when more than 500 mm of rain falls this favours the growth of trees; and subsequently the interdependence of grass and woody plants becomes inverted.

The largest part of the northern half of South Africa is covered by Bushveld, including virtually the entire province of Limpopo and large parts of KZN, as well as about half of the North West Province and the northern section of the North Cape Province right up to the Orange River. Towards the coast it stretches up to the Eastern Cape and can occur from sea level up to an altitude of 2 000 m. Annual rainfall varies from 200-1 000 mm, depending on the region. The great variety of species – more than 5 700 plant species and approximately 600-700 tree species – is only surpassed by the fynbos region.

Trees, too, are present in the Bushveld; their types and density depending on the local precipitation and the types of grass growing in the specific areas, as these have a bearing on the amount of water available to the trees during and after the rainy season. Recurrent fires are of great significance in the bushveld, as in any area with grass covering, since they regulate the way it is partitioned into patches of grass or wooded areas. Fire has always been an important ecological factor. These days, fires are deliberately set in the winter months in the large nature reserves as a probate way of ensuring the survival of different species in symbiotic relationships.

Elephants in the lurch

Elephants play a key role in natural symbioses. Were they not present, ecosystems would undergo dramatic changes as they would have – for instance – a huge impact on the food chain on which numerous other species are dependant. Only 300 years ago elephants were part of most ecosystems in South Africa. But this has changed radically, because towards the end of the 19th century their numbers were reduced by big game hunters to just a few hundred. In the mean-time the basic stock has increased to about 20 000, the impressive result of excellent conservation measures, and it is increasing at an annual rate of 4-6 %.

Although the elephant population in South Africa today is less than one twentieth of its original distribution its ecological functions and the influence on the vegetation has increased. This in turn has an influence on the biological diversity as well as on the biological goals, as determined or envisaged by humans. The spectre of culling is looming. Another factor is the conflict between elephants and humans, as it occurs along the borders of conservation areas and rural villages. It has to be borne in mind that elephants constitute a vital element in the growing ecotourism that cannot be done without.

Morning surprise at Mkhuze Game Reserve, Zululand

The wild life in the Bushveld also needs to be balanced between browsers and grazers. Under normal natural conditions there is an optimal equilibrium. Without its wild life, the savannah could not exist, but overgrazing can also destroy it. Agriculture and tree felling have already changed the face of the Bushveld to a great degree.

The largest and most important nature conservation areas lie in the savannah or Bushveld and have become the greatest attraction for ecotourists from near and far. Apart from the big game parks there are numerous private reserves and many game farms. More and more sections of Bushveld are taken up by human settlements. Huge plantations have been laid out with sugar cane and subtropical fruit; ever shrinking water supplies and pollution of rivers also has a great impact on the nature reserves.

The various forms of savannah have one thing in common: the ground is always covered with grass that dries well, thanks to a highly effective photosynthesis, and they have adapted to the intensive radiation factor of the sun prevalent in that climatic region. In the more humid areas the grasses may reach a height of one metre or more, even to a maximum of six metres.

Nature reserves that have been in existence for a long time show that with ongoing conservation and protection from human interference the density and diversity of trees begins to increase. It is, however, not known what extent the open grasslands originally had. Less than 5 % of Bushveld falls officially under nature conservation.

Arid savannah of the Kalahari

This almost desert-like arid savannah covers the southwestern part of the huge Kalahari sand bowl. Precipitation is very low. It increases towards the north where the arid thorn bush vegetation of the infertile sandy soil changes into the Bushveld with trees that grow on the richer soils of granite rocks and sediment.

GRASSLANDS

The South African grasslands are similar to those vast landscapes of the world like the North American Prairies, the South American Pampas and the Eurasian Steppes. Grassland covers a large part of the eastern half of the country, including the Highveld of Gauteng, parts of KZN, the Eastern Cape, the Free State and Limpopo. The grasslands stretch from the coastal plains inland into regions with an altitude of 3 000 metres. The height of grasses and their density does not only depend on the rainfall, as grazing, reaping of cut grass, frost and veld fires also have an influence on the dominance of grass. Trees are rare.

Eland herd moving through subalpine grassland of the Drakensberg

A birdhide enhancing Rietvlei Dam Nature Reserve near Pretoria, in altered Highveld grassland

Grasslands are much older and more complex than the indigenous woodlands. It is assumed that three million years ago grasslands covered more than half of the African continent. Perhaps a prehistoric global warming had been the cause of the proliferation of other plants and trees that led to the evolving of the Bushveld or savannah. According to the latest research the South African grasslands have only come about during the last Ice Age, about 18 000 years ago, and at its peak it covered possibly 25 % of the land surface. Even today it is the habitat of the herds of big antelopes and numerous bird species that have adapted to it.

In South Africa the term grassland encompasses all regions that are covered with grass and include the montane grasslands and those on the high plateaus, in spite of some significant variations. The grass on the high plateau is predominantly short which makes the landscape appear monotonous, although it contains up to 3 370 species of plants, including many delightful flowering plants. In the high lying area of the Drakensberg Mountains a flora has evolved that is different from the other grassland in its composition and the number of its species.

More than 50 % of grasslands are today utilised for growing maize and other agricultural plants. On the Highveld around the Witwatersrand that forms part of the grasslands and has the highest population density on the whole subcontinent, gold and coal mines are also found. Yet the pitiful remnant still sustains a diversity of fauna and flora, especially numerous flowering plants. Red Grass, Common Thatch Grass and High Turpentine Grass are the most important of the numerous grass species. Amongst them grow up to a hundred indigenous plants and thousands of others, many of which are spread over the entire continent. More than 30 highly specialised butterfly species can survive only in the grasslands. The same holds for the typical birds of the grasslands like the Drakensberg Siskin, the Sentinel Rock Thrush, the Eastern Long-billed Lark and the Drakensberg Prinia.

Only a few nature reserves afford this vegetation some protection if one discounts the wilderness areas of the KZN Drakensberg Mountains. Less than 2 % fall under nature conservation.

FRESHWATER ENVIRONMENT

This sphere encompasses all inland lakes and streams, from the tiniest rivulet to the largest rivers, like the Limpopo, Vaal, Fish and Orange. Wetlands, dams and small water reservoirs also form part of it. All of these ensure the supply of fresh water to the country and are therefore of vital importance.

The predominantly arid character of the country and the erratic rainfall make South Africa permanently susceptible to water shortages and this can only become worse due to the increasing demand for water. This makes conservation and protection of fresh-water resources of vital importance, and to this effect ample long-term planning and education of the public is imperative, because the future demand for water will far surpass the existing water reserves. Presages of the growing problems can be observed in the 96 species of freshwater fish that repeatedly make their appearance on the Red Data List.

A brook snakes through Wetland in the foothills of the Drakensberg Range

Bushman's River near Giant's Castle Tourist Camp, KZN Drakensberg Range

Cape Agulhas, southernmost spot of Africa where Indian and Atlantic Ocean meet

Sunset at Swartvlei, the heart of the Garden Route

Mangrove swamp

COASTAL AREAS AND COASTAL WATERS

Along the often turbulent west coast of South Africa runs the cold Benguela Current while the warm Agulhas Current, coming from Mozambique, turns eastwards again south of the Cape Peninsula at the Agulhas Bank. Both of these ocean currents produce a multitude of ecosystems that span from tropical coral reefs in the east to cool kelp forests along the west coast. Furthermore the Agulhas Current sweeps along towards the south a huge number of sea organisms from the Indian- and Pacific Ocean that include fish and corals. Along this coast line of almost 3000 km there are 12 marine reserves to protect the unique fauna and flora.

The Benguela Current is still one of the big fishing zones of the Seven Seas. Strong winds often blow the upper layers of the water off-shore and this results in the colder, deeper layers of the Atlantic, that are rich in nutrients, welling up closer to the shore whereby a spectacular growth of plankton is stimulated. This in turn is the basis of rich sources of nourishment for fish, sea birds, seals and marine mammals.

Indiscriminate exploitation of the seemingly inexhaustible fish reserves, especially by foreign fishing fleets, has long had a negative influence on the South African fishing economy and is proving a great threat to the very existence of the small fishing communities along the coast. This ransacking of the oceans has reached such proportions that not only are the natural resources extremely endangered, but, according to scientists, the whole of the natural fish population might be exhausted by the middle of this century. This highly unsettling trend is traceable in the fast diminishing numbers of Angelfish, Red Abalone and Rock Lobster.

Counting both oceans there are at present about 2 200 species of fish and 56 marine bird species, some 30 mammal species and 7 species of reptiles, as well as approximately 9 000 different invertebrates.

ESTUARIES – RIVER MOUTHS

More than 260 estuaries along South Africa's extended coastline provide contact with the sea. In contrast to estuaries in other parts of the world the funnel shaped river mouths of South Africa are intermittently sealed up by sandbanks for shorter or longer periods. The frequent and ongoing mixing of fresh water and sea water brought about the emergence of unique biomes. Both fauna and flora evolved here that were adapted to and dependent on a blend of aquatic as well as terrestrial conditions and manage to survive in the fluctuating biotope.

The estuaries are situated either in the subtropical, warm temperate or cool temperate zones; the greatest variety of species is found in the subtropical zone and diminishes gradually in a westerly direction. Also the number of endemic species is at its highest in the warm temperate region.

Among the most important estuaries are iSimangaliso Wetland Park (Greater St. Lucia Wetland Park), Knysna Lagoon, Olifant's River Mouth (West Coast), Kosi Bay, Gariep and the Bot/Kleinmond. In a poor condition: Estuary of the Amanzimtoti River and many others.

Estuary of Mzamba River near the Eastern border of the Wild Coast. This largely unspoiled part of Pondoland is threatened by a toll road with a 330 m long high level bridge crossing a picturesque gorge

Hunting and Fishing

In the past, until well into the 1980's, Nature Conservation had practically given away its surplus game, but since then the country has become the most sought after hunting ground on the African continent as destination for international hunting tourism. Commercial game farming is booming in South Africa. The growing number of hunters has convinced many farmers and landowners that more money is to be made with game farming than with stock farming or crops. Almost 7 000 trophy hunters from overseas, predominantly from the USA, Germany and Spain, come annually to hunt both big and small game and shoot up to 55 000 animals, while the 200 000 local hunters concentrate more on hunting for meat. There are approximately 9 000 game farms in South Africa. A further 15 000 are combined stock and game farms. Hunters from overseas are keenest on the Eastern Cape which boasts 1 300 game farms and ranches. It is estimated that three times as much game is to be found on private property than in state wildlife reserves. "Money is saving the wild animals of Africa", has become the motto of the hunting fraternity. Game farms generate an annual turnover of several hundred million Euros.

Game that can be hunted includes Buffalo, Kudu, Impala, Giraffe, Warthog, Zebra, Blue Wildebeest, Waterbuck, Bush Pig, Grey Duiker, Blue Duiker, Gemsbok, Springbuck, Eland, Grysbok, Red Hartebeest, Grey Rhebok, Bontebok and numerous game birds like Guineafowl, Francolin, Quails, Egyptian Goose, Spur-Winged Goose, Rock Pigeon and wild ducks. Some pigeon species may be hunted right through the year and without restrictions, but otherwise the hunting season for game birds applies, stretching from the beginning of May to the end of September.

South Africa is well known for hunting safaris aimed at grassland animals. Black Wildebeest, Impala, Springbuck and Kudu are numerous. Even the White Rhino that had been on the endangered list till quite recently may be hunted again. Probably even the rare Black Rhino will soon reappear on the hunting menu.

Obviously the Big Five constitute the supercup, although the price of a big game hunt – preferably in the savannah near the Kruger National Park – can be mind-boggling. The main argument in favour of this steadily increasing business is that hunting constitutes a great asset for the preservation of wild life. Hunting, as sport, is geared at trophies and often considers killing as a tiresome, but unavoidable collateral issue.

"You kill, when you are hunting, but you don't hunt in order to kill", so says the Spanish cultural philosopher, sociologist and essayist Jose Ortega y Gasset. The classic big game hunt – searching for and tracking, then challenging and outsmarting a formidable opponent in his natural habitat – has been all but lost. Comment of a well-known professional hunter: "Some clients don't care how they acquire their trophies, as long as they enhance their collection."

Those that oppose hunting claim that these arguments ignore the right to life of the individual animal. If killing the animal is not the motive for hunting then why not rather make use of the camera instead of rifle, shotgun, or even crossbow and bow and arrow? Hunters with bows and arrows or crossbows are welcome in South Africa.

These saltwater fish species may not be caught:

English Name	Scientific Name
Basking Shark	Cetorhinus maximus
Brindle Bass	Epinephelus lanceolatus
Coelacanth	Latimeria chalumnae
Dageraad	Chrysoblephus cristiceps
Great White shark	Carcharodon carcharias
Natal Wrasse	Anchichoerops natalensis
Pipefish and Seahorses	Family Pristidae
Potato Bass	Epinephelus tukula
Sawfish	Family Syngnathidae
Seventy-four	Polysteganus undulosus
Whale Shark	Rhincodon typus

Top: Khoi people capturing elephants by impaling them (woodcut, about 1710)

Centre: Canned hunting – trophy of an amateur huntsman

Below: Rangers with Impala and assegai, taken from a runaway poacher

Left: Dageraad, an odd fish species under threat   Right: White Steenbrass

The organisers of hunting with bows or crossbows declared the country to be a veritable paradise for such hunters. It is, however, expected that the archer can really handle his weapon professionally. Arrows are shot from a distance of 20 m – or less. Greater distances might result in precious hunting time being squandered on the lengthy tracking of wounded animals.

Men have made use of bows and arrows for more than 12 000 years, both for hunting and also for warfare. A crossbow is much easier to handle and requires less practice than a conventional bow. Both may also be used for big game hunting. Even elephants have been brought down that way, sometimes with a single shot, as has been proudly related.

Permits are not required when bringing in bows and crossbows. On the other hand it is forbidden to bring more than one fire arm (this includes shotguns) into South Africa, and no more than 200 bullets. Semi-automatic weapons may not be brought in at all, and so-called "pump guns" are sure to raise the suspicion of the security personnel at the airport.

Angling and Fishing

Fishing as a sport is very popular both on the coastline and on lakes. Angling has long been established as a national sport and at least 500 000 South Africans have taken it up one way or another. About 10 % even make a living from it. Whereas those that practise fishing seriously, either part-time or full-time, usually take to the sea from small fishing harbours during the night in their boats, sport fishermen stand on the shores of lakes, estuaries, streams and dams or on sandy beaches and rocks along the coast and cast their lines into the breakers. Alternatively they make use of modern motor boats to go to the sea. Diving and spear fishing is also possible.

The coastal waters of South Africa are home to innumerable species of fish – from Sardines to Zebra fish – as well as mammals and invertebrates, including the prehistoric Coelacanth, the feared Great White Shark, Sea Horse, Rock Lobster, Dolphin, Whale, Seal and many other animals.

Although the quotas for sport fishing have been drastically reduced and new minimum sizes laid down, the number of angling fish continues to dwindle at a dangerous rate. Among the reasons for this are inadequate controls and unbridled commercial over-fishing. According to the Fish Protection Authority more than twenty species of fish are highly endangered. These include well known and popular species like silver Kob and Dusky Kob (*Argyrosomus* spp.), Seventy-four (*Polysteganus undulosus*), White Steenbrass (*Lithognathus lithognatus*) and Dageraad (*Chrysoblephus cristiceps*).

Experts demand far stricter controls to halt this negative trend.

For some fish the reason for their predicament might be sought in nature, as for instance with the highly sought after Dageraad: these long-living fish mature when they are about 10 years old, when some females transform into males and continue to increase in size, thereby developing into the prized trophyfish for anglers. This results in a reduced reproduction of the species.

Tip: Permits for fishing can be obtained from all state nature conservation authorities.

Fishing in inland waters

Trout fishing is very popular. Crystal clear streams in higher lying areas are usually well stocked with Rainbow- and Brown Trout that had been brought in from overseas. They have increased to such a degree that they often displace indigenous species. Areas for trout fishing are to be found in the Drakensberg and in the Cape.

Exotics

The Rainbow Trout (*Salmo gairdneri*) can be found all over the country where the water is cool. They grow up to a length of 50 cm long and can be easily identified by their shimmering pink band stretching from head to tail. In South Africa their life expectancy is no more than four years. Fishing is only permitted with artificial flies as bait. The European Trout (*Salmo strutta*) is to be found in the Western and Eastern Cape, in KZN and Mpumalanga in mountain streams and high-lying reservoirs. They can be identified by their pale encircled black to dark red spots on their brown bodies. In South Africa they are often bred artificially, as they also flourish in warmer water and grow to a size of up to 75 cm in length and 7,7 kg in body weight.

The Carp (*Cyrinus carpio*) is said to have been introduced around 1 700 and is widely distributed, except in the mountains and low lying plains (Lowveld). It grows to a length of about one metre. The fishing record in South Africa is 22 kg. Carp continues to be one of the most important sport fish, but disliked by ecologists.

The Bluegill (Centrarchidae-family) is present in many lakes in South Africa. Three species had been imported from North America between 1928-1939.

Western Cape

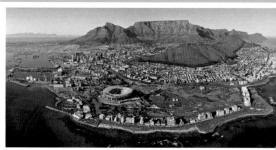

The countryside around the Cape of Good Hope with its majestic landscapes and the unsurpassable Sixth Floral Kingdom is one the most spectacular natural sites in the world. The 1 087 m high Table Mountain (see picture below) brings the natural environment right into the suburbs of one of the most beautiful cities in the world.

Photo left: Preparation of the stadium for the 2010 World Soccer Cup Tournament. Source: http://namibsands.wordpress.com/2009/07/01/green-point-stadium/; July 2009

Table Bay

The old harbour basins "Victoria and Alfred" have been developed as the V&A Waterfront with premier shopping malls, restaurants and residences. It draws the greatest number of visitors of any location in South Africa.

For the ecotourist the large Two Oceans Aquarium, presenting South Africa's underwater world, is well worth a visit.

Table Mountain National Park

This is the seventh national park of the province and constitutes without a doubt the most important part of the Cape Floral Kingdom. It comprises a mountain range that starts with Table Mountain and stretches over an area 50 km long and 16 km wide right down to the Cape of Good Hope. The original 50 km^2 of wilderness have been combined with Cape Point, Silvermine and the Boulders Beach Penguin Colony, as well as other nature reserves on both sides of the peninsula to become the Table Mountain National Park (TNP) – the largest nature reserve in the province stretching over 220 km^2.

A drive around the peninsula to the Cape Point and back is the highlight of any trip to South Africa.

Kirstenbosch Botanical Gardens

The largest botanical garden in Africa, the world famous Kirstenbosch Botanical Gardens, is an important research centre for the endangered Cape Flora. About 20 000 plant species from all over the subcontinent are collected, cultivated and displayed in magnificent surroundings. Right through the year there is something in bloom in the extensive garden. Numerous bird species live and nest here, including Red-chested Cuckoo, Orange-breasted Sunbird, Cape Reed Warbler, Cape Sugarbird and Forest Canary.

Hout Bay

Behind Kirstenbosch, Rhodes Avenue winds up to Constantia Nek and then continues with many curves and shaded by oak trees down to the valley of Hout Bay (Wood Bay). Details about the development of the bay can be gleaned from the Hout Bay Museum and the South African Sea Fisheries Museum.

It is possible to explore the Hout Bay by kajak. In good weather you can even paddle around the 330 m Sentinel to Duiker Island, where fur seals lie drowsily on the rocks or drift about on the swell and move around the boats out of curiosity. Sightseeing boats operate to a timetable and offer 40 minute trips. These are especially sought after during the season when seals have their young (November and December).

Chapman's Peak Drive

Where the beach of Hout Bay comes to an end, one of the most spectacular scenic coastal drives commences. The road that cuts deep into the granite and sandstone rock was opened in 1922 and over the years it has been improved and stabilised; lately it

Table Mountain is a national monument, a nature reserve and a World Natural Heritage Site. It encompasses a unique treasure of centuries been enticing botanists from all over the world. The magnitude of plant species has been scientifically grouped as the Cape Floral Kingdom – by far the smallest, but at the same time by far the richest in relation to its size as compared to the other floral kingdoms of the world.

Gliding up the mountain

Ascending the mountain was a taxing expedition in days gone by, and few undertook it. Today it takes less effort by cable car and as the floor of the cable car rotates each passenger is afforded a 360° view of city and mountain.

Walking and climbing

For others a walking tour is a more satisfying way to experience the grand wilderness. More than 350 routes lead to the top, the easiest of which can be tackled by a reasonably fit outdoor enthusiast in 3-4 hours. The mountain climate is so capricious that you can experience all four seasons during one ascent. Walkers and climbers need to get informative details, safety precautions and addresses from the Cape Mountain Club.

Conservatory in Kirstenbosch

The Conservatory is like a museum of living plants where rare plant species of southern Africa are displayed under appropriate conditions in simulated environments. The majority of these plants would not survive outside in the lovely garden, because they either need an arid desert climate or a subtropical environment, dark forest glens or high altitude. Conducted tours (including groups) are offered daily.

1. & 7. Kirstenbosch, Africa's leading ecological Botanical Garden
2. Cape Point, the disputed southernmost part of Africa
3. Silvermine Nature Reserve, an important centre of fynbos vegetation
4. At weekends, Table Mountain is illuminated.
5. Family outing at the top of Table Mountain
6. Beautiful view over Chapman's Peak and parts of Noordhoek Beach

has been made a toll road, much to the annoyance of the people living in the area. The official stops along the roadside provide panoramic vistas. Walking around offers further perspectives, but it can be dangerous, as no provisions have been made for pedestrians.

The beaches of Noordhoek, Scarborough and Soetwater are among the prettiest on the Atlantic coast. The narrow road leads through the southern part of the as yet incomplete Mountain National Park. Fantastic views over the silvery blue Atlantic alternate with views of the Cape Mountains with varying shades of green of the Fynbos vegetation. Scattered along the coast are settlements in natural conservancies such as Misty Cliffs and Scarborough. Schuster's Bay is frequented by whales between June and November.

Cape of Good Hope – Cape of Storms

And finally you stand at Cape Point. A footpath or the funicular take you up to the remnants of the old lighthouse with grand views all around. There is another footpath winding its way down to the Cape of Good Hope. This can also be reached by tarred road that turns off at the Vasco da Gama Peak towards Platboom Bay, the latter being sought after by surfers. One travels through coastal fynbos with Ostrich, Bontebok, Mountain Zebra and Baboon, while Kelp Gull, Cape Cormorant and terns sit on the rocks near the sea. There are footpaths leading to viewpoints along both coasts. Black Rock, Buffel's Bay and Venus Pool are favourite picnic spots where angling and bathing in the False Bay are possible.

The drive back to Cape Town along the False Bay meanders between mountains and sea and offers beautiful vistas like Smitswinkel Bay, where many ships came to grief.

Penguins have right of way

At Boulders Beach, as you enter Simon's Town, South Africa's only penguin species has procured a safe haven between exclusive villas and massive granite boulders, living among the coastal vegetation and small dunes, close to access roads leading to the main street. Other coastal birds share their living space, e.g. Oystercatcher, Crowned Cormorants and Kelp Gull, as do some songbirds. Seals, sharks and Killer Whale hunt the birds, but even greater is the danger from land, where Genet, Mongoose and domestic dogs and cats prey on them.

It all started with two pairs – joined for life, as all penguins do - that in 1982 settled on the narrow beach in front of the elegant holiday homes. Nowadays there are more than 3 000 penguins and tourists can observe them from elevated wooden walkways which allow such a close interaction that it became necessary to put up a warning: Don't tease the penguins, as they have sharp beaks and can inflict serious bites!

Simon's Town

South Africa's naval base has quaint Victorian houses, a waterfront and the dockyard with the naval museum.

Baboons behaving badly

The baboons at the Cape belong to one of the subspecies of the Chacma Baboons. They have not only adapted to living off seafood, but also to begging from tourists as an easy alternative to foraging in the wild. They have become a real pest, and even their sex life has been affected by the treats that are supplied by well-meaning visitors. As these treats often consist of sweets, the baboons have developed caries in their teeth and now find it difficult to chew normal baboon food like fruit, roots, scorpions and other small creatures. Nature Conservation now endeavours to put an end to this by threatening draconian penalties for those caught feeding the baboons, in order to give these animals a better chance of survival, as they are so much part of the area.

Robben Island – where Mandela was incarcerated

Daily boat trips are conducted from the Waterfront to the offshore island where Nelson Mandela, the country's most famous person was jailed for many years. The trip is not only of interest for political reasons as the island is also a nature reserve and has been proclaimed a World Heritage Site. Tourist guides on the island are generally made up of previous convicts. Booking is essential.

Ocean excursions

The ocean around the Cape of Good Hope has such a multitude of sea birds that the South African Pelagic Excursions are counted among the best in the world. Good starting points are Simon's Town on the False Bay and Hout Bay on the Atlantic side.
The greatest diversity of sea birds can be seen during the wintertime (April-September), among them Shearwater, Petrel and Giant Petrel and various types of Albatross.

1. & 2. Cape Point
3. & 6. Penquins at the Boulders Nature
   Reserve
4. Entrance to Hout Bay's harbour from
   Chapman's Peak View
5. Chapman's Peak Drive, one of the
   most beautiful marine drives of
   the world

7. Cape Baboons are
   normally known as
   very aggressive
8. Boulders Beach, part
   of False Bay, renown for
   swimming with Penguins

Behind Simon's Town there is a turn-off to Ou Kaapse Weg, the oldest road linking the mother city to the coast that leads past the Silvermine Nature Reserve with wetland areas and footpaths through the fynbos, including the magnificent King Protea.

From the Boland to the Great Karoo

Wine Routes in the Boland

The wine lands adjoining Cape Town are internationally famous. The various wine routes lead to both historical and modern wine estates. They are well signposted and can be enjoyed on your own or on an organised tour.

Paarl Nature Reserve

This small nature reserve lies above the town and is known for its huge granite boulders that are more than 500 million years old. It affords a magnificent view of the surrounding wine lands and the Du Toits Kloof Mountains which rewards one for the somewhat strenuous ascent. From here the N1 takes you through the mountains into the Great Karoo.

Karoo is Khoi and means "stony arid area". That is a good description of the Great Karoo – a semiarid plain stretching from the Cape Fold Mountains to the Orange River and thereafter merging into the Kalahari Desert. Its approximately 500 000 km² take up almost a third of the landmass of South Africa. Rainfall is scant and the vegetation is accordingly so. The Little Karoo occupies the southwestern part of the Cape Province and the Swartberg Mountains form its boundary.

Karoo National Park

Its location in the semidesert and arid savannah in the west and southwest of the country enable this 800 km2 National Park to present multi-facetted attractions. The huge prehistoric freshwater lake changed to a semidesert and numerous primitive amphibians and mammal-like reptiles have been preserved in fossilised form in this largest ecosystem of South Africa with its diverse fauna and flora.

The reserve protects part of the extensive Karoo plain and the Nuweveld Mountains (1 800 m) with the typical Karoo landscape of grass, succulents and shrubs. Extensive hiking trails, the picturesque Klipspringer Pass and gravel roads for 4x4's provide the opportunity for leisurely exploration. Guided night tours are also available.

Among the more than 50 mammal species are the endangered Riverine Rabbit and Cape Mountain Zebra (with obvious signs of decades of attempts to rebreed the extinct Quagga). Black Wildebeest, Eland, Kudu, Springbuck and Red Hartebeest are also present. Cape Buffalo and black rhinos have been re-introduced. In the early morning you can meet Klipspringer near the Klipspringer Pass and excellent game watching is possible on Lammertjiesleegte (plain of the lambs). Bird watching is best in and around the tourist

Wine, Cheetahs and Raptors

The famous Spier wine estate is known for its excellent music productions, but it also has a heart for animals. Apart from a bird park, it has made space for breeding Cheetah. The Cheetah Outreach Programme draws attention to these increasingly endangered wild cats that are still able to roam freely in southern Africa. Barely 10 000 Cheetahs are left worldwide, of which only about 600 live in South Africa. On the Spier estate about ten adult cheetahs and up to twelve young ones are kept. For a donation people may pat them and have their photo taken with them.

The adjoining Bird of Prey Centre provides the opportunity to learn about South Africa's most important raptors. Interactive displays introduce falconry or provide the opportunity to accompany a Secretary Bird on a simulated snake hunt, or owls, harriers, buzzards and hawks tackling their prey, or to admire the acrobatic flight of Africa's largest eagles.

Karoo Botanical Gardens

This specialised botanical garden near Worcester is geared to the display of various succulents, most of which occur in the Karoo. Fascinating are Lithops, the "Living Stones", quite rare in South Africa, that are - outside of its flowering season - so perfectly camouflaged on the dry stony ground. The well-known *Aloe ferox* also grows here; its medicinal usefulness was appreciated and utilised by the original inhabitants. Nowadays it is used world wide in the cosmetic industry.

1. Typical landscape inside Karoo National Park
2. King Protea, South Africa's national flower
3. Cyclists on the popular track of Silver Mine Nature Reserve
4. Klipspringer found a secure home in the Karoo National Park
5. Mountain Zebra Park in the Little Karoo
6. Grape harvest in the Boland
7. The Paarl koppies, massive rounded granite rocks, a main attraction in Paarl Nature Reserve

camp. The birdhide at the man-made lake in the tourist camp is a favourite.

Location: Along the N1 – 500 km north of Cape Town, 1 000 km south of Johannesburg and 10 km south of Beaufort West.

Climate: Hot on the plains in summer, higher lying areas are cooler. Annual rainfall is 175-400 mm, depending on altitude. In midwinter the mountain peaks in the reserves are often covered with snow.

The West Coast

The bracing air and stark coastline impact from the time you start the drive at Bloubergstrand and follow it along the R27 along the Atlantic coast. Beyond the West Coast National Park to the north lie a modern industrial region around Saldanha Bay and some picturesque fishing villages on the coast.

West Coast National Park

Langebaan Lagoon, 90 km north of Cape Town, lies at the centre of this nature reserve along the Atlantic coastline. It is surrounded by brackish marshland, reed beds and dunes. As a wetland it has global significance and is registered with the Ramsar Convention. Numerous wading birds from the Northern Hemisphere migrate here in winter; they arrive exhausted and famished after the long transcontinental flight.

The Postberg region presents itself in colourful splendour in springtime when the limestone and granite foothills that are covered with Fynbosthat has burst into flower. After good winter rains (May – August) walks with a flower guide are available. In the Strandveld-vegetation around the lagoon endemic birds are numerous, including Black Korhaan, Black Oystercatcher, Greywing Francolin, Southern Grey Tit and Cape Penduline Tit, Ant-eating Chat, White-throated Canary and Yellow Canary, Karoo Lark, Bokmakierie and Cape Bunting and often even the African Marsh-Harrier and the Black Harrier.

Small islands, like Malgas Island that is open to tourists, constitute ideal breeding colonies for thousands of sea birds like Cape Gannet, Cape Cormorant, Kelp and Hartlaub's Gull, Jackass Penguin and various species of terns. Boat trips to Malgas Island (Gannet Island) are on offer.

The old Geelbek homestead has been restored and refurbished into an environment centre. There is an excellent birdhide that can be reached via a wooden walkway across the brackish marsh.

Overnight accommodation in beach cottages, houseboats (some double-storied), dormitories and camping sites.

Information on houseboats: www.houseboats.cjb.net. Hotels, chalets and guest rooms are available in nearby Langebaan at the entrance of the reserve.

Flower Tours: Booking in the reserve. The Postberg section is open during the flower season (August-October) from 09h00-17h00.

Ramsar Convention

The international convention for the protection of wading and water birds in wetlands was ratified in December 1975 in Ramsar (Iran). South Africa was represented among the five founding states with the wetlands Barberspan and De Hoop. In the meantime a further 110 states have joined the agreement. South Africa has 20 wetlands covering a total area of approximately 500 km² registered, among which uKhahlamba Drakensberg Park, Ndumo Game Reserve, Nylsvley and Verloren Vlei.

ECO HOTSPOT

Decoy Gannets

Bird Island, South Africa's most important breeding colony for more than 30 000 Cape Gannets, lies within a few steps of the small harbour of Lambert's Bay. During the breeding season, in spring and summer, breeding pairs congregate on the site that is about the size of a soccer field and proceed to incubate their eggs on nests made of their own guano.

When the amount of fish began to diminish rapidly in recent years many gannets left the colony, because the fur seals living here were substituting their dwindling food source (fish) by preying on gannets and ruining their breeding season. Nature lovers placed 50 gannets made of plaster at strategic spots in order to entice the birds back. Within a few months about 10 000 birds had returned. Cape Provincial nature conservation has employed a fulltime conservationist to prevent a repetition of the tragedy. So far this is proving successful: The acrid smell of guano is again hanging in the air.

It is possible to visit Bird Island. Booking is not essential. There is also an aquarium, a penguin pool and a café.

1. Gnarled tree of the Great Karoo
2. & 4. Paternoster, a picturesque
fisherman's Village on
the West Coast
3. Gannet Colony at Lambert's Bay
5. The West Coast has become
a Mecca for windsurfers from
around the world

Cedarberg Wilderness Area

The Cedarberg Wilderness Area (700 km²) starts at the Middelberg Pass near Citrusdal, about 170 km north of Cape Town. This inhospitable mountain region forms part of the Cape Fold Mountain Range and has grandiose landscapes and spectacular rock formations of weathered Table Mountain Sandstone. The area lies in the winter rainfall region and the Cape fynbos is well represented with numerous flowering plants, shrubs and trees.

The endangered evergreen Clanwilliam Cedar grows in the so-called "Cedar Zone" at altitudes above 1 000 metres. It attaches itself in the rock crevices and ravines. About 8 000 yearlings are planted out annually. On the highest cliffs the attractive endemic Snow Protea grows and there are several types of Erica. The most famous plant meanwhile is the Rooibos Tea (*Aspalathus linearis*) that only grows in the Cedarberg and can often be found under the sheer cliffs. It is known worldwide as excellent health tea.

Among the animals commonly seen are Klipspringer, Grysbuck, Duiker and Rock Hyrax (Dassie), whereas Leopard, Cape Clawless Otter, Aardvark, African Wildcat, Brown Hyena, Caracal and Cape Fox are rarely spotted. About 100 bird species live there, such as Black Eagle, Red-necked Buzzard and Rock Kestrel. The endemic Giant Girdled Lizard (*Cordylus giganteus*), known in South Africa as Sungazer, is rather surprisingly, also present. Among the 16 snake species the Spitting Cobra, Mountain Adder and Puff Adder are common – and dangerous.

Climate: Winters are cold and wet with snow in the higher lying regions, summers are warm and dry with the danger of veldfires.

Tip: Trips by donkey-cart lasting several days can be undertaken through parts of the Cerderberg Wilderness Area with overnight stops at Heuningvlei, once the outpost of the mission station at Wuppertal. About 20 families work on small farms producing organic potatoes, sweet potatoes and beans. Rooibos Tea is also produced in the traditional ecological way.

Eastwards over the mountain

Sir Lowry's Pass, traversing the Hottentot's Holland Mountains at an altitude of 400 metres, was a much frequented game track. The Khoi-San called it "Pass of the Eland" and in 1839 a road was constructed that opened up the fruitful hinterland, the "land over the mountain" (Overberg), and thereby also opened up the Garden Route and on to Port Elizabeth and Durban. Sightseeing spots on the pass afford a panoramic view across the Cape peninsula. For the ecotourist happy to travel around a bit the route between the coast and the Kogelberg is also very attractive. It commences just behind Gordon's Bay (R44) and avoids the mountain passes. The magnificent scenery and diversity make it one of the most fantastic routes in South Africa.

Kogelberg Nature Reserve

The wilderness area Kogelberg is a prime spot for the diversity of Fynbos species and it is considered the "heart of the Cape Floral Kingdom". Being positioned between the southern sections of the Hottentot's Holland Mountains down to the Indian Ocean it remained inaccessible and pristine for a long time.

Steep gorges, deep valleys, clear brooks and streams enhance the primal beauty of the mountain world whose grandeur had already been mentioned by travellers in the 18th century. Stone-age hunters had survived here for 100 000 years up to modern times. Farmers considered the mountains too uninhabitable for agriculture and animal husbandry.

More than 1 600 plants have been classified, about 10% of them as endemic. The hidden treasure of rare Protea species is remarkable. Along secluded mountain slopes the Marsh Rose (*Orothamnus zeyheri*) blooms, as well as several Pagoda species. In well preserved areas of original woodlands Yellowwood, Stinkwood, Wild Almond, Red Alder and Cape Beech grow.

The animal world has undergone a dramatic change since the end of the Khoi period. Game has virtually disappeared. Leopard, Cape Clawless Otter, Klipspringer and Grysbuck have become rare. Only baboons and hare are common. Fish Eagle, Black Eagle and Peregrine Falcon nest all over the reserve. Wild horses from the time of the Anglo Boer War survive near Rooisand at the mouth of the Bot River.

Mountain climbers must prepare themselves for rugged terrain and changing weather conditions. White water excursions by canoe are permitted on the Palmiet River during the winter months. However, participants must show proof of their competence, as the river can be dangerous.

Apart from two plain wooden huts no overnight accommodation is available. Entrance: about 8 km southwest of Kleinmond (R44) turn to right (signposted) and carry on for 3 km on a gravel road through private property to reach the entrance to the reserve.

1. & 5. The Cederberg is famous for its spectacular sandstone and shale rock formations like the Wolfberg Cracks, Wolfberg Arch, Maltese Cross and Stadsaal Caves

2. The famous rare San rock painting of elephants near the "Stadsaal" impress like many other subjects in the Cederberg area. It was created 8 000-200 years ago

3. & 4. Cederberg plants

6. The Wilderness area of the Kogelberg range borders the R44 between Gordon's Bay and Hangklip

More penguins

Betty's Bay, a village of individualistic residential and holiday homes, has been invaded by new inhabitants in "dress suit". Since 1982 the number of penguins on the tiny peninsula of Stony Point has increased at such a rate that nature conservationists feel quite baffled. In the beginning it was difficult. Leopards, genets and mongoose preyed on the growing colony. In one night a leopard killed 50 penguins, and some time later another 15. Thereafter the colony was fenced in and the area around the penguin colony proclaimed a nature reserve. After wooden walkways had been constructed the number of visitors increased tremendously. A museum, a restaurant and an ecology centre are planned. Stony Point lies east of Cape Hangklip, about 90 km from Cape Town.

Ecological success: Penguin colony at Betty's Bay

Harold Porter Botanical Garden

Behind Betty's Bay lies the Harold Porter Botanical Garden on the slopes of the Kogelberg. For travellers under time pressure a short stop in the aromatic fynbos can be most relaxing and restorative. Harold Porter, an architect and town planner in Johannesburg found his Arcadia here. He transformed the picturesque piece of earth at the foot of the Kogelberg into a paradise of wild flowers and named it his Shangri-La. His heirs bequeathed the magnificent place to the National Botanical Gardens.

The garden communicates lively impressions of the diverse biospheres of the Cape Floral Kingdom. A great variety of Fynbos plants can be admired and photographed in their seasons, including King Protea, Prince of Wales Heather (*Erica perspicua*), Sugar Bush Protea and Restios that are used for thatching.

Several hiking routes – some of them even suitable for wheelchairs – lead into the Kogelberg Biosphere Reserve and to ravines with endemic trees and sparkling waterfalls. Numerous small mammals and baboons live here, as well as Puff Adder and Boomslang.

The garden lies directly on the R44 south east of Betty's Bay. There is a Fynbos Eco Centre, a fynbos nursery, a restaurant, and on mild summer evenings concerts by candlelight are performed.

Whale watching

In spite of restrictions on hunting them – in force since 1937 – numerous whale species were close to extinction. Only the ongoing protests of animal and environmental activists led to a change in attitude. The widespread education about the intelligence, ability to learn and highly developed social relations of the giant mammals hugely increased their popularity. Once tourists began to open their hearts to the friendly giants the blossoming "Whale Tourism" took off worldwide and whale watching became a serious pasttime. The new ecotourism accelerated this enormous transformation even more. South Africa certainly profits from this as more than half of the 70 species of whales living in the oceans come regularly into South African waters. The most frequent visitors are the 3 000-4 000 Southern Right Whales whose numbers have meanwhile grown to about 6 000 and are continuing to increase at an annual rate of about 7 %. The whale season along the Cape coast, from Saldanha, around Cape Point and along the Garden Route lasts from July to November.

1. Landscape near Hermanus   2. Agulhas lighthouse   3. Hermanus

Hermanus to Cape Agulhas

Hermanus (120 km from Cape Town) is the centre of a striking stretch of coastline. Every year whales visit the coast to mate, give birth and just to hang around, especially in Walker Bay. A well laid-out path of 12 km leads to the various viewing points on the rocks. The best place for whale observation from the land is the Old Harbour, according to the Whale Watcher who announces their presence by blowing his kelp horn.

Meeting on the high seas

Much more dramatic is a meeting with whales on the open sea. The skipper of the Southern Right Charters takes the enthusiasts by catamaran – a 42-seater with an elevated viewing deck – to a quiet cove and takes up his waiting position, keeping to the prescribed distance. It is now up to the whales whether they want to come closer or not. Usually their curiosity gets the better of them and they swim right up to the boats, to the delight of the watchers who are not put off by an occasional squirt from the blowhole.

Gansbaai

This small fishing village, 45 km from Hermanus, has – together with Kleinbaai – become the centre for the controversial cage-diving to observe the feared Great White. These days Gansbaai is also called the "Bay of the Big Two", because not only the Great White can be observed under water from the steel cages or plexi-glass diving contraptions, but also the Southern Right Whale that frequents the calm bays.

Cape Agulhas

Another fishing village that has developed into a remarkable holiday resort and whose inhabitants claim with pride that the Indian and Atlantic Oceans meet on their doorstep – the most southerly point of the African continent lies only 1 km to the west of the lighthouse. The early Portuguese seafarers called the promontory l'Agulhas, the "needles", because their compass needles pointed exactly north. The lighthouse and adjoining buildings have been built from the local lime stone and in there you find the only lighthouse museum in South Africa and a restaurant where the same type of fish is freshly available that were centuries ago caught by the Khoikhoi with their cleverly constructed fish traps. The latter can be viewed in the museum.

Cape Agulhas National Park

This is one of the most recent developments and begins at the lighthouse. Apart from coastal fynbos, the wetlands of the Agulhas plain also form part of it. Further inland Mediterranean type of flora and fauna are to be found. So far there are few larger animals, but rare smaller ones abound, like the Platanna frog, and this windy and lonely coast is home to bird species like the Black Oyster Catcher and the Damara Tern.

Struisbaai

It is claimed that the "Bay of Ostriches" (Struisbaai) has the longest beach with white sand in the Southern Hemisphere. The little town is a perfect combination of pretty beach and picturesque fishing harbour. But fresh fish is only on offer at the fishmongers near the beach. "We are sliding into poverty!" groan the old fishermen who have been following their trade for generations. They feel severely disadvantaged by the new quota system. Catches in the coastal area have also diminished tremendously.

In Arniston/Waenhuiskrans, where other hardened fishermen have been plying their trade for more than 200 years, it is today the estate agents who haul in the big catches. But you can still pick up your fresh fish here and haggle about the price, until the fishermen become irritated. The picturesque houses in the part of the town known as Kassiesbaai have been restored in the traditional style of a Cape fishing village, and there is also a historic graveyard. In the vicinity are several rock caves that have been excavated by the sea, the largest of which has led to the common name of the town: Waenhuiskrans means wagon-shed cliff. The official name of "Arniston" stems from a ship that sank on the coast.

Good accommodation, both for preplanned and casual visits, can be found in Agulhas and Struisbaai. Water sports and angling are also on offer. It is an easy 230 km drive from Cape Town via Caledon (R316) or Swellendam.

Bontebok National Park

Many nature lovers like the small, 3 200 ha reserve because of its convenient position for a leisurely drive through the Garden Route with all its natural beauty, framed by the Langeberg and the Breede River. Originally this park was created in 1931 to save the endangered Bontebok, a typical antelope of the Cape Floral Kingdom. The surviving 17 antelope have increased to more than 3 000 and excess numbers are annually distributed all over the country. A core population of 300 animals remains in the Bontebok National Park. In addition to them there are now also Cape Mountain Zebra, Red Hartebeest, Grysbuck, Duiker and Steenbok that often hide in the riverine forest and in the low growing fynbos.

The more than 200 bird species include the rare Stanley's Bustard, Secretary Bird, Cape Francolin, Blue Crane, Black Korhaan and numerous inconspicuous small songbirds that are the delight of all bird lovers. Fish Eagle, Heron, Moorhen,

1. Typical homestead in the 200-year old restored Cassiesbaai Fishing Village in Arniston
2. Waenhuiskrans Cave is only accessible at low tide, when, according to lore, an ox wagon and a team of oxen can turn around inside the cave
3. The rare once endangered Bontebok is now protected in the Bontebok National Park near Swellendam

Egyptian Geese and darters frequent the riverbanks. All are mentioned on the list that is handed out on registration. It also gives details about the park and its historical background.

De Hoop Nature Reserve

This reserve, a scant 600 km², is administered by the province and half of it consists of marine protection area. The other half is made up of coastal fynbos with Bontebok and Mountain Zebra. Along the 13 km long coastal path Southern Right Whales may be observed between July and November. The Windhoek Grotto is the most important breeding place for bats in the Cape. About 300 000 bats live in

Mosselbay seascape

the caves and annually they catch approximately 100 tons of insects.

Whale Maternity Ward

Whales often come to St. Sebastian Bay to give birth to their calves. It can be reached from Swellendam via Malgas, where the country's last hand-operated car ferry shuttles back and forth on the Breede River. The R324 leads on to Witsand and St. Sebastian Bay. But watch out for the sand road! It is easier to stay on the N2 until just before Heidelberg and then turn right into the tarred R322 to St. Sebastian Bay.

Garden Route

Fantastic in spring and summer. From Mossel Bay onwards one reaches an area with impressive vegetation of the Cape Floral Kingdom. The view from the lighthouse and the cave that has been converted into an open-air museum on the highest peak of Cape St. Blaize is breathtaking. The lighthouse is also the starting point of the 13,5 km long Oystercatcher Trail that takes 3-5 days and leads through one of the most beautiful coastal stretches in the country.

Botlierskop Private Game Reserve

The 25 ha game park in the mountainous terrain near Mossel Bay was named after a rocky ledge where a navigational fire was lit as soon as a ship was nearing the harbour so that farmers of the surrounding area could make their way there with food and drink for sale, while the captain manoeuvred his sailing ship safely into the harbour.

Nowadays the game reserve with riverine forest, marshlands, Fynbos and grassland has become a haven for Black-faced Impala with wholly black coats. The present owner, Dr. Dirk Neethling, had found these antelope in the Waterberg Mountains. They have a recessive gene just like the White Lions of Timbavati. Since predators like Lion and Leopard perceive their prey in black and white the Black-faced Impala had no chance to reproduce on a reasonable scale, so Dr. Neethling bred them in order to preserve them for future generations. There are already more than a hundred in the reserve, living together with Rhinoceros, Lion, Buffalo, Giraffe, Eland, Zebra and Elephant. The latter are also available for riding safaris.

Wilderness National Park

Mountains, forests, lakes and wetlands with several

rivers winding through the area may not sound like African habitats, and the area in the heart of the Garden Route is, to be honest, focused mainly on stimulating family holidays. However, nature lovers do come into their own right with venues for bird watching and boating facilities as well as canoe trips through the area lasting up to three days.

Overnight accommodation for all tastes is available inside and outside the reserve. Inside the park there are two sites with rondavels (round huts), blockhouses and family cottages as well as a camping site for campers, caravans and tents along the banks of the Touw River.

It lies 415 km from Cape Town, 315 km from Port Elizabeth and 15 km from George.

Knysna National Lake Area

The landscape is awesome – the view over the Knysna Heads can be dramatic, especially at sunset or at high tide when the boats return to their moorings on the big lagoon. City life revolves around the 17 km² lagoon. Water sports are controlled by the department of nature conservation as some the 200 species of marine animals are endangered, e.g. the Sea Horse (*Hippocampus capensis*). The Heads, two sandstone cliffs, form the narrow entrance to the lagoon and to the old harbour from where in days gone by wood was shipped that came from the Outeniqua Mountains rising up in the background. Today the remaining woodland, including some very tall Yellowwood trees, is protected.

The countryside around the picturesque town is not a proper nature reserve, but is looked after by the National Parks Board nevertheless. Sandbanks and the salty marshes are home to a variety of marine life and the tiny Knysna Sea Horse is especially guarded.

The town is geared for tourism and there is plenty of accommodation in the vicinity. Sailing, fishing, boardsailing and even motor boats are permitted in some areas of the National Lake Area.

Distances: 500 km to Cape Town, 250 km to Port Elizabeth, 70 km to George where there is also an airport that links up with the main centres in South Africa.

Little Karoo

Oudtshoorn is the tourist centre of the Little Karoo and still an important breeding area for ostriches which led to the "feather boom" at the turn of the 20th century. Today meat and hides are of more importance. The well-known Cango Caves with impressive stalagmites and stalactites are not far from the town.

Swartberg Pass

This historical pass was constructed around 1885 by Thomas Bain and the narrow gravel road leading along hairpin bends with steep cliffs and surrounded by multi-coloured sandstone rocks still forms the bridge between the Little and the Great Karoo. The Swartberg Pass is considered to be the most spectacular mountain pass in Africa and compared to the famous Darjeeling Pass in Asia.

ECO HOTSPOT
Mischievous meerkats

The first rays of the sun enter the burrow system of the Ungulungu Clan in the Little Karoo. Soon the sun entices Rafiki, the dominant female of the group, to venture outside. She stands motionless on her two hind legs and attentively observes the visitors. While the clan starts to warm up, Grant McIlrath approaches with soothing sounds. He has been studying Suricates (Meerkats, Stokstertjies) for 12 years and is able to entertain ecotourists with surprising insights into their lives. With their cute faces, large eyes and pointed noses and playful ways they delight all visitors. Some young were born recently, and these little ones are growing up quickly. Their devoted helpers teach them all the tricks that a Suricate needs for survival. Scientists speak about the bidirectional – real learning – of Suricates, apparently the only proven example in the animal world.

They live mainly in the arid Kalahari, but McIlrath, who is known as the "Meerkat-Man" in nearby Oudtshoorn, found his clan in the Little Karoo at the foot of the Swartberg Range. He made them the main subject of his conservation and research project which he finances with the income from his Meerkat-tours and donations.

Now that the animals have warmed up a bit, they follow the matriarch on the morning hunt. Again and again she stands up and sniffs the soft morning breeze. The protruding nose has developed from the perky little nose of the suckling young into a Pinocchio-type organ that is the most important implement for the daily foraging.

With her highly developed sense of smell she localises the first morsel and quickly digs it out with her front paws and then leaves the squirming lizard to the young that followed her eagerly.

The visitors are enraptured while following the foraging excursion through the 4-5 km² hunting territory of the clan. The prey consists of all kinds of insects, spiders, termites and even birds, small snakes and rodents. Suricates stay in constant contact with each other through soft twittering sounds. The young instinctively stick to the most successful hunters that will selflessly give them even the most desired bits.

1. The Cango Caves with its stalactites and stalagmites are widely known as one of the most famous and biggest limestone caves around the world. They are situated near Oudtshoorn
2. Oudtshoorn, once known as the "feather capital" of the world, still produces leather and meat from the world's biggest bird
3. Swartberg Pass landscape
4. The Knysna Heads, two magnificent sandstone cliffs, guard the mouth of the lagoon. A lookout on the Eastern Head commands spectacular views of the lagoon and Knysna
5. The major parts of the Knysa Lake area will soon be incorporated in a new National Park

Eastern Cape

A great diversity of magnificent landscapes attracts many adventure and ecotourists and provides a variety of habitats. Among them is the wilderness of Baviaan's Kloof (gorge), the coastal areas of Cape St. Francis, Jeffrey's Bay and Port Elizabeth, the Wild Coast (pictured below at sunrise) along the erstwhile Transkei with innumerable picturesque coves and estuaries, the Little and Great Karoo, the Eastern Cape section of the Drakensberg Range as well as the 700 km coastal area between Tsitsikamma and the Wild Coast which is part of the Garden Route.

Tsitsikamma Marine National Park

The Tsitsikamma Marine National Park protects an 80 km narrow stretch along the coast with the last big natural indigenous forests and deep ravines as well as the coastal waters with a rich marine life. Tsitsikamma means "clear water" in the Khoi language. Near the road leading to the reserve stands the 800 year old "Big Tree", a giant Yellowwood tree. The indigenous forest is an ideal hide-away for the rare Knysna Lourie. Other forest birds are the Emerald Cuckoo, Narina Trogon, Knysna and Olive Woodpecker, Chorister Robin and Grey Cuckooshrike.

Baviaanskloof

An extensive wilderness, 120 km west of Port Elizabeth, that consists of rugged mountain terrain and forms part of the Cape Floral Kingdom. In the diverse biotopes Mountain Zebra, Leopard, Bush Pig, Cape Buffalo, Kudu, Bushbuck and other wild animals occur. Hiking trails lead into the mountain area with more than 1 000 plant species and offers game and bird watching, Mountain Biking excursions and roads for 4x4 vehicles. Overnight stays are available on simple camping sites in the wilderness or in mountain huts and chalets for self-caterers.

Van Stadens Wildflower Reserve

The 500 ha Wildflower Reserve lies 35 km west of Port Elizabeth on the N2 towards Cape Town. It preserves the indigenous flora (Lowland Fynbos and Coastal Forest) at the southern rim of the Cape Floral Kingdom. It is also a paradise for birds of the fynbos species that can be observed at leisure, among them the Cape Sugarbird, Orange-breasted Sunbird, Protea Canary, Red-necked Francolin as well as four other Sugarbird and six Canary species. In the ravines breed Jackal Buzzard, Gymnogene, Crowned Eagle, Lanner and Peregrine Falcon, Fish Eagle, Black Sparrowhawk and Booted Eagle. The coastal forests are inhabited by Sombre Bulbul, Olive Thrush, Terrestial Bulbul, Bluemantled Flycatcher and Paradise Flycatcher, Knysna Lourie, Cape Robin, Crowned Hornbill, Tambourine Dove and Cinnamon Dove and in the summer time the shy Narina Trogon may be heard, while down at the river the Half-collared Kingfisher (*Alcedo semitorquata*) is fishing.

There is a picnic area and a nursery that specialises in indigenous plants. Hiking trails and roads for jeeps are suitable for family outings. Cycling is permitted.

Port Elizabeth

The friendly port in Algoa Bay was founded in 1820 by British colonists. Sheltered beaches and the placid emerald green sea are family-friendly and invite swimmers, divers and sun worshippers. Water sports such as windsurfing, sailing, angling, surfing and snorkelling are also possible. Lifesavers are on duty on the official beaches during the summer season.

Otter Trail

The five-day Otter Trail is one of the most favoured hikes in South Africa. The hiking path leads along 42 km in the National Park's tidal zone along the steep coast through forests and flowering fynbos to caves and waterfalls and sites with breathtaking views of the Indian Ocean. Lagoons and coves tempt you to take a swim. Along the way one wades or swims through the Bloukrans River. Occasionally a Cape Clawless Otter crosses the path. Overnight accommodation in block houses with bunk beds, simple toilets and grill facilities with fire wood. Bookings have to be made up to a year in advance. The 60 km five-day Tsitsikamma Hiking Trail is also well worth the effort. It runs inland, parallel to the Otter Trail, through dense forest. The two trails may be combined.

Spekboom/Purslane Tree

The Spekboom is characteristic of the succulent thicket biome. These succulent trees or shrubs form impenetrable thickets in which the last elephants managed to hide until the thickets had to make way for orange groves. At some stage the excess fruit was fed to the grey hunks that became so addicted to it that they started to pinch oranges out of visitor's cars thereby damaging them, so that the orange-feeding had to be discontinued and the elephants weaned back onto the nourishing Spekboom that today supplies about 80 % of their food requirements.

1. & 3. & 5. The changing faces of the wild Tsitsikamma coast
2. Knysna Louries can be heard and watched in the coastal forest of the Tsitsikamma Marine National Park
4. Erica, prominent among the many flowering plants of the Tsitsikamma Forest

Bayworld

The excellent marine aquariums have daily demonstrations with dolphins, seals and penguins from local coastal waters. The performances of the dolphins may also be enjoyed from an underwater perspective. Sharks, stingrays and other fish endlessly swim around in the large tanks together with sea turtles. In the Snake Park demonstrations with South African poisonous snakes are presented, while in the Tropical House you enter an artificial jungle where indigenous birds and colourful exotic species abound.

Outings along Algoa Bay

Cape Recife Coastal Reserve

The 370 ha coastal resort on the southwestern corner of Algoa Bay offers prime conditions for snorkelling with its sandy beach and rocks. There is also a revered old lighthouse. The peninsula is a perfect place for bird watching since a lot of seabirds frequent it. In the winter time Roseate Tern and Antarctic Tern can be seen and in summer the Damara Tern, Jackass Penguin, Black Oystercatcher and other coastal bird species. The turn-off from Marine Drive is clearly signposted.

Tip: From the comfortable raised hide you can tick off within a few hours 50-70 of the 190 bird species that occur here.

Addo Elephant National Park

The Addo National Park, 70 km from Port Elisabeth, has been experiencing ongoing expansion and renewal for decades. The small sanctuary for the last Addo elephants has developed into a large reserve with a notable diversity of species. The "Big Five" were upgraded by the addition of the Southern Right Whale and the Great White Shark into the "Big Seven". Other attractions are Black Rhino, Cape Buffalo and a rare species of dung beetle. The Spekboom/Purslane Tree (*Portulacaria afra*) is the most important food source of the Addo Elephants.

During the day the elephants like to visit the water holes Domkrag and Hapoor. Domkrag (jack in English) was a huge Mountain Tortoise that used to crawl under high-wheeled cars and then jacked itself up. It came to a pitiful end in the burrow of an Aardvark. Its carapace can be seen in the Tourist Hall together with the enormous head of Hapoor (ear with a piece missing), the elephant that had his one ear pierced by hunters. He was one of the lucky seven that survived the killing in the Addo forest and which subsequently formed the ground stock of the new reserve.

Addo has been enlarged to 3 600 km² and now stretches from the arid Karoo to the Indian Ocean. Elephants have thereby returned to the borders of the Karoo after an absence of 150 years. In the central areas Lion and Spotted Hyena have been reintroduced. Wild Dog and Cheetah are destined to follow. In the southernmost parts some coastal area has been incorporated into the reserve, including Bird Island and the island of St. Croix with colonies of Cape Gannet and Jackass Penguins.

Apart from the traditional cottages of the National Park in different sizes there are also bush camps in the various habitats. Really nice are the guesthouses Hapoor and Domkrag with views over the floodlit water hole where Elephant and Rhino blink in the bright lights while Burchell's Zebra, Blue Wildebeest, Red Hartebeest and Eland bid each other "good night".

Camping and caravan sites are also available. Apart from shared ablution and kitchen facilities every site has electricity and a wooden table with seating. Overnight accommodation in luxury tents is also available. Those who want to enjoy Africa in five-star comfort can book at the private Gorah Elephant Camp.

Shamwari Game Reserve

The exclusive reserve lies near the Addo Elephant National Park. The large number of animals are distributed over 200 km² in five different eco-systems. For five years in a row Shamwari has been nominated as top "Conservation Company" of the world. Six individually spaced luxury lodges are meant to ensure the privacy of visitors.

Amakhala Private Game Reserve

Professionally restored ox wagons carry you back in time to the dangerous life of pioneers on the border areas of the Eastern Cape – at least in your dreams. They have been converted into cosy double bedrooms with bath en suite. Obviously, the colonists and Voortrekkers of bygone days did not enjoy such comforts, neither were they served traditional menus in thatched guesthouses. But one thing they had in common with present day visitors – breathtaking views across the plains where all kinds of wild life roamed, which they promptly decimated almost to extinction.

1. & 5. Addo Elephants and their troubled past are the biggest draw card of the Addo National Park

2–6. Typical Karoo Boer-Bean (2), Spotted Dikkop (3), the Greater Kudu (4) and the Addo Blood Flower (6) are also easily spotted

7. Buffalo at Addo Elephant National Park

Their descendants reintroduced the game and increased it through careful nurturing. That is why you are bound to take home some good photos when you go on game drives in the early morning or at dusk, provided you haven't fortified yourself too much at the sundowners with cheese and wine. You can also study the distinctive characters of Rhino, Elephant, Buffalo, Giraffe, Blue Wildebeest and Zebra. Experienced rangers detect rare and shy nocturnal animals like Caracal, Porcupine, Spring Hare and Cape Otter. Bird watching can be especially rewarding on a leisurely cruise down the Bushman's River.

Amakhala lies on the N2 between Port Elizabeth and Grahamstown.

Kariega Game Reserve

This private reserve of 5 000 ha of predominantly pristine wilderness lies only 14 km from the pretty beach of Kenton-on-Sea. Apart from the Big Five – Lion, Leopard, Elephant, Buffalo and Rhino – there are Hippos, Giraffes, Zebras, Wildebeest, Eland, Waterbuck and numerous other antelope as well as abundant bird life. Martial Eagle, Crowned Eagle and Fish Eagle breed here. Experienced rangers bring visitors as close as possible to animals and birds during game drives by day or at night.

Accommodation in luxurious lodges and environmentally friendly chalets in blockhouse style, some with own pool, all with views of the picturesque Kariega River.

East London

South Africa's smallest commercial harbour on the mouth of the navigable Buffalo River lies on the Indian Ocean with a coastal strip of great variety and kilometers of white beaches. There is not much of note in the city, but the East London Museum houses an example of the famous coelacanth. This primitive bony fish was caught in the ocean here in 1938; it was believed to have died out 50 million years ago. Recently specimens were found living in an undisclosed location in the ocean.

Wild Coast

South Africa's most beautiful coast with incredible potential for ecotourism has been termed the "most spectacular wilderness on earth". The homeland of the Xhosa stretches from the border with KZN via Port St. Johns in the direction of East London up to the mouth of the Kei River. A tarred road running near the coast will soon connect the far flung coastal villages between Durban and East London and further promote the development of ecologically important areas.

Hiking along the Wild Coast

Hiking trails connect the most spectacular parts of the coast between Port Edward and the Mtanvuna and Great Kei Rivers in

The beetle as gardener

Large black Dung Beetles, the size of Stag Beetles, assist in protecting fragile ecosystems. One specie is particularly numerous in the Addo Elephant National Park. Like gardeners they ensure the even and extensive distribution of natural fertiliser and simultaneously take care of the distribution of seeds that survive the coarse digestive system of elephants. They take elephant dung to form balls the size of golf balls, then roll these up to a distance of 50 m before burying them as nourishment for their offspring.

Cape Mountain Zebra

Only a few animals had survived when desperate measures were taken in 1937 to save them. Thanks to good preservation methods they quickly multiplied. Today the local population consists of more than 300 animals. Excess numbers are transferred to other suitable reserves. There is every reason to be proud of this achievement.

Mountain Zebra eat mainly grass and live in small family groups of 2-8 animals, led by a stallion. The surefooted animals have hooves that regrow quickly and are thereby able to regenerate from the great wear and tear on the rocky terrain. They are smaller than their cousins in the savannah and can be distinguished by their protruding dewlap, the reddish brown nose, the white belly with no stripes and a barred pattern on the rump.

1. A spectacular Wild Coast sunset
2. Basket Maker
3. Adventurous horse riding along the Atlantic Ocean
4. Hole-in-the-Wall
5-6. Evidence of prehistoric creatures at the East London
   Museum: Coelacanth (5), fossilised spiral shell of an
   Ammonite, an extinct marine mollusc (6)

the west. One route leads in six stages from the Mtanvuna River up to Port St. Johns (ca. 110 km) and further on via Coffee Bay to the famous rock formation Hole-in-the-Wall (ca. 170 km). River mouths and estuaries have to be crossed. One can pick individual stages or tackle the whole tour of more than 300 km in about 25 days.

Tips for drivers: Please drive with great care and lookout for the so-called "Big Five of the Transkei" – donkey, goat, pig, dog and cat.

Mkambati Nature Reserve

With 8 000 ha Mkambati is the biggest nature reserve on the Wild Coast. It stretches over 10 km along the beautiful rocky coastline, bordered by grasslands and cut across by three rivers with deep gorges and picturesque water falls. In the subtropical rainforests Sugarbirds swarm around flowering Strelitzias and the rare Pondoland Palm (*Jubaeopsis caffra*).

Where originally only Eland and Hartebeest occurred, Wildebeest, Blesbuck, Zebra and Gemsbuck (Oryx) from the Kalahari were also introduced. The very rare Samango Monkey, Rock Hyrax (Dassie) and Golden Mole also live here. Fascinating birds like Red-shouldered Widow, Yellow-throated Longclaw, Cape Parrot, Common Waxbill, Croaking Cisticola, Gurney's Sugarbird, Greater Double-collared Sunbird and the majestic Fish Eagle can be seen in forest and grassland. The rare Cape Vulture breeds in colonies along the Msikaba River. Among the many diverse trees are 34 species that only occur in the woodlands of Pondoland which has been ranked among the most important hotspots of species diversity.

With its crystal clear water the Mkambati River tempts you to take a dip on the way to the spectacular Horseshoe Falls. The flow of the river is interrupted by more water falls downstream, until the waters in a grand finale plunge down from the rocks into the sea. A path through the grassland unexpectedly offers a view into the breathtaking Msikaba Gorge with evergreen woods where the Trumpeter Hornbill utters his nasal call and the Rameron Pigeon coos enticingly. Wetland forests and the world of birds can be experienced from close-up during a canoe trip upstream.

The Mkambati Reserve can best be reached from Port Edward: Drive over the bridge on the R61 in the direction of Bizana and approximately 20 km after the town turn left, towards the Holy Cross Mission. The route is well signposted.

Accommodation: Lodge with 5 double rooms, swimming pool and sea view. The simple rondavels and cottages are self-catering. The Lagoon Lodge offers sociable accommodation for up to 20 people. You can also pitch a tent.

Karoo and Drakensberg Region

Camdeboo National Park

The small town of Graaff-Reinet is surrounded by a National Park (145 km²) that evolved from the Karoo Nature Reserve which was created in 1979 to preserve the original ecosystem. Spandau Kop,

Wetland forests

These have never been plentiful in the overwhelmingly arid South Africa, and now there are only small pockets left in the coastal area between Maputaland and the Wild Coast near Port Grosvenor. The rest have been drained, with no consideration for the valuable eco-system and converted into agricultural land. Up to that time accumulation and filtration of the water had prevented the bogging up of estuaries and coastal waters.

The areas that are permanently or temporarily submerged under water consist mainly of sandy, muddy soil, thickly encrusted with rotting plant material. They create the indispensable habitat for a unique and unusual world of plants. It is not particularly diverse and is dominated by trees including five fig tree species and two types of palms. Also growing here are *Ficus trichopoda, Barringtonia racemosa, Cassipourea gummiflua, Syzygium cordatum, Phoenix reclinata* and *Raphia australis* as well as climbers, epiphytes and *Hibiscus tiliaceus* bushes. The latter dominate the undergrowth where ferns and orchids grow. Surprisingly species that prefer a more temperate climate also occur here, such as *Podocarpus, Rapanea, Burchellia, Halleria, Ilex* and others.

Old Man's Beard

Mountain landscapes of the Eastern Cape:
Rock formation near Barkley Pass (1),
Karingmelkspruit (2) and Bastervoetpad (6)
between Ugie and Barkly Pass
3. & 4. Xhosa boys during circumcision
5. Xhosa woman adorned with traditional
    headdress

a hillock immediately northeast of the town is a typical Karoo mountain with erosion-resistant top, in stark contrast to the weathered rock pillars of the Valley of Desolation (14 km west of Graaff-Reinet), some of which are more than 100 m high. The reserve is situated at an altitude of 700-1500 m on the slopes of the Sneeuberg Range. In this impressive landscape with semi-desert characteristics live 43 types of mammal like Klipspringer, Mountain Zebra and Red Hartebeest in the higher altitudes and Kudu, Oryx, Steenbuck, Springbuck, Black Wildebeest, Blesbok and Cape Buffalo further down; 13 smaller predators such as Bat-eared Fox and Suricate also occur. They can be observed from the car or on short (or longer) hikes. There are picnic sites as well as an information centre. An enlargement to 5 200 km² is on the cards and this will merge Camdeboo with the Mountain Zebra National Park.

Mountain Zebra National Park

The 6 500 ha reserve lies in the mountainous area between arid Karoo and temperate grassland and is covered with extensive carpets of wild flowers in spring. Plants are mainly a mixture of low growing shrubs and grass. Some larger bushes and trees grow in the rugged valleys of the Bankberg Mountain (2 000m) and in the sparse riverine forests of the Wilgerboom River. Mountains and high plateaus afford sweeping views in all directions.

The Mountain Zebra Park is the protected home of the largest population of Mountain Zebra in the world. Good roads enable you to follow these rather shy animals and to spot them repeatedly. Observation of Cape Buffalo, Black Rhino, Eland, Black Wildebeest, Red Hartebeest and Springbuck made for diversity on the high plateaus. Mountain Reedbuck and Grey Rhebock prefer the higher lying slopes, whilst Kudu rather take to the lower lying green valleys and ravines. The only predator of note is the Caracal. A variety of birds are present like the Blue Crane and the rare Stanley's Bustard as well as Dusky Sunbird, Ostrich, Rock Kestrel, Cape Eagle Owl (several breeding pairs), Black Eagle, Black Harrier and Booted Eagle.

Guided hikes over short distances or lasting several days are on offer, as are game drives by night and excursions on horseback. Summers are hot, winter nights sometimes very cold with snow at higher altitudes. The average annual rainfall of 390 mm falls predominantly in early summer and winter.

Accommodation in eighteen 4-bed cottages; Doornhoek is a restored Victorian style farmhouse.

There is a well appointed caravan and tent site as well as a petrol station, restaurant and swimming pool. The reserve can be reached via the Middelburg-Graaff Reinet road. Another 12 km takes you to the picturesque Karoo town of Cradock.

Rhodes

The Victorian village lies in the northeastern part of the province on the border of Lesotho at the end of the Drakensberg Mountains. It is surrounded by mountains of up to 3 000 m and crystal clear rivers. The Bell River – a paradise for trout anglers – runs through the village. In 1997 Rhodes was declared a National Monument and the area surrounding it became a reserve. The landscape and the indigenous flora attract visitors from around the world into this high altitude region where Kniphofias, Ground Orchids and thousands of other wild flowers bloom.

There are some wonderful drives, e.g. to Naudesnek (30 km), one of the highest mountain passes in the country, or on the road along the border to the winter sports resort of Tiffindell (22 km). Really fit hikers can undertake the 3-5 day hike starting at Rhodes to the 3 000 m high Ben McDhui Mountain. Horse-riding and cycle tours are also available.

The tent sites have hot and cold water, but no electricity! More comfort is on offer in the Rhodes Hotel and a number of B&B's, including Rubicon, housed an old school building dating back to Sir Herbert Baker and built from sandstone. Farmhouses in the vicinity also offer overnight accommodation.

The once endangered Mountain Zebras found a safe home at the Mounta Zerbra National Park near Cradock

1-3. The versatile reserve (Moutain Zebra National Park) is home to
many different species, among them: Bush Rat (1), Leopard Tortoise
(*Geochelone pardalis*)(2) and a herd of Mountain Zebra (3)
4. Camdeboo National Park: Valley of Desolation
5. Eastern Cape Drakensberg foothills near Elliot: more and more visitors
discover the extraordinary shapes and hues of peaks and buttresses

KwaZulu-Natal

Durban, Africa's biggest and most important harbour is a good starting point for travels through Zululand, into the Drakensberg Mountains – pictured below (Amphitheater) – and along the coast.

uShaka Marine World

The huge aquarium complex, complete with a ship wreck, is inhabited by an abundance of marine creatures that live along the coast of Zululand. You can see marine turtles like the loggerhead turtle that lays its eggs on the coast as well as sharks and stingray and numerous indigenous fish species. The dolphinarium is especially geared to the large Bottlenosed Dolphin that frequent this coastline.

Meeting up with nature in Durban

The metropolis has more than 50 nature reserves, parks and public gardens of which the municipal Botanical Garden in Lower Berea – the oldest botanical garden in Africa (1849) – is famous for its collection of rare cycads, orchids and palms as well as trees from all over the world. The Hawaan Forest has rare indigenous trees and is the last relic of the coastal forest of the region, while the Beachwood Mangroves Nature Reserve on the mouth of the Umgeni protects the only mangrove swamp near a city. The Umgeni River Bird Park is one of the biggest and best in the world due to its picturesque setting and the diversity of indigenous and exotic birds in walk-through aviaries. Every day South African raptors display their skills in flight. In the Fitzsimmon's Snake Park snake phobias can be overcome by watching the most important poisonous snakes of Africa and other reptiles up close. Saturdays is feeding time.

Zululand

After crossing the Thukela – 110 km beyond Durban – you enter the world of the Zulu and the most magnificent game and nature reserves of Southern Africa. The first real town you reach is Eshowe that used to be a holiday home of Zulu kings and is surrounded by sugar cane and the beautiful Dlinza Forest. It attracts bird lovers from around the world since a wooden walkway in the treetops was erected.

Hluhluwe-Imfolozi Park

Sunsets over the Imfolozi River – silence, solitude in pristine nature, wild animals around the next turn being the only "stress factor" – the tropical home of the rhinos in the game parks of Zululand is the highlight of any holiday in Africa. The 960 km² Hluhluwe-Imfolozi Park, Africa's oldest game reserve (1895), can hardly be surpassed as far as biological diversity is concerned. It became world-famous through the "Save the Rhino" campaign to ensure the survival of the remaining South African rhinos. Today more than 2 500 White Rhino and 500 Black Rhino are again living here. More than 4 000 have been relocated in the wilds. A similar success story was the reintroduction of elephants from the Kruger National Park.

Observation points in areas with traffic much game are an additional attraction during the winter. Every day a real kaleidoscope of African wild life is enacted before your eyes. Game reserves in Zululand are home to a great number of wild

Birds of prey fly over a thousand hills

The spectacular flying skills of South African raptors are demonstrated by bird expert Shannon over the Valley of a Thousand Hills. Her meticulously prepared demonstrations are performed solely by birds than can not be rehabilitated into nature and are based on the uniqueness of a bird's natural flight technique. It takes concentration to observe the dedicated hunt of a sparrow hawk or the silent flight of an owl, or to take pictures of a falcon in swift flight bearing down on his prey. After the demonstration one can take a close-up look at the great variety of birds and have one's picture taken while posing as a "falconer".

Some types of animal and plant species in KZN	Qty.
Land mammals	165
Marine mammals	28
Bird species	693
Snakes	78
Reptiles	75
Freshwater fish	79
Butterflies	382
Trees	708
Proteas	17

Impressions of the varied Garden Province:
1. Mighty Thukela Falls
2. Valley of a Thousand Hills
3. Loggerhead Turtle (*Caretta caretta*)
4. Bearded Vulture at Vulture Restaurant Giant's Castle
5. Zululand White Rhino with calf
6. & 7. uShaka Marine World, one of the biggest marine aquaria systems in the southern hemisphere offers insights into the open ocean, rocky reefs, coral cardens and the deep zone

animals. Apart from White and Black Rhino, other mammals are also plentiful: Bushbuck 750, Duiker 500, Elephant 500+, Hippo 15, Cheetah 40, Giraffe 800, Wild Dog 25, Impala 23 600, Buffalo 3 000-3 500, Kudu 1 400, Leopard 200, Lion 100, Red Duiker 100, Steenbuck 100, Burchell's Zebra 3 120, Blue Wildebeest 2 035, Nyala 8 100, Spotted Hyena 500, Warthog 4 000, Waterbuck 800.

With more than 400 species – more than in the whole of Europe – the bird life in Zululand is exceptionally rich. Four of the seven vulture species occurring in Southern Africa, are present here: Cape Vulture, White-backed Vulture, Lappetfaced Vulture and White-headed Vulture. Cape Vultures nest on the cliffs of the Lebombo Mountains to the north. The most common vulture, the White-backed Vulture, nests predominantly in riverine forests on rivers and streams in Sycamore and Acacia trees. The Lappetfaced Vulture (*Torgos tracheliotus*) is South Africa's biggest vulture species, building their huge platform nests in the crowns of large trees in the open bushveld, preferring Knob-thorn and Black Monkey Thorn. The Red-throated Wryneck lives in the Mpila Camp, where guests are woken in the mornings by the "toktoktok" of Rudd's Apalis and the noisy chattering of francolin and guineafowl.

European migrants like to spend the winter in Zululand. At the beginning of the rainy season Black (Yellow-billed) Kite swoop down on the termites swarming in their thousands. From January to March White Storks live in the open grasslands, some birds even stay on during the winter. Their numbers are dwindling due to encroaching bush; this also leads to the reduction of the European Bee-Eater that is present between October and March. The European Nightjar can be heard between December and March, and from October to April the European Swallow is the most common swallow around.

Summers are hot and humid; temperatures often rise to above 35 °C, especially in the valleys. Heavy thunderstorms don't always bring the desired rain and frequently ignite dangerous bush fires. All reserves in Zululand are open throughout the year, but the best times for game watching are during the dry winter months between May and October when the animals come to the watering holes.

NOTE: Malaria prophylactics are recommended for the entire region, especially in summer. Grasslands are known for bilharzia and ticks. Make use of Vaseline or insect repellent (see Ecoadviser).

Hiking in the wild
Hikes lasting several days through 25 000 ha of unmarked, pristine wilderness in Imfolozi have been on offer since the middle of last century and have to be booked months in advance. You are virtually guaranteed to meet rhinos. The "trail record" lies at 112. But it is usually easier to take pictures of animals from the window of a car. The armed rangers that accompany the groups are very concerned about keeping a safe distance. Their knowledge of animals and plants in Imfolozi ensures that you meet up with birds, insects and other small animals that you would never have spotted on your own. It is wonderful to experience the soothing solitude of the wilderness and listen to stories like the one about the lizard (*Mabuya quinquetaeniata*) of which the Zulu say that it eats the lightning and this enables it to be so quick.

Learning about nature
"Auto-trails" and "Self-guided trails" are a bit like courses in nature study. One can undertake short excursions without a guide (at your own risk) to observation points and observe nature close-up. This enables you to take creative photos of the scenery, flowers, etc. The "Auto-trail" brings the motorised visitor to ecologically significant parts of the reserve. Interesting stops are clearly marked and explained in detail. Night drives with experienced guides deepen your knowledge of nocturnal animals. From the high seats you can observe Leopard, Hyena, Blue Wildebeest, White-tailed Mongoose, Aardvark and owls. Other animals are also caught by the beam of the headlights. Game drives at night are very popular, so it is advisable to book early.

Lammergeier Hide at Giant's Castle Game Re

View from inside the hide, in big demand by watchers from around the world

Lammergeier (Bearded Vulture) leaving its lai

1. Warthogs at Mkuze
2. Wild Dog at Mfolozi-Hluhluwe
3. Giraffe with calf
4. Black rhino
5. Butterfly on foothpath, sucking moisture from baboon droppings

Lammergeier Hide

The well-camouflaged Lammergeier hide on a spur in the central Berg offers excellent raptor viewing from May to September. Black Eagle, Cape Vulture, Jackal Buzzard and Lanner Falcon as well as baboons are regulars. The highlight of any visit is the sudden arrival of one or two Bearded Vultures (Lammergeiers), attracted by bones laid out by rangers on top of the cliff in front of the hide. Photographers from all over the world queue up for a chance to photograph such rarities close up. To share this wonderful experience, book as early as possible as the hide is often fully booked up to a year ahead.

A comprehensive bird list of the area includes more than 170 species, including raptors such as Bearded Vulture, Cape Vulture, Black Eagle and jackal Buzzard.

Bush hikes started in 1958 in Imfolozi and St. Lucia; today they are offered in all the larger reserves. Participants walk, ride on horseback or go by canoe. In Zululand wilderness hikes take place between March and October. During the hot season bush hikes are undertaken from base camps. Experienced rangers explain the environment and the animal world during half-day excursions. Night drives especially need to be booked ahead of time at the reception office.

Huts and Lodges

The modern, rustic, elegant Hilltop Camp lies in the Hluhluwe Block on the edge of a wooded slope. Even during the hot and humid summer the veranda of the restaurant catches a cooling breeze. Accommodation in the tourist camps is in simple, thatched huts or modern lodges. European visitors consider the bush lodges ideal, because they are positioned far from the day-to-day hustle and bustle, secluded in an attractive environment where guests can be among themselves with their own cook and personal ranger.

Greater St. Lucia/iSimangaliso Wetland Park

The town of St. Lucia is the headquarter of a conglomerate of highly diverse reserves with six different ecosystems and an impressive fauna and flora that has been declared a World Heritage Site. The largest estuary and coastal reserve in Africa is a wetland of high international ranking. Two species of marine turtle lay their eggs here. There are hippos and crocodiles and numerous antelope, as well as rare dune forests, 12 species of heron, many water birds and frog species and also coral reefs. Since seawater and fresh water mingle in this huge lake it presents exceptionally differentiated and nutritious foods and is therefore an ideal habitat for seabirds and waders. Lake St. Lucia is an important spawning site for many fish species. The varying landscape surrounding it supports many organisms.

The coastline of St. Lucia and further north up to the border with Mozambique is the largest marine reserve of Africa, reaching 5,6 km into the deep blue sea of the Indian Ocean and warmed by the Agulhas Current; it contains reefs and soft coral (the most southerly coral reefs in the world). The latter developed about 80 000 years ago and are the habitat of a multitude of marine invertebrates and colourful fish. The endless sandy beaches are only broken by the odd river mouth and are to some extent still quite pristine.

Hippos, crocs (Crocodile Centre) and birds

Hippopotamus (700-800) and Crocodiles (1 500) are among the most numerous in southern Africa and are very accessible. The Nile Monitor is very prevalent here – it likes crocodile eggs. Several breeding pairs of the Fish Eagle give the area an African feeling. Of special interest are also the bird species that use the evergreen dune forest as habitat. Among these are the Knysna Lourie, Rudd's Apalis, Brown Robin, Green Coucal, Green Twinspot and Grey Waxbill. About a dozen heron species live around the lakes. Both flamingo species arrive in their thousands during the breeding season. 1 000 or more pairs of Great White Pelican

South Africa's world-famous Wetland Park and biggest natural inland lake

Lake St. Lucia is 28 km wide, 40 km long and approximately 1 m deep. Due to a 20 km long canal in the inter-tidal zone it is directly connected to the ocean. The funnel-shaped mouth becomes periodically clogged up with alluvial soil and mud so that the salinity fluctuates greatly and as a result of evaporation it can be up to three times as strong as seawater. Inland, Lake St. Lucia is fed by the Imfolozi, the Mkuze, the Hluhluwe and other rivers that have greatly diminished as a result of the extensive plantations of sugar cane, so that the natural water supply to Lake St. Lucia sometimes dries up these days

Hippos under pressure

South Africa's hippopotamus populations are carefully nurtured and reproduce well. But for more than a decade the numbers in over half of the other African reserves have been dwindling and the situation is therefore disturbing, even serious. The hippos are especially endangered by being illegally hunted for their meat and their huge teeth that are sought after as ivory since the trade with elephant tusks has been prohibited. In the Democratic Republic of Congo only a scant 5 % of the original population have survived the ongoing insurrections. Added to this is the pressure that is exerted on the few remaining wetlands. The increasing water consumption of the growing human population brings the needs of the clumsy giants more and more into direct conflict with that of people. All the more reason for South African conservationists to carry on their nurturing.

A look at the Wetlands and some of its creatures:
1. Africa's largest lizzards, the Nile Monitor (*Varanus niloticus*) stays close to water where he hunts part of his food. He can stay under water for up to one hour
2. South Africa's only breeding colony of Pink-beacked Pelicans, Nsumo Pan, Mkhuze
3. Wetlands in Drakensberg foothills where the threatened Wattled Crane breeds
4. Crocworld; 5. Spider during morning dew

flock together in breeding colonies on inaccessible small islands. There you can also find the majority (up to 290 pairs) of the approximately 400 pairs of Caspian Terns breeding in southern Africa. Yellow-billed Storks, Woolly-necked Storks and Saddle-billed Storks are often spotted, as are Ruffs, Turnstones and Plovers, as well as Swifts, Sandwich and White-winged Tern and more.

Mkhuze Game Park

The diversity of discernible habitats with a multitude of bird life is impressive. We find such rarities as Pink-throated Twinspot, Rudd's Apalis and African Broadbill as well as the Lesser Black-winged Plover. On guided walks with a ranger one can see Pel's Fishing-Owl in the riverine forest and in the vicinity of the Nsumo Pan and in summertime spot several bee-eater species in their burrows in riverbanks. Along the Nsumo Pan you can be almost sure to come across Yellow-billed, Saddle-billed and Open-billed Stork, African Spoonbill and up to ten species of heron. Also look out for the Woodland Kingfisher and White and Pink-backed Pelicans.

This reserve (340 km²) is a special trip for serious bird lovers, because here the tropical and the temperate zones overlap and therefore species of both the tropical north as well as the temperate south can live here. Biotopes in Mkhuze profit from this versatility that includes several types of forest, dense bushveld and thorn savannah, lush evergreen subtropical shrubland, dry woodlands with sandy soil, riverine forest and flood plains, open grasslands and coastal plains with rich, marshy, alluvial soil as well as prehistoric coastal dunes. The original flora is complex and dynamic, and in itself worth a visit.

Wild figs, for instance, are important trees in Africa; among them the Sycamore that grows to a height of 25 m takes a special place as source of food and remedies. These huge Sycamores grow in rich alluvial soil that is very valuable for agriculture. For this reason, the 1 400 ha fig forest in Mkhuze is one of the last untouched areas in Africa. The tasty wild figs grow in large clusters and ripen at different times on the various trees. So the larder remains well stocked for the fruit eating mammals and birds. The Green Pigeon also enjoys the ripe fruit that is surrounded by fruit flies, which in turn attract Fantailed Flycatchers and other insect eaters.

You feel as if being transposed to a different world. The sweet musty smell of figs under the spreading canopies is intoxicating and the strange barking and screeching of baboons cuts through the air – they can't seem to stop fighting in spite of the glut. This is interspersed with the off-key trumpeting of the Trumpeter Hornbill. Fishing Owl, Southern Banded Snake Eagle, Green Coucal and Broad-billed Roller that find shelter and nesting sites in the Sycamores.

Nsumo Pan

The pan is situated behind a row of old coastal dunes. The large hide stands next to the picnic site from where one can also watch birds and hippos. The hippos grunt and yawn in the murky water usually just beyond the reach of the camera. Open-billed Stork fly past and the occasional Squaco Heron hovers, ready to strike its prey. In July hundreds of Spur-winged Goose meet for moulting.

WARNING:
Always treat hippos with great respect! They can move much faster than you might imagine (30 km/h) and are considered Africa's most dangerous animal. In the case of an unexpected meeting one should stand quite still and then carefully retreat. When you perceive the animal to be aggressive, you must move fast - either climb a tree or stand behind its trunk. A shrub does not offer sufficient protection! Luckily hippos usually flee from humans, especially at night, provided their way to the water is not cut off.

Beautiful flower of the Sickle Bush (*Dichrostac cinerea*)

First sign of spring in Zululand: Blood Lily (*Scadoxus puniceus*)

Zuland's Nature and Game Reserves rank as South Africa's most diverse wildlife sanctuaries:

1. & 4. Highly poisonous Gaboon Adder, very well camouflaged, up-close (4) the adder looks extremely frighteningly
2. Black Eagle hunt by surprise attack, often in pairs
3. Rhino calf chasing adult baboon, Mkhuze Game Reserve
5. Cheetah, looking for prey, Mfolozi, Game Reserve
6. Trunk of a mighty Sycamore. Rangers rounding a huge Sycamore on their way to inspect the famous Mkhuze Fig Tree Forest
7. Blue Wildebeest and many other species are watched with ease from the fantastic hide at Kumasinga water hole in Mkhuze

On the opposite side of the pan large breeding colonies of Pink-backed Pelican sit in the high Fever trees.

Ndumo Game Park

This 10 000 ha game park and nature reserve protects an important wetland in southeastern Zululand. Tropical and subtropical habitats overlap and sustain an exceptionally rich bird life. Thickets with large fig trees and fever trees grow around the ponds and clay pans where a sizeable number of Hippopotamus and Nile Crocodile dwell. Nyala, Bushbuck and Black and White Rhino are well represented. One can travel by car on your own, or hike under the leadership of a ranger. Trails through the wetlands with expert guidance are on offer. Accommodation is in thatched cottages that have to be booked well in advance. Inhabitants of the surrounding area run a camping and caravan park. The summers are very hot and humid.

Maputaland's dream coast

The 100 km long, pristine coastline of northern KZN has magnificent sandy beaches, surrounded by dune forests. Sodwana, Rocktail and Kosi Bay offer a very diverse marine habitat. One can dive and snorkel all year among the coral reefs and in blue lagoons. From October to February the Loggerhead Turtles and the Leatherback Turtles seek out the warm dunes at Kosi Bay and Sodwana to lay their eggs. Camping or accommodation in lodges is available in various places.

Ithala Nature Reserve

In the mountains of northern KZN, outside the subtropical belt, lies this 30 000 ha reserve that has changed exhausted farmland into a blooming nature reserve. The Ntshondwe Tourist Camp is one of the most magnificent and modern in southern Africa. There's a pond in front of the veranda of the restaurant, which is frequently visited by the reintroduced big game (unless it happens to have dried up). Elephants, Rhino, Sassaby, Red Hartebeest and Nyala are often to be seen. Also birds can be observed very well. The fantastically positioned swimming pool is a refreshing haven, especially on hot summer days.

Apart from cottages and camping sites three rustic bush camps, Mhlangeni, Mbizo and Thalu, offer genuine African atmosphere in secluded solitude. Two are situated on the rocky riverbed of the Pongola. Angling and swimming are permitted, and safe. Night drives in an open vehicle afford close-ups of nocturnal animals and the star-studded night sky of Africa. Three-day-hikes right through the heart of the wilderness bring a chance to switch off and dream around the nightly campfire.

South Coast of Natal

The coastal area between Port Edward on the Umthamvuna and Amanzimtoti near Durban is especially popular because of the annual Sardine run that begins on the Wild Coast and ends at Amanzimtoti. Tightly packed shoals of sardine,

Bottlenose Dolphins swim in front of a skiboat

The South Coast's attractive laid-back style:

1. Uvongo Beach sports Blue Flagg status
2. The annual Sardine run is a big attraction, especially for scuba diver
3. A fabulous sun rises behind a stand of Natal Strelitzias/Natal wild Banana (*Strelitzia nicolai*), common in costal dune vegetation and evergreen coastal forests
4. Surffishing
5. Catching the big ones from ski boats
6. Further inland monotonous sugar plantations abound
7. Explore one of of many South Coast lagoons

15 km long, 3 km wide and up to 40 m deep, move – often close to the shore – and attract sharks, dolphins, other predatory fish and seabirds that follow the easy prey in a frenzy. The spectacle can be observed either from the beach or on a special diving safari.

Oribi Gorge Nature Reserve

The Umzimkulwana River has eaten its way through massive layers of sand stone and thereby created a 27 km long ravine, the Oribi Gorge. The impressive landscapes are partially protected in a small nature reserve and are accessible by clearly signposted hiking trails. This is the best place for bird watching on the south coast of KZN (270 species). Various antelope also occur. The rare Oribi, however, is no longer present. Accommodation is available in cottages and huts. It can be reached from Port Shepstone in half an hour's drive.

Umtamvuna Nature Reserve

The 3 257 ha reserve protects one of the last colonies of Cape Vulture in the province. They nest on the sheer cliffs of the river that constitutes the border between KZN and the Wild coast. Wooded ravines, lots of trees and a total of 1 300 plant species, among them 25 orchids, complete the picture. On beautiful hiking trails, offering fantastic views, one sometimes sees Peregrine Falcon, Crowned Eagle and Gurney's Sugarbird, as well as Duiker and Bushbuck.

Mountains like the back of a dragon

In the KZN Drakensberg Mountains the South African Escarpment reaches its highest peaks of more than 3 000 m. The jagged peaks reminded the Trekboers of the back of a dragon. The Zulu called them uKhahlamba, the "Barrier of Spears". The new name "uKhahlamba-Drakensberg Park" does justice to both. It was introduced when the UNESCO Natural- and Cultural Heritage Award was granted. The area stretches over more than 300 km from north to south and comprises more than 2 400 km² of impressive landscapes and wilderness. Here the unique fauna and flora is protected together with the cultural heritage of the San (Bushmen).

Breathtaking sheer cliffs that glow in the morning light like Alpine panorama and at the foot of the mountains the marvellous pristine wilderness form part of the "face of the earth like the creator

had intended it" as Henry Miller described such grandiose landscapes. In this country they have to date hardly been recognised by poets, nobody made a song about them; but ecotourists and other visitors enjoy the deep silence of nature, occasionally broken by rolling thunder, and in summer the 2 000 species of wild flowers and groves of proteas.

In the secluded humid ravine where the veldfires don't reach, there still grow natural forests of colossal, centuries old Yellowwood trees. They are the last survivors after the devastating attack on natural resources in the early colonial period, when men – standing in trenches – sawed up the huge trunks of the fallen giants to produce beams and planks. In old farmhouses they can still be seen as roof beams and floors, and furniture made from Yellowwood continues to be highly prized.

Northern Drakensberg area

From the 4 km long rock face of the Amphitheatre in the Royal Natal National Park (88 km²) the Thukela River falls in several stages over 614 m down vertically, squeezes through the Thukela Gorge and then continues it's way, gurgling and foaming, towards the Indian Ocean .

Royal Natal National Park

From the camping site on the Mahai River and from the cottages of the Thendele Camp hiking trails lead to the narrow Thukela Gorge. When it is shallow one can wade across the rocky tunnel. At its end lies a rock pool with a small waterfall. A further 28 routes of varying degrees of difficult terrain lead to waterfalls in the reserve, rock paintings, or to the cascades, where in 1947 Queen Elizabeth II as a young girl cooled her feet. That is the origin of the "Royal" in the name of the reserve and of the short footpath called "Queen's Causeway". The ascent to Policeman's Helmet, a sandstone formation, is also breathtaking. The Gudu Falls and the Gudu Bush can be reached within an hour from Thendele or from the camping site. The paths and trails are well signposted.

Ascent to the plateau

The longest and most difficult mountain hike leads behind the escarpment to Mont-aux-Sources (3 282 m). Not only the Thukela has its origin here, but also the Orange River. The ascent begins at the Mahai Camp and takes about 9-10 hours (22,5 km) Along the way two chain ladders ascending the vertical rock face have to be braved. It is permitted

1. Oribi Gorge, a 24 km ravine, carved out by the Umzimkulwana River
2. The famous Cascades, princely landmark of Royal Natal National Park
3. Basket weavers show their skills, Champagne Valley
4. Cathedral Peak range with Didima Camp in foreground
5. Rocky pools are filled during the rainy saison and a rich life develops here for a short period
6. Cathkin Peak range, one of the best-known landmarks of the Berg. The nearby Didima Gorge shelters one of the richest clusters of San Rock Art
7. Basket weaver preparing grass for weaving baskets

to tent on the plateau, but pilfering by Basotho herdsmen does occur.

Tip: Before setting out you must definitely make an entry in the Mountain Register at the visitor's centre.

The Mahai campsite in the lower part of the park is one of the prettiest in the country. Thendele Camp has such a magnificent setting that in high season even the most expensive cottages need to be allocated by drawing lots. There are also several hotels in the surrounding area. Bathing in the rivers is permitted virtually everywhere. It is also possible to undertake half-day rides on horseback into the adjoining areas.

Cathedral Peak

In this region the latest and most luxurious camp in the KZN Wildlife is positioned. It is Didima and has a breathtaking view of the Cathedral Range. Adjoining it is a world class cultural centre of San art. Fascinating hiking trails start nearby and a path for mountain bikers has been cleared on the upper end of Mike's Pass. Highly recommended is the not too difficult trail to Rainbow Gorge that is only 10 km both ways. The path, along the eNdumeni River, leads through lush mountain forest with impressive Yellowwood trees and passes crystal clear mountain streams and rapids. Centrepiece is a huge rock that is jammed between the walls of rock faces in the narrow gorge.

Central region of Drakensberg Mountains

This mountain range commences with the delightful Champagne Valley, at the top end of which lies the Monk's Cowl Mountain Reserve. In between, exclusive hotels with golf courses have sprung up.

Giant's Castle Game Reserve

The game park in the heart of the Drakensberg Mountains has been created to preserve the Eland antelope. Today it is famous for its marvellous hiking trails, rock paintings that can be easily reached on foot and also for the excellent, modern – yet blending in with the environment – chalets, lodges and mountain huts. The world-famous Lammergeier Hide is fantastic. During winter one can observe here at close range the rare Bearded Vulture, as well as Cape Vulture, Black Eagle, Jackal Buzzard and other inhabitants of the mountains that have been lured with meat. This is also enjoyed by baboons. Open from 1 May to 30 September. Bookings are accepted from November of the preceding year.

From the wide sun terrace one can also watch for Lammergeier (Bearded Vulture), while listening to the Bushman River roaring in the valley. Upstream, the rock with a sandstone overhang that is marked by smoke is visible; it was once the dwelling of a San clan and today it is a museum that exactly replicates their way of life, that was in harmony with nature.

Landmarks of the Central Berg: 1. Giant's Castle 2. Cathedral Peak and Bell 3. Aerial view of Centr Berg, 4. Top of Cathedral Peak 5. Champagne Ca range 6. Berg fires are laid selectively towards th end of winter

1. Christmas Bells (*Sandusonia aurantiaca*) in full blossom during summer time
2. Devil's Tooth
3. Stand of *Agapanthus campanulatus* sp. blooms in 1 800-2 350 m height during Jan/Feb, mainly in the Northern Berg
4. Cosmos fields abound in the Mnweni area between Royal Natal and Cathedral during late autumn
5. Flap-neck Chameleon (*Chamaeleo dilepsis*) photographed in the Thukela riverbed, Amphitheatre in background

Kamberg Nature Reserve

A short drive on a tarred road brings you from the village of Rosetta to the Kamberg Nature Reserve with fascinating rock paintings, among them the one known as "Rosetta Stone", also known as the Stone of the Wise.

Southern Drakensberg region

The Cobham Mountain reserve, approximately 12 km from Himeville, is appreciated by campers that don't set a great store on comfort. An old farmhouse with double bunks and log fire serves as halfway house for participants of hikes that last several days and lead along the contour path. Shorter hikes with overnight stays in Bushmen's caves are also possible.

In the marshy area near Himeville lives the large Wattled Crane that is endangered by the draining of the wetlands. Blue Crane and Crowned Crane are also quite common in this area. Around Christmas time the Crowned Crane gets company from the European White Stork that spends the northern winter in large numbers on the grazing areas on the slopes.

Sani Pass

An adventure trail has evolved from the mule track where donkeys and tough Basuto Ponies carried cornmeal and people across the Sani Pass (2 895 m) into the barren highlands of Lesotho to the remote district of Mokhotlong. The road is also used by trucks and at the moment still poses a challenge for four-by-fours, but a tarred mountain road is on the cards that will ring in the end of an era. At present the most high-lying watering hole in Africa – at the top of the Sani Pass, opposite the border post of Lesotho – is still an important halfway stop. On foot it takes about two and a half hours from the South African border post at the bottom of the pass up to the border with Lesotho. It can be done the easier way by booking a guided day tour with a 4x4.

Trekking on horseback

The rugged highland of Lesotho can also be explored on horseback. Horses are part of everyday life of the Basotho and in some areas they still constitute the only means of transport, although there are hardly any of the surefooted, hardy little Basuto ponies left. You can rent horses privately on the Sani Pass or book a "Horse Trail" in Underberg according to your own wishes.

Red-hot Poker (*Kniphofia caulescens*) in bloom during Christmas time at the foot of Sani Pass

1. Multi-coloured, highly agile Appaloosa horses are used by a mountain guide to take tourists on a trail through the Northern Berg

2. Amphitheatre with Thukela River – Royal Natal National Park

3. Wattled Crane raised in captivity by Enzemvelo rangers

4. Blesbok battling with deep snow at Himeville Nature Reserve

5. Natal Calendabra Flower (*Brunswigia natalensis*)

6. Policeman's Helmet, a mighty sandstone rock, landmark of the Royal Natal National Park

7. Access road to Sanitop, will be tarred in the near future.

Mpumalanga

This province offers breathtaking landscapes and a vast variety of animals and plants – from the Blyde River Canyon (pictured below) to the Kruger National Park.

Nelspruit

When the railway line reached the Crocodile River in 1892 it marked a new era for the malaria infested Lowveld as the station that was built on Nel's farm grew into a village, a town and finally a city, now the capital of Mpumalanga. During December and January it is aflame with the brilliant scarlet and orange blossoms of the African Flame trees.

Lowveld National Botanical Garden

This pleasant garden is laid out on both sides of the Crocodile River, where it makes a narrow ford that cuts deep into the granite rock and then crashes down as a waterfall before it joins the Nel River. About 600 indigenous plants grow in the garden and form a natural wood just like the mountain forests of the Drakensberg range. An additional 2 000 other plant species and 650 indigenous trees were grown. A unique plant collection presents the rapidly disappearing tropical rain forests of Central and West Africa.

All South African species of cycads grow in the garden – it is the best collection of its type in the whole country – and it also boasts the largest cycad collection in the world.

Several hiking trails lead through the various parts of this diverse and extensive garden; the highlight is undoubtedly the African Rainforest.

Barberton Walks and Trails

Fortuna Mine: The hiking trail of 2 km starts at Lone Tree Hill and leads past a copse where more than 80 tree species grow. The trail ends at an old tunnel that used to be used for transporting gold. A flashlight is a must for this excursion. Rose's Creek: This is a leisurely walk of approximately 1,5 km with a picnic site at the end. Another picturesque hiking trail leads to the ghost town of Eureka City and on to the Pioneer Reef and Agnes Mine that boasts a waterfall.

4x4's and quad bikes are organised by Rassie Schoeman: Forget the gold – around Baberton other "nuggets" can be found: Quad bike trips are Rassie's speciality. They take you through the 14-arm river, tree plantations and grassland up to mountain peaks and floral attractions. In the Blue Swallow Nature Reserve that lies in the vicinity efforts are under way to save this endangered swallow from extinction.

Barberton Nature Reserve

Here various types of protea grow, including African White Sugar-bush (*Protea gaguedi*), Clusterhead Sugarbush (*Protea welwitschii*) (hybrid), Common Sugarbush (*Protea caffra*) as well as the Broadleaved Beech and the Transvaal Beech.

Songimvelo Game Park

The 49 000 ha provincial game park lies hidden in the folds of the ancient Barberton Mountains where visitors walk on rocks that are several billion years old. Archaeological sites point to habitation as early as 400 B.C. Misty highlands, sheltered valleys and wooded ravines between grassy plains and mountains and the broad band of the Komati River shelter a highly diverse wildlife. Herds of Buffao,

The Olifants River Cycad belongs to the comple[ ] collection of South African cycads, growing in t[ ] famous Lowveld National Botanical Garden

"Swallow Blues"

1. Jock of the Bushveld statue in Barberton
2. Barberton Daisy (*Gerbera Jamesonii*)
3. Quad biking takes you from Barberton through the 14-arm River and grassland up to the mountain peaks,

Among the many flowering plants of the fantastic Lowveld National Botanical Garden are many indigenous species like the:
4. Drooping Clivia (*Clivia gardenii*) and
5. Blood Lily (*Scadoxus puniceus*)

Burchell's Zebra, Waterbuck, Blesbuck, Blue Wildebeest and Hartebeest have been introduced. Giraffe, Kudu and Impala are still quite common in the bushveld. There are also a few elephants from the Kruger Park and some White Rhino as well as Black-backed Jackal and Leopard filling the predator niche. Brown Hyena are rarely sighted.

Among the bird species are Golden-breasted Bunting, Shelley's Francolin, cisticolas, shrikes, pipits and warblers. The raucous calls of the Knysna Lourie sound through the forest and Olive Bush-Shrike, Grey and Collared Sunbird are also around.

The Komati River flows through the reserve and creates pleasant conditions for hikers, canoeists and those wishing to tent. Game drives and bush hikes are also possible.

Protea and Beech species in Songimvelo: Beechwood, Broad-leaved Beechwood, Transvaal Beechwood, Soapstone Pincushion, Common Sugarbush and subspecies, Saddleback Sugarbush, African Sugarbush, Dainty Sugarbush, Silver Sugarbush and Dwarf Grassveld Sugarbush.

Chrissiesmeer

The little village in Matotoland (Frogland) celebrates a Frog Festival each year in November. Participants swarm out day and night hunting frogs of every description, of which at least 12 species occur in the vicinity. Experts, like herpetologist Jerry Theron of the regional nature conservation, identify the findings and give talks around the camp fire on the situation of frogs, while all around their nocturnal croaking can be heard.

The Chrissiesmeer lake is the largest freshwater lake in South Africa (1 500 ha) and heartland of an extensive wetland comprising 270 lakes and ponds with a big population of water birds including 20 000 flamingos. Bird watching is therefore rewarding all year round.

The lake was named after Christina, daughter of Martinus Wessel Pretorius, first president of the South African Republic (old Boer Republic). The Tlou-tle, a San clan, were the first people who settled in the area and lived on rafts on the larger lakes.

Chrissiesmeer offers excellent B&B and overnight accommodation on farms.

Holnek Game Park and Nature Reserve

Here you can see Oryx Antelope and Springbuck – even in Mpumalanga. Naturally there are also the indigenous game species like the Black Wildebeest, Kudu, Burchell's Zebra, Blesbuck, Reedbuck, Eland and Waterbuck. The reserve is situated near Chrissiesmeer on the road to Swaziland in a varied environment and is an ideal weekend break for nature lovers from Gauteng.

Northwards to the Blyde River

Tip: This route saves the toll on the N14 in the direction of Nelspruit.

Verlorenvallei Nature Reserve

This is a rather unique nature reserve in the cooler parts of the country, lying at a subalpine altitude (2 150-2 331m) on the

Bull frog

Reed frog

1. One of the rare protea species thriving in the mountains near Barberton
2. & 3. The mysterious Barberton mountains, a geological wonderland
4. The Barberton Museum's most ancient rock, dating back around 3,5 billion years when the famous Barberton was formed, which represents the earliest geological events on Earth. What is more, layers within the greenstone revealed traces of minute blue-green algae, being one of the earliest life forms

Steenkampsberg Plateau, 15 km north of Dullstroom. Erosion caused marshes to develop around the furrows. The high-lying grassland is an important wetland biotope and the catchment area for the Crocodile, Elands and Steelpoort Rivers.

The vegetation, classified as northeastern sandy high plateau, consists of alpine grass species as they are common in the Drakensberg region of KZN up to an altitude of 3 000 m. Species of Festuca, used for weaving and thatching, are prevalent and sedge reeds dominate the marshland.

Among the numerous wild flowers are more than 50 types of orchid and other rare species like the endemic *Aloe graciliflora*. The "Ploughbreaker", related to the Coral tree, is resistant to cold which is common here.

The main goal of the reserve that was founded in 1984 remains the preservation of the Wattled Crane that is dependent on wetlands. Blue Crane and Crowned Crane also occur, as do other interesting species such as the White and the Black Stork, Bald Ibis, Cape Vulture, Stanley's Bustard, Cape Eagle Owl, Spike-heeled Lark, Cloud Cisticola, Yellow-breasted Pipit and House Martin. Malachite Sunbird and Gurney's Sugarbird often visit the flowering aloes and proteas.

Mountain Reedbuck, Grey Rhebuck and Blesbuck are common, but the Oribi is rare, and so are Grant's Golden Mole, Spotted-necked Otter, Cape Clawless Otter, Yellow Mongoose and Suricate. It is also worthwhile to look out for the numerous species of reptiles and amphibians.

There are several hiking trails enabling you to explore the reserve, but at this stage it has to be under the guidance of a ranger.

Gustav Klingbiel Nature Reserve

The reserve is situated on the slopes of Mount Anderson and became world-famous for the "Lydenburg Heads" – seven ancient terracotta sculptures that were discovered by a schoolboy. More information can be found in the Lydenburg Museum that forms part of the reserve. The excellent exhibition provides insight into archaeology, history, ethnology and the local culture. A system of footpaths leads to a complex of ruins dating from the late Stone Age. Antelope and birds can be observed en route.

Bird watching in the forest

Bird watching is difficult in a dense forest. Luckily there are many fig trees bearing fruit in the Shebam Reserve. If you take your time here you can soon spot and hear quite rare local birds like the Purple-crested Lourie, the Knysna Lourie and the Trumpeter Hornbill, as well as perhaps meeting up with a troupe of Samango Monkeys, a Thick-tailed Bushbaby or a Duiker.

Tip: For serious bird lovers a drive along the Blyde River from Pilgrim's Rest to Vaalhoek and Bourke's Luck (26 km) can be very rewarding. The gravel road is generally in a good condition and it crosses the river at least six times. It is always worth your while to stop there and scan the area for Giant Kingfisher, Pied Kingfisher and Malachite Kingfisher. To see a magnificent Half-collared Kingfisher or a Cape Clawless Otter would be a real bonus.

Top: Jacarandas flourish in Barberton
Centre: Woman at Blyde River lookout selling souvenirs, Common Coral tree (*Erythrina lysistemon*) in background
Bottom: Common Tree Fern at Berlin Falls

1. Landscape near Badplaas after a veld fire
2. Feral horses surviving around Kaapse Hoop
3. The 65 m high Mac Mac Falls, a National Monument, situated about 13 km north of Sabie just off the R532. Gold miners blasted the riverbed and split it in two. Since then two waterfalls roar down the slope towards the Blyde River
4. Aloes and Old Man's Beard (left) at Blyde Krantz

Panorama Route

8 km behind Graskop the view from God's Window makes you almost dizzy as you look from the 1 900 m escarpment into the lush evergreen eastern Lowveld. The hot humid air rises almost 1 000 m and cools down in the process. You notice its freshness. On clear days you can see beyond the Kruger Park as far as Mozambique. Stimulating views can also be enjoyed from the Pinnacle next to it. The free-standing rock is framed by sheer cliffs. Both of these tourist attractions lie on the border of the Blyde River Canyon Nature Reserve and mark the start of the most important part of the Panorama Route.

Blyde River Canyon Nature Reserve

The R532 leads past grassy slopes to the Tourist Centre at Bourke's Luck Potholes, at the confluence of the Blyde and Treur Rivers whose waters have eaten deep holes – like solidified whirlpools – into the stony riverbed. Tom Bourke, a legendary figure from the time of the gold rush, is supposed to have found his luck in these potholes. There are few traces of all the other gold diggers that were less lucky. Only the inscriptions on the tombstones report something of the hard life of a gold digger.

Lisbon and Berlin Waterfalls

Both waterfalls are on private property, directly outside the nature reserve. The Lisbon River branches out into three beds, before it drops from a 92 m sheer cliff. It is the highest waterfall in the country and also carries water in winter. The grassland sprouts a variety of pretty wild flowers, even before spring has arrived. The Berlin waterfall is 45 m high and is protected as national monument. Its feeding river, the Waterval Spruit, has churned away the softer rocks and created a picturesque ravine.

Climate and Rainfall: Temperatures in the canyon area average between 9-25° C. The average rainfall of approximately 1 500 mm falls mainly between October and April. God's Window gets up to 2 660 mm, Graskop 600 mm, Bourke's Luck 1 230 mm, Swadini 650 mm. The summer is pleasant; winters cold with frost at night and sometimes snow falls. Mists can occur on the escarpment all year round.

Tip: Never leave your car unattended!

Meandering through the Canyon

From God's Window long hiking trails lead through dense forest, grassland and plantations along the edge of the canyon, where one is surrounded by wild scenery with the staccato sound of the Samango Monkeys and the raucous call of the Knysna Lourie.

Echo complex

This extensive sequence of caves that is a national monument lies in the beautiful Molopong Valley on the border with the Province of Limpopo. The caves are surrounded by a large number of different indigenous tree species and impressive cycads. The historical value including a collection of tools from the Stone Age by far exceed the value of the partially damaged stalactites and stalagmites. It is reached on a side road of the main route between Lydenburg and Tzaneen.

The Canyon

In the course of 400 Mio. years a mighty river sculpted fascinating scenery. The waters snaked along a fault line, cut through basalt formations and uncovered ancient subterranean rocks on the floor of the canyon. The raging waters that created the 26 km long and 700 m deep canyon, are still busy. The gorge is surrounded by grassland and shrub savannah. Species like Red Grass, Heartseed Lovegrass and some others dominate. They alternate with copses of different protea species and mountain woodlands of impressive Yellowwood trees, Broad-leaved Beech and Transvaal Beech, White Stinkwood, Rock Cabbage tree and others.

Jumbos are no mountaineers

Scientists have found out that elephants try to avoid regions with hills and mountains. The reason being that the heavyweights would have to expend too much energy. They worked out that an elephant of four tons would have to feed at least an extra half an hour to make up for the energy expounded in ascending a 100 m hill. Life in mountainous countryside would cost about 40 times more energy than on the plains. Added to this would be danger of injury, scarcity of water and overheating, according to the zoologists. That demonstrates what an enormous achievement the crossing of the Alps must have been for the African Elephants of Hannibal. So it is better to circumvent a mountain than to climb it. With these new insights the researchers hope to find ways to create spaces for the grey giants that ensure their survival.

1. Bird's eye view of the upper parts of the Blyde River Canyon
2. Lisbon waterfall, a few kilometres north of Graskop, with a 92 m drop is the highest in the country. Be careful, the rocks are very slippery!
3. Minerals found in the Blyde River Canyon
4. Breathtaking vista from the main observation post

Climate: Annual precipitation along the escarpment is about 1 600 mm. Winters are severe with severe frost and occasional snow. Dense mists can occur on the Escarpment all year round.

Those wanting to continue on the Panorama Route can turn around here and drive back in a southerly direction on the R36. The entrance to the Echo Caves comes into view shortly after the turn-off. These dripstone caves in the dolomite walls of the Escarpment were inhabited in the Middle and Late Stone Age by the San; their rock art is well preserved. The extensive cave complex is still not much explored. The caves are up to 100 m long and 50 m high. Visits are possible.

Connecting with to the Kruger National Park

One travels on the R36 from Lydenburg onwards via Ohrigstad. Near the Echo Caves complex the tarred road meets up with the connecting road (R532) that leads back to the Panorama Route.

Kruger National Park

With an area of 20 000 km² the Kruger Park is one of the largest and oldest nature reserves in the world and harbours a great multitude of animal species. The oldest and largest game park in South Africa forms part of the huge Limpopo Transfrontier Park and is a dream location for friends of the wild from all over the world. Nowhere else can African flora and fauna be experienced as undiluted as in the "Kruger", and nowhere else can man and beast meet so peacefully as in this "Garden of Eden".

The Kruger Park has an average width of about 60 km and stretches along its western side for more than 350 km along the borders of Mpumalanga and Limpopo. Both provinces form part of the southern savannah biome. South Africans call the combination of grassland, shrubs and trees "bushveld"; it offers an amazing number of habitats, as do the adjoining subtropical "Lowveld" and the Escarpment.

The convergence of subtropical and temperate climatic regions coupled with extreme differences in altitude and diverse geological structures favour the biological diversity and the great number of endemic species of animals and plants. This region boasts the largest number of nature reserves and game parks, private game farms and other environmentally friendly establishments.

Tip: Even when you queue at the gate in the early morning there's every chance that some lions will cross your way or even a leopard returning from a night hunting baboons.

Kruger's Wealth

80 dams of various sizes that have been constructed along the main rivers and their tributaries are favoured habitats of birds and hippos and attract numerous other animals as well. Five big rivers flow through the large reserve from west to east – Crocodile, Sabie, Olifants, Letaba and Luvuvhu Rivers are all perennial rivers. Their springs lie outside of the park. Only the Sabie River is still relatively free of external interference and for that reason it is a favoured spot.

The fantastic variety of species is incomparable and encompasses innumerable forms of life. There are about 400 trees among the

1. Grinding stone found in the Echo Caves, lead to their early declaration as National Monument. Many of the once quite impressive stalactites and stalagmite formations still carry the marks of early local people, who found refuge inside the extensive cave system

2. Bourkes' Luck Potholes are found along the Panorama Route, where the Treur River plunges into the Blyde River. Here swirling whirlpools grinded potholes deep into the riverbed with sand and stones. They are named after the gold digger Tom Bourke who prospected here without success

3. The Three Rondavels on the eastern side of the Blyde River Canyon are rich in history

approximately 2 000 plant species; 150 mammals and more than 500 types of birds, including 14 eagles, 12 flycatchers, 11 owls and 10 cuckoos occur, as well as 120 reptiles, 35 amphibians and up to 50 types of freshwater fish. In the summer months more than 60 000 insect species are active and often a nuisance, but only the female of the *Anopheles* mosquito constitutes a danger to humans as carrier of malaria.

The number of mammals is amazing. All are accounted for, from a few hundred tiny Steenbuck to the 150 000 Impala and 12 000 Elephant. There are also 150 Mountain Reedbuck, 25 150 Buffalo, 500 Bushbuck, 300 Eland, 3 000 Hippo, 200 Cheetah, 9 000 Giraffe, 350 Wild Dog, 5 000 Kudu, 200 Sassaby, 1 000 Leopard, 1 500 Lion, 350 Black Rhino, 5 000 White Rhino, 70 Roan Antelope, 550 Sable Antelope, 300 Reedbuck, 32000 Burchell's Zebra, 17 000 Blue Wildebeest, 300 Nyala, 2 000 Spotted Hyena, 3 800 Warthog, 5 000 Waterbuck and 5 000 Crocodile. 17 comfortable to luxurious Tourist Centres are distributed among all the habitats.

The South – where tourists congregate

The southern half of the Kruger Park stretches from the Crocodile River in the south, across the Sabie River in the north and right up to the Baobab trees to the north of Tshokwane. On the Sabie River lies Skukuza, the biggest rest camp, where the headquarters of the park, as well as the administration and research centres are situated. You will also find a supermarket, a fast-food kiosk, an econursery and a dog cemetery. The ecogolf course, originally only for the use of rangers, is now open to tourists.

In the mountainous region in the southwestern corner are the highest rises, up to 840 m, some granite "kopjes" and grass-covered rocky cliffs with wooded gorges (kloofs). A broad swathe of riverine forest, alternating with open, interesting flood plains, waterfalls, little islands, rapids and interwoven side streams make the Sabie River one of the prettiest and most diverse of rivers.

The wooded savannah (bushveld) is rich in plant species and is a preferred living space of the White Rhino. Early in the morning they like to graze on shade-loving grass and later they rest in the shade of riverine forests. Apparently rhino avoid crossing river beds in a northerly direction, although these do not pose an impediment. In order to get a wider distribution of them, the heavyweights are caught and transported northwards across the rivers. The great growth potential of both rhino species makes the Kruger Park today one of the most important rhino protection areas in Africa.

Numerous fruit-bearing trees and shrubs that attract mammals and birds dominate. Acacias and various Bush Willows, as well as Marula trees, Sickle Bush, Tamboti and Teak, Knob-thorn and giant Sycamores are plentiful. Many of the trees have thick, corky or scaly barks that have developed as protection against bush fires. Riverine forests with impressive numbers of fig trees are to be found along the Crocodile and Sabie Rivers together with broad swathes of dense thorn bush. Here the smaller, shy antelope live, like the Common Duiker, the Grysbuck and the Reedbuck. Klipspringers often stand on the granite rocks near the commemorative plates in the Kruger Park.

The route from Skukuza to the rest camp at Lower Sabie that leads along the Sabie River is particularly popular, because it brings lots

1. Crocodile with captured mature Warthog near Sunset Dam

2. Greater Galago visits camp at night

3. Dinosaur sculpture at nearby Sudwala Caves

4. Satara: Southernmost occurence of Baobab tree in natural habitat

5. Bushbuck visiting Letaba camping site at night

6. Soles of a dead young elephant

of sightings without much effort and the swanky sedan cars don't even have to leave the tarred road. That is the reason why it is quite hectic here even early in the morning.

The Lion's Heart – in the centre

Satara, the "Lions Heart" of the game park lies amidst open grassland. Once sufficient rain has fallen here on areas that have been burnt during the winter months the largest animal herds of the reserve gather here, followed by many predators. That is the reason why we find the largest herds of grassland animals together with the highest concentration of lions in southern Africa in the centre of the park. The main prey of lions are Zebra and Blue Wildebeest. But Impala, Buffalo, Kudu, Hartebeest, Waterbuck and Roan Antelope also need watch out. The best time to observe lions is prior to the rainy season in August and September. The five vulture species that occur in the Kruger Park can all be seen in the grasslands around Satara. Other raptors like Steppe Eagle, Tawny Eagle and Martial Eagle are also present, as are many species of typical grassland birds.

Typical trees are the Marula and Knob-thorn that are symbiotic with the Leadwood as well as the Red Bush Willow and the Delagoathorn that grows only in this region. Masses of the small blood-red flowers of the Flame Creeper signal the approach of summer along the river beds and side streams in September and October. Then the Kruger Park becomes a green paradise.

Early birds see more

Those who don't want to make early rising a rule while in the reserve should at least attempt one of the versatile round trips, e.g. the Nwanedzi River Game Drive that commences 3km south of Satara on the left with the dirt road S100. Morning light, beautiful landscape and numerous animals – those that have not retreated from the increasing tourist traffic – can be seen close-up. At the stops under the high trees one can observe at leisure the animal life in and on the edges of the river. Among them you often find Buffalo, Burchell's Zebra, Waterbuck, Warthog, Kudu and Black-backed Jackal, while near the Mavumbye pond on the S90, about 5 km before it merges into the tarred road, a big group of lions tend to rest and lie in wait. Herds of buffalo come here to drink and elephant bulls roll in the mud at the edges.

Where lions come to drink

From the popular picnic site near the Timbavati River a gravel road winds for 30 km along the river. Small roads lead into the dense riverine forest from where one can look down on to the river bed where not only lions like to drink. Shortly before the road ends the marvellous viewpoint Goedgegun lies surrounded by dense Mopane-savannah. With a bit of luck you can see – besides elephants – Eland, Roan and Sable Antelope and the rare Tsessebe (Sassaby).

Northwards through elephant country

50 km north of Satara runs the Olifants (Elephant) River. This is the real elephant country. From the bridge that leads across the river right down to the turn-off to the Olifants Camp there are animals along the river. The best chance to observe Hippo is from the parking lot under the high Sycamore trees on the river's edge.

Surprise sightings

Watching animals requires patience. Early risers often wait for the gates to open just before sunrise. It is advisable to look for a quiet spot where no enthusiastic visitor shares his experience by mobile with loved ones far away. Even at the Sunset Dam, the end of the popular stretch between Skukuza and Lower Sabie, one is able to seek out a quiet spot. Up to 50 Hippo often laze around here, swim or snooze, unperturbed by Egyptian Goose, Stilt, Saddle-billed and Yellow-billed Stork and Marabu Stork. In the trees Fish Eagle perch or devour their prey. Just below the African Harrier-Hawk raids the thorny nests of the Red-billed Quelea. Appearing like knobbly wooden logs, Crocodiles lurk motionless.

Their tail hairs reveal their life-cycle

The black, wire-like tail hairs of elephants that can grow up to 50 cm long were to date only used to make bracelets for ecofreaks or as amulets, maybe as magic items for hunting. Today interesting scientific knowledge may be obtained from them that provides more insight into the behaviour of the animals. By analysing the chemical isotopes in the tail hairs it is possible to track their extended movements. It can be worked out where they met up with poachers or came into conflict with humans and how quickly they move through the bush. By virtue of the fact that the hairs grow about one millimetre per day even information about their feeding habits may be gleaned.

Elephants, Impala, Waterbuck and other big game also appreciate the fresh water. Hippo bulls that weigh up to 3 tons carry on their fights unperturbed by the tourists. Mothers and their offspring avoid the turbulent water and prefer to stay in quiet side streams. On one boulder it is even permitted to leave the car. That way you can enjoy the magnificent view across the wide river even better, especially at dusk. The Olifants Camp, high above the river, is for many visitors the best rest camp in the whole park. From the shady benches on the rock terrace you can watch all sorts of drama in the river below. Binoculars are indispensable.

More than half of the approximately 12 000 elephants live along the rivers and presently breed uncontrolled. The debate on necessary decimation is in full swing.

Only the large rivers like the Olifants, fed from an area of 50 000 km^2 make the survival of the large numbers of hippos and the numerous water birds possible. 60 % of the hippos live in the Olifants, Letaba and Shingwedzi Rivers and in the Tsendse and Mphongolo that are dependant on rainfall and regularly run dry in the winter months, but at least retain some adequate pools. Not only hippos succumbed to drought in the past, but also other animals that are dependant on water. Only the construction of large dams avoided this.

Elephant Walk
The new hike along the Olifants River – paradise on earth for hippos – avoids trodden out paths and leads through pristine wilderness. Each hiking group picks its own trail. A noisy 4x4 takes the participants 100 km to the start in the vicinity of the Phalaborwa Gate.

From there they set off with provisions, tent and backpack for three days in a southerly direction along the meandering riverbed in the direction of Olifants Camp. Competent rangers additionally carry a gun, navigation system, short spade for excretions and a walkie-talkie. They patiently comment on what their visitors see (or don't see) and warn them: "In a dangerous encounter with lion, hippo, buffalo or similar animals freeze and await instructions." It is easy to find tracks, but rarely can you track down the relevant animal. Hippos are an exception.

For three nights a camp is pitched in a protected location, usually in a semicircle around the fire where the communal meals are prepared. "Don't worry about the wild animals", the rangers keep on reassuring, "It is not in their nature to simply attack humans. They head off even when they only catch the scent."

The wilderness trails take place between April and October. Only persons between 16 and 65 may participate. A relative sound physical condition is essential; this has to be proved by a recent medical report.

The North – Where the big rivers flow
Distances between the tourist centres become greater. Savannah with Mopane trees and shrubs or Mopane woodlands dominate the monotonous landscape. Elephants feed on Mopane – either as tree or as shrub – and large buffalo herds make use of it as camouflage or resting place. The Tropic of Capricorn is Mopane-country.

Above: Red-billed Oxpecker attack cancerous growth on Buffalo horn
Right: Monkey business

The Letaba Camp is laid out under wonderful old trees. The Engelhard and Mingerhout Dams in the vicinity provide excellent viewpoints to observe animals. The riverine forests along dams and rivers offer a varied animal life in the giant Sycamores, Apple-leaf, Tamboti and Jackal-berry trees. Elephant and buffalo herds emerge from the Mopane trees on their way to drink and surprise the visitors on the picturesque paths along the river. There are also Waterbuck, Impala, Kudu, Bushbuck and even the shy Nyala, ever wary of hidden predators and noisy people. Grey-rumped Swallow and Brown-throated Martin sweep up and down.

A viewing point near the Shingwedzi River provides interesting observation of crocodiles in the Kanniedood Dam and birds in the air.

The Punda Maria camp in the northern corner of the Kruger Park, known in spite of its dense vegetation as "Sandveld", is less hectic. Here you might see Baobab giants and among them often lurk the otherwise rare African Wild Dog.

The most northerly picnic spot is Pafuri that lies in the corner where the three countries – South Africa, Mozambique and Zimbabwe – meet up and the parts of the Transfrontier Park lock into each other like pieces of a puzzle. On the way there one crosses the Luvuvhu River where giant crocodiles sun themselves and lazily watch the hippos. The fig tree forest along the almost tropical Levuvhu is also impressive.

Precipitation is lowest in the north at 500 mm. This is the result of the high pressure area over the Limpopo Province that prevents the moist air from the coast from moving in. This makes for semiarid conditions. Only the "Sandveld" of Punda Maria boasts an average of 800 mm rain per year. Further north the savannah of trees and shrubs becomes more varied again. Baobab, Fever trees, Palms and other plants point to the climate being ever more tropical. The "Sandveld" around Punda Maria is an extension of the Kalahari bowl that takes up a large part of southern Africa. This arid savannah with deep sand and diminishing sandstone goes over into flood plains and riverine forests with a tropical character along the Luvuvhu near Pafuri. Here Sycamores, Fever Trees and Baobab are plentiful. The northern part of the Kruger Park is said to be the best area for bird watching. For several species of birds from Central Africa this is the most southern region of their distribution.

Private Game Reserves – Luxury in the wilderness

A number of exclusive – and expensive – private game reserves lie along the western boundary of the Kruger Park. Their attraction lies mainly in the exclusive sleeping and catering offers, including dinner under the African sky around the open fire in a boma. Visitors are taken around in open 4x4's. The drivers communicate with each other by radio about special viewings. Both nightdrives and game watching on foot with a guide is offered. Predators are quite often enticed with meat. The 150 km long game fence that separated private game reserves from the Kruger Park has been removed. This provides enlarged living space of several thousand square kilometres for the wild life between the Sabie and Olifants Rivers. Drives directly from the private reserves into the vast Kruger Park are not permitted.

Bush-etiquette

Be sensitive towards other visitors, animals and habitat.

If you only dash through the bush you will miss a lot. It is advisable to drive slowly, not only because of dust clouds and stones on gravel roads, but also not to miss out on tips that you collect when meeting up with other "scouts". Advance slowly and stop discreetly without bothering others. If somebody is kind enough to let you pass, thank him with a smile and a wave. When you notice a queue of cars ahead of you, because a predator is lying on the road or there is perhaps a "kill" in the vicinity, consider in time whether it is worth your while to squeeze in. It might be better to look out for another road to approach from the other side. Don't irritate the animals by driving around noisily. Lions move away quickly and elephants might become aggressive. Never feed the animals – not even the cutest baby monkey. Game Parks and Nature Reserves are no zoos. Primates quickly get used to their "cousins", the humans, and might have to be killed, because they might become a nuisance and a danger.

Immediately switch off your engine when you stop at a viewing point, even – or especially – if your air condition is running. Always see to it that others are also able to see.

In the large reserves you are, strictly speaking, not even permitted to lean out of the window. Never open car doors or get out. Keep an eye on children who have a tendency to unknowingly get into dangerous situations. Loud talking annoys, irritates and frightens off the animals. Try to be as inconspicuous as possible. Local visitors often take a snapshot of the number plates of "irresponsible visitors" and report them to the parks administration. This is easily done with a digital camera these days. Any flaunting of the regulations can lead to expulsion from the "Garden of Eden". In the early morning there is often a queue of cars at the gate. Don't dash past; rather give the early risers a chance to observe the last nocturnal animals.

Don't expect to be let off a fine when you enter the camp after official closing time just because you are an ignorant visitor from overseas – your foreign currency is very welcome.

In some areas elephants may be exceptionally aggressive and cheeky. It is best to get out of their way, more so if you are not very experienced. Retreat carefully from any elephants that head directly for your car. As long as you remain in the car the animals view vehicle and occupants as a unit and aren't bothered by it. The moment you leave the car elephants and lions tend to become aggressive and other animals usually flee immediately. Never drive fast and never directly towards any animals. That always disturbs them and makes them flee. "Problems occur because of lack of knowledge", say the game wardens. They are especially concerned that visitors from overseas lack respect for wild animals and don't keep their distance.

1-4. Giraffe (1), Impala (2), Hyena (3) and herd of Buffalo (4) all found in the Kruger Park

Limpopo

In the northern parts of the province destinations that get you close to nature lie within the precincts of the N1, after passing towns and villages whose names have recently been changed, travelling becomes interesting. One can also reach the Limpopo region from Lydenburg-Ohrigstadt (R36/R527) over the Abel Erasmus Pass into the Valley of the Elephants and via the Baobab Route to Hoedspruit and on to the large private reserves and the Kruger Park. The photo below shows The Northern Drakensberg range near Blydepoort.

Bela-Bela

The town with the hot springs lies 100 km north of Pretoria along the road to the north. It is a good place for resting and recuperating and it also has several attractions for the ecotourist. There are several attractive private game parks and nature reserves in the vicinity. Some of them offer game drives to view the Big Five. To follow the fresh trail of elephants under the guidance of an experienced ranger is a thrilling experience. Thaba Kwena, the largest crocodile farm in South Africa is worth a visit, as is Mokopa Reptile Park.

Bela-Bela became well known for the healing power of its hot springs of which the Tswana had been well aware long before European settlers changed the name from Bela-Bela "the water that cooks itself" to Warmbad. Now again called Bela-Bela, the town has developed into a favourite holiday and spa centre. Hourly almost 20 000 litres of hot mineral water with a temperature of about 50° C bubble up from the earth. The water is rich in sodium chloride, calcium carbonate and other mineral salts. The healing baths available in a modern thermal spa and are said to be beneficial for sufferers of rheumatism, arthritis, myalgia, skin problems and chronic headaches.

Nylsvley

The largest and most impressive bird paradise in South Africa – unfortunately usually only for a brief period – lies between the towns of Modimolle (Nylstroom) and Mookgophong (Naboomspruit), close to the N1, about 150 km north of Pretoria. When the rains are plentiful the Nylsvley (clay pan) becomes flooded by the northwards flowing Nyl and its tributaries. At times flood plains of about 70 km develop that cover up to 160 km² farmland. Only about 40 km² form part of the Nylsvley Nature Reserve and are permanently protected. The existence of this ecological treasure is therefore continuously endangered.

To date more than 400 bird species have been recorded; among them are more than 100 species of water birds, wild ducks and crakes, often in great numbers. Storks and raptors add diversity to the population of about 43 000 crakes, 19 000 ducks (17 species) and 12 000 herons, that in good years may swell to 80 000 birds. Eleven species of heron form breeding colonies together with cormorants and ibises. Sometimes Great White Heron, Black Heron and Squacco Heron that all breed here constitute the largest breeding population of their kind in the whole country. Also other rare species, some of them endangered, like Rufous-bellied Heron, Bittern and Little Bittern, Lesser Moorhen and Lesser Gallinule.

This lively bird life can be observed from the car or on foot or from various birdhides, both within the reserve and outside. Even small predators are still around including Black-backed Jackal, Aardwolf, Honey Badger, African Wildcat and Aardvark, and from time to time a Leopard or Rock Python is spotted. The Nylsvley Nature Reserve nurtures Roan Antelope and Sassaby for breeding purposes.

Mokopane Nature Reserve

A sanctuary close to the town and known for its mixture of indigenous and exotic wild life that is under the auspices of the

Three-banded Plover

Lesser Moorhen

Pygmy Kingfisher

Egyptian Geese

1. Riding an Elephant in a Limpopo Game Reserve
2. Wild Dagga (*Leonotis leonurus*), also known as Lion's Tail. The robust shrub is used in traditional medicine and was used as garden plant in Europe as early as the 1600's
3. A magnificent Leopard in a Limpopo Game Reserve

centre where animals are bred for their worldwide distribution to zoos. The Arend Dieperink Museum on the fringe of the town is also worth a visit. It has an excellent cultural collection and a garden with 4 000 aloes of 212 different species, most of which are in flower during June-July.

Percy Fyfe Nature Reserve

This is mainly a breeding centre for the rare Sable and Roan Antelope and the Sassaby, but various other game can be observed when driving around the reserve. Several hiking trails cross the grassland with rocky outcrops. The reserve lies about 35 km to the north east of Mokopane.

Makapan's Gat

It is situated just 23 km west of Mokopane close to the N1. It was the hiding place of Sotho Chief Mokopane during his conflict with early Boer settlers. Later it became an important archaeological site that proved that early hominids knew fire as early as 1,8 to 1 million years ago.

Polokwane

The capital of Limpopo Province – called Pietersburg before – has some impressive nature reserves in the vicinity. On the city borders lies the Polokwane Game Park, one of the biggest nature reserves belonging to a town. Here the quite unique Pietersburg-Plateau-False-Grassland-Biotope is protected, home to rare bird species and plants. On a 20 km hiking and game watching trail one can meet up to 20 different types of game. Overnight stays are possible inside the reserve. More than 280 bird species live in the Polokwane Bird Sanctuary. Observation is possible from strategically placed birdhides. In the Moletzie Bird Sanctuary the rare Cape Vulture is protected. A visit to the bird and reptile parks is also worthwhile

At Polokwane one can turn right towards the Lowveld or continue on the N1 in a northerly direction towards Makhado (Louis Trichardt), the Soutpansberg mountains and the vaVenda, right up to the most northerly section of the Kruger Park and to the border with Zimbabwe.

Tzaneen

The pleasant drive from Polokwane through the evergreen forests of Magoebaskloof with its secretive footpaths leads partially through the original rain forest and partially through areas with exotic plants and ends in subtropical Tzaneen on the Letaba River.

Grootbosch Nature Reserve

The best way to enjoy this reserve with its picturesque waterfalls, indigenous rain forest and the ravines of the Magoebaskloof is by doing the 3-day Magoebaskloof Hiking Trail.

Wolkberg Wilderness Area

An area of largely pristine wilderness, more than 200 km² in size and mainly serving as important catchment area, but also as a hotspot

OLD AND NEW NAMES
Warmbaths – **Bela-Bela**
Pietersburg – **Polokwane**
Potgietersrus – **Mokopane**
Naboomspruit – **Mookgophong**
Soekmekaar – **Morbeng**
Nylstroom – **Modimolle**
Ellisras – **Lephalale**
Louis Trichardt – **Makhado**
Messina – **Musina**
Dendron – **Mogwadi**

Above: Hand-reared Hippo Jessica fed by Tony Joubert, who saved the day-old hippo from drowning

Fascinating Limpopo:

1. Clivias growing at God's Window
2. Start of morning game drive at Kapama Game Reserve near Hoedspruit
3. Tame hippo Jessica on the farm near Hoedspruit
4. Young Elephants being trained for tourist riders
5. The graceful lounge of Kapama Lodge
6. Cabbage trees (*Cusonia* sp.) grow along the Blyde River Canyon in profusion

of biological diversity. It is situated to the south west of Tzaneen and 60 km west of Polokwane. The extensive grassland, interspersed with rain forest, still has quite a bit of game and the 320 bird species make it compulsory for the serious bird watcher. About a hundred of the rare Cape Parrot survive here.

Note: Nature-in-the-raw for experienced nature lovers: no huts or other accommodation and no signposted hiking trails.

Ivory Trail

This adventure route follows the legendary trails of big game hunters and gold diggers in the olden days. Experts mapped out the Ivory Trail for ecotourists and for those that seek excitement and adventure off the beaten track. Where once ox wagons and stagecoaches wound their way through difficult terrain there now exist proper tracks and gravel roads in sweeping curves through areas of wilderness that are not much frequented as yet. These include game parks, either private or run by the provinces. Moving roughly from west to east you cross rugged mountain ranges like the Strydpoortberge, the Waterberg range, the northern Escarpment and the Lebomboberg range.

The trail does not require 4x4's and can be undertaken on your own. You can either plan your own tour or choose one of the Ivory Trail Tours on offer by tour operators.

Rain Queen Modjadji and Modjadji Cycad Reserve

500 years ago a young vaVenda princess settled with her clan in the Molotsi valley, about 30 km north east of Duiwelskloof. The secret of rainmaking is handed down in the female line and practised even today by the young queen Modjadji VI. Tourists pay for an audience, although her magic is hardly needed in the humid subtropical region, but a visit to the neighbouring Modjadji Cycad Reserve (530 ha), where the extremely rare Modjadji Cycad (*Encephalartos transvenosus*) that has been growing on these sacred misty slopes since the times of dinosaurs, is worth a visit. The little cycad forest – unique in the world – is crisscrossed by four attractive hiking trails. A small museum informs about the ancient plant and the rain queen.

Swadini-Khamai Reptile Park

The aim of this unique collection of indigenous and exotic reptiles is the preservation of South African reptiles by means of research and education. On display are mainly indigenous poisonous snakes like Black and Green Mamba, Boomslang, Puff Adder and Spitting Cobra, but also various types of scorpions and dangerous spiders that were feared even by people in bygone ages. The intention is to help people overcome their deeply rooted phobias by watching demonstrations of live animals by snake handlers with scientific knowledge and also by encouraging participation in the milking and feeding of these dangerous animals. First aid demonstrations are also presented.

Baobab Route

Behind the Swadini-Khamai Reptile Park is the turn-off to the lower part of the Blyde River Canyon National Park and the private reserve of Swadini. Straight on, the road leads to Hoedspruit, from where direct air connections are available to Eastgate International Airport. The town is also the starting point for visits to the private luxury game parks near the Kruger Park.

Mariepskop

From the highest and most significant rise in the Mpumalanga-Limpopo Escarpment you can see, on a clear day, the coast of Mozambique and at night the lights of Maputo. Mariepskop is known for the biological diversity of its plants (some still unprotected). The mountain range boasts more then 2000 plant species, including 78 endemic herbs that grow on quartzite rocks.

The Mariepskop Dwarf Chameleon and the Three Rondavels Flat Gecko are also of interest. Both reptiles occur only in the "magic mountain", probably isolated due to the loss of normal habitats. It is also amazing that about 50 % of all South African butterfly species occur here, including endemic ones like the rare Mariepskop Swallowtail and the endangered *Papilo euphranor.* Among the numerous bird species the striking Narina Trogon can often be heard, but is seldom seen in the 3 000 ha pristine mountain forest.

Note: You can climb up to the peak or drive up. The view from the picnic site is superb. Collect a permit from the forester near the peak.

River Rafting and Canoeing

Blyde River Canyon: Exciting Wild Water rafting through the canyon, lasting two days or less, commences at Mariepskop camping site and leads into one of the most pristine wilderness areas in the country where impressions of the earliest geological periods on earth are revealed. These excursions are offered by a private firm that works in conjunction with the administration of the park.

1. Crested Guineafowl (*Guttera pucherani*) ruffling its feathers
2. Road to Forever Swadini Resort at the foot of the Blyde escarpment on the Blyde River
3. Baobab blossom

4. African Sausage tree (*Kigelia africana*), Letaba Camp
5. Flowering Blyde River Protea (*Protea laetans*)
6. Age-old Baobab on farm Dublin in the Olifants Valley

Olifants River: This is a comparatively easy two-day river-rafting trip on the Olifants River between Manoutsa and Penge leading through narrow gorges and between steep cliffs to remote camping sites.

Hoedspruit

The town lies in the middle of the Lowveld and is surrounded by extensive, largely intact savannah covered by Marula trees, typical acacias and rocky outcrops. The diverse habitats are still sustaining a great number of different game species.

In this region the R40 runs partially through private reserves and game farms or along their borders. Furthermore there are several Game Lodges, some of which serve lunch and dinner and often provide accommodation without prebooking. The cheetah project of the Kapama Game Reserve, on the right side of the road before reaching Hoedspruit, conducts scientific research and breeds cheetahs. Rare animals like Wild Dog and several vulture species can also be observed.

The Moholoholo Rehabilitation Centre is well-known and concentrates on raptors and their reintroduction into the wild. Prime attention is focussed on the "Magnificent Seven": Fish Eagle, Black Eagle, Bateleur, Martial Eagle, Crowned Eagle, Tawny Eagle and Giant Eagle-Owl. The Hoedspruit Research and Breeding Centre conducts scientific research, breeding and keeping of cheetahs in captivity. About 80 Cheetah are on view. A place for sick and orphaned animals forms part of it. Some representatives of the Big Five as well as less common animals like Wild Dog, African Wild Cat, Caracal and Serval are also around. Several species of vulture regularly visit the Vulture Restaurant.

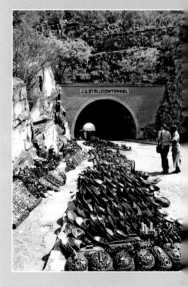

Musina Nature Reserve

Numerous game and bird species live among the impressive ancient baobab trees and an approximately 3 852 million year old rock that graces this beautiful reserve. In the neighbouring Erich Mayer Park, named after a famous South African artist, is a bizarre baobab, known as the elephant trunk.

Mapungubwe National Park

South Africa's youngest national park lies in open grassland, about 70 km west of Musina. The attraction of Mapungubwe, since 2003 a Cultural Heritage Site, lies in its historical, cultural, archaeological and ecological significance, and in its impressive landscape. Apart from the archaeological and San rock painting sites the 280 km² national park protects the fauna and flora in the catchment area of the Limpopo and Shashe Rivers. A wooden walkway at treetop height leads through the beautiful riverine forest to a well-camouflaged birdhide on the Limpopo and affords unusual perspectives. About two kilometres upstream two terraces overlook the confluence of Limpopo and Shashe. There are probably Elephant, Leopard, White- and Black Rhino, Wild Dog and possibly even Lion around, as well as up to 400 bird species and a variety of magnificent trees including 24 species of acacia and a huge Baobab with a circumference of 31 m.

Local people offering handicraft (from top to bottom): Carvings near Abel Erasmus Pass, pottery near Blyde Rivier, various crafted items at J.G. Strydom Tunnel, Venda woman with cycad cone near Thohoyandou

1. Limpopo landscape with three rondavels in the background
2. Blyde River before entering the canyon
3. Common tree Euphorbia (*Euphorbia ingens*), at Mookgophong, formerly Naboomspruit
4. Escarpment, widely known as the Northern Drakensberg, from the North

Accommodation is available in new rondavels, cottages and lodges. There is a tree-camp in the riverine forest on the Limpopo. A 45 km ecotrail is meant for 4x4's but can also be used by other cars. Bring your own food. The nearest petrol station is in Musina. Summer temperatures in the hot Limpopo valley can easily top 40 °C. Malaria is endemic. Information and bookings: SA National Parks.

Marakele National Park

Marakele (Tswana) means "place of refuge" and that is a fitting name for this new national park positioned in the intermediate zone between the bushveld of the drier west and the humid areas in the east, in the heart of the Waterberg range. Attractive mountain scenery alternates with undulating grasslands and hidden ravines. Among the 765 plant species grow occasional yellowwood trees and cedars and tall cycads, like the rare Waterberg Cycad.

Practically all grassland mammals find refuge here or will be coming in the near future, among them Elephant, Rhino, Lion, Buffalo, Leopard, Cheetah, Wild Dog and Brown Hyena, Kudu, Waterbuck, Sassaby, Roan Antelope, Impala and Eland. Baboon and Vervet Monkeys can be a pest.

Due to its position in the transitional zone, birdlife is very diverse as species of both habitats live side by side, e.g. Arrow-marked and Pied Babbler, Pin-tailed and Shaft-tailed Whydah, Southern- and Tropical Boubou, Black-eyed and Red-eyed Bulbul, Southern Black and Cape Penduline Tit, Tawny-flanked and Black-chested Prinia, White-browed and Kalahari Robin. A great attraction is the colony of Cape Vultures, probably the biggest in the world with 800 breeding pairs. A narrow tarred road brings visitors via a mountain pass to the crest near the Sentech Towers.

Please note: Most roads in the reserve are only suitable for 4x4's.

Marakele lies about 250 km north of Johannesburg and may be reached via Bela-Bela or Brits from neighbouring Thabazimbi. The Waterberg biosphere adjoins the reserve in the northeast.

Overnight stays are possible in a comfortable tent camp on the Apiesrivierpoort Dam; camping site next to tourist office.

A collection of trees, representing in miniature the great plant diversity of Limpop Province:
Top to bottom: The Strangler Fig kills other trees; Euphorbia along the Blyde River, Cabbage Tree
Left: Enormous tree and cycad cone

Leading exponents of the Limpopo animal kingdom: Vervet Monkey eating flowers of Flame Creeper (*Combretum paniculatum*) (1), Elephants at a waterhole at night (2), Male lion at Kapama (3), Sable Antelope (4) and Giraffes (5) at a private game reserve and Pied Kingfisher at sunset (6)

Gauteng

Gauteng is the smallest province in South Africa with the highest population density. It takes up the largest part of the 1 500-1 800 m high plateau of the Witwatersrand. (Picture below: Hot-air balloons with Magaliesberg mountain range in background)

Originally Gauteng was inhabited by tribes that had migrated from Central Africa. Later the seminomadic pastoralist Voortrekkers moved into the area as it comprised mainly grassland. In the 1880's the Australian prospector, George Harrison, discovered the greatest gold reef on earth here. Within a very short time the unhygienic gold-digger's camp grew into a city of 10 000 inhabitants – Johannesburg. Today they talk about "Jozi" or "Egoli" (the place of gold). The gold rush passed, but the province and metropolis remained the economic hub of the country, and of Africa. More than 25 % of the country's GDP is produced here, using up 40 % of the electricity that the continent of Africa generates

Any sanctuaries in such an environment are usually small and under ongoing pressure. The region around Johannesburg and Pretoria with the highest population density in southern Africa is no exception. Apart from a few small bird sanctuaries it is mainly the Magaliesberg range and the Suikerbosrand Nature Reserve where whatever remained of the original natural environment was salvaged. There are big zoo's in both these cities.

Bird Sanctuaries

On the cliffs of the Magaliesberg range are several colonies of Cape Vultures that benefit from strict protective measures, active nurturing (by means of the so called "vulture restaurants") and ongoing education. Interesting bird sanctuaries within or on the peripheries of large cities are Blesbokspruit Bird Sanctuary, in the middle of the goldmine on the eastern Witwatersrand (East Rand); Austin Roberts Bird Sanctuary in Pretoria; Rolfe's Pan Nature Reserve near Boksburg; Rondebult Bird Sanctuary near Germiston.

Walter Sisulu National Botanic Garden

This relatively new botanical garden definitely merits a visit. In the last 25 years a succulent collection of note has been created here. It not only includes South African and Namibian species, but also collections with species from Ethiopia, Kenya, Madagascar, Somalia, Tanzania, Zimbabwe, as well as from America, Asia and Europe. One section has been devoted to medicinal plants from Africa. What remains of the original vegetation of the region is also protected, and there is a compilation of the cycads of southern Africa.

Gauteng Snake Park

The snake park displays many snakes and other reptiles. It is situated on the R101 near Halfway House, between Johannesburg and Pretoria.

Suikerbosrand Nature Reserve

This pretty Highveld Nature Reserve of 13 337 ha is situated only 50 km south of Johannesburg (N3) and is ideally suited for ecological excursions over the weekend. It derives its name from the Sugarbush Protea that is widespread here (*Protea caffras* subsp. caffra). The vegetation is varied with mountain grassland and undulating savannah, wooded ravines, marshes and even Fynbos and therefore suitable as habitat for a great number of mammals like Mountain Reedbuck, Oribi, Blesbuck, Duiker, Eland, Kudu, Hartebeest, Baboon, Springbuck, Steenbuck, Black Wildebeest and Zebra. Among the predators are Cheetah, Brown Hyena, a few – usually not visible – Leopard and some smaller types. More than 200 bird species have been listed so far. They can be observed from the car on an 80 km circular drive or on shorter or longer hiking trails including a six-day-nature-route with overnight huts. There is also a meditation hut for unwinding.

Both endemic and other bird species that live in grasslands and mountains are present: Mountain Chat and Mocking Chat, Jackal Buzzard, Yellow Canary, Grassbird, Greywing, Redwing and Orange River Francolin, Black Eagle, Desert Cisticola, Orangethroated Longclaw, Cape Weaver, Cape and Sentinel Rock Thrush, Cape Longbilled Lark, Red-eyed Bulbul, Layard's Titbabbler, Red-throated Wryneck, Red-collared Widow, Secretary Bird, Wailing Cisticola and White-quilled Korhaan.

Pretoria

Groenkloof Nature Reserve

This is probably the oldest nature reserve in Africa and it lies only 5 km from the city centre of Pretoria. As far back as 1894 hunting was forbidden here, mainly to protect the Oribi (*Ourebia ourebi*). President Paul Kruger proclaimed the valley as a game park. Around the turn of the century Kudu, Blue Wildebeest, Impala, Ostrich, Roan Antelope, Giraffe and Red Hartebeest were reintroduced. Currently attention is given to salvaging the original intermediate zone between high plateau and bushveld. There is also a wonderful copse of trees with White Stinkwood (*Celtis africana*) and Sugarbush (*Protea Protea caffra*).

The 6 km Interpretation Route can be followed with an ordinary sedan, but there is also a 15 km

1-3. Hot-air ballooning, one of the main tourist attractions of the Magaliesburg area

4. Pollution is still a problem in the industrialised part of Gauteng

5. Johannesburg skyline

6. Puff Adder (*Bitis arietans*) at a snake park near Halfway House/Midrand

7. Springtime in Pretoria, 60 000 Jacarandas in full bloom, Union Buildings in the background

road reserved for 4x4's, as well as shorter (4 km) and longer (10,5 km) hiking trails and a 20 km route for Mountain Bikers with an overnight hut. Bikes may be hired. Entrance is via the Fountains Valley Resort.

National Botanical Garden

Research, education and relaxation are the three pillars of the National Botanical Garden that is under the auspices of the faculty of botany of the University of Pretoria. More than 3 000 plant species have been brought together here, including a collection of indigenous trees with some large ones that were planted more than 60 years ago. Of special interest is also the complete collection of cycads including Wood's Cycad that has died out in the wild. A newly laid out footpath leads to more than 140 remarkable plant species.

Rietvlei Nature Reserve almost in Pretoria

Even before construction work for the dam commenced the city councillors had decided to develop the farming area ecologically and create a nature reserve into which game would be introduced. Today the reserve comprises almost 4 000 ha and is well stocked with game including Eland, Waterbuck, Blesbuck, Black Wildebeest, Oribi, Burchell's Zebra, Buffalo, White Rhino and even Brown Hyena. Added to this are smaller mammals and various bird species like Cormorant, Goliath and Black-headed Heron, Fish Eagle, Grass Owl, Marsh Owl, Ostrich, Secretary Bird and others. There is a well-placed birdhide for observation. The terrain consists predominantly of open grassland and marshes, broken by copses with about twenty different indigenous tree species. Today Rietvlei provides 15 % of the water requirements of the capital.

An ecological information centre provides details about the reserve and footpaths (with overnight accommodation), horse riding, night drives, yacht club, camping site and facilities for socialising (Lapa) for 30-200 people.

Tswaing Crater, Museum and Nature Reserve

More than 200 000 years ago a meteorite hit the bushveld 40 km north of present day Pretoria with an impact of more than 60 atom bombs and left a crater with a diameter of 1 100 m and a depth of 200 m. During the course of millennia the crater that is encircled by hills, filled up with saline water and that probably attracted people of the early Stone Age. Much later it was intensely utilised by the Tswana who settled here. They named the crater Tswaing, place of salt. Later it became known as Soutpan (Salt Pan). Salt and soda were produced commercially in the first half of the 20th century. After that a research farm tested the bushveld ecology on its suitability for cattle farming. In 1993 the National Cultural History Museum took over the complex and changed it into the impressive Crater Museum with themes of geology, environment, history and culture. A path leads from the museum that is situated on the rim of the crater, down to the salt lake. Four new footpaths have been laid out. They also lead to the nature reserve (20 000 ha)

Pretoria Botanical Gardens has a large collection of indigenous cycads. Among them is the Giant Cycad and Cycad cone

Secretary Birds are often seen at the Rietvlei Nature Reserve, Pretoria

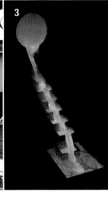

1-3. Gold Reef City, exibition of early gold mining
4. Mine dump in Johannesburg
5. Dancing in traditional garb at Gold Reef City
6. Stand of indigenous and exotic trees at Jan Smuts's Doornkloof home, Irene, a historical monument

that has become very popular, especially with bird watchers. Various mammals have been re-introduced. Camping sites are available.

Hartbeespoort Area

Hartbeespoortdam

Apart from water sports, there is also a reptile park and some private game parks where Lion, Cheetah and Leopard are present among other animals, including Elephant that are even available for a ride through the bush.

Sailing through the air

The experience of rising up in the air in a hot-air balloon is nothing short of sensational. When you start at dawn the burner hisses menacingly, but soon you can watch the sun rise while gliding over the landscape and have a bird's eye view of the Highveld and Hartbeespoort Dam.While you are enjoying your balloon ride you can't help to notice to what an extent agriculture and other human developments have changed the original country side for ever, and these changes are on-going. Bill Harrop brought balloon flying to Gauteng's skies more than 25 years ago with his "Original" Balloon Safaris and is regarded and trusted as the doyen of the South African balloon tourism.

Cradle of Mankind

The Sterkfontein Caves are the absolute Eldorado of palaeontologists. Fifty years ago the first proof was unearthed here that some 5-7 million years ago the human ancestry tree split off from that of the large primates. Meanwhile 35 % of known hominid fossils in the world have been discovered in the Sterkfontein, Kromdraai, Swartkrans, Drimolen and nine other caves. Among the 6 different hominids are Mrs Ples and Little Foot. Further great finds are expected in the coming decades and many unresolved questions about the origin of man may find answers.

Maropeng, a supermodern interpretation centre at Mogale's Gate, near the Sterkfontein Caves, has seen a great increase in the number of visitors. It is to be expected that one of the biggest tourist attractions of South Africa is in the making here.

Maropeng

"The place where we once lived" is a new multi-faceted interpretation centre at Mogale's Gate, a scant 7 km from Sterkfontein, where the first traces of today's human race have been discovered. After further finds in other parts of Africa – and some controversy – palaeontologists declared Africa as the Cradle of Mankind

Right from the entrance to the partially subterranean exhibition one enters another era. It has been constructed like a Tumulus, those pre-historic graves with earth and rock mounds that were reserved for heroes and other dignitaries from Early Stone Age up to the time of the Vikings.

Down there one can now trace by means of interpretation and proofs the evolution of life on earth right up to the present time.

Maropeng is a good place of orientation for novices to get their bearings. The excavation sites, with the world famous Sterkfontein Caves as the nucleus, were declared a World Cultural Heritage Site by UNESCO in December 1999. Today the prehistoric excavation sites of Taung and Makapansgat form part of it.

The cave system of Sterkfontein that is far from being extensively explored is more for knowledgeable visitors and serious ecotourists. The public may visit the caves and this is best done under competent guidance. A laboratory where hominid findings are being prepared is also open to visitors, and furthermore there is a hominid display.

Where and What: Interpretation Centre, Cave Tours only with registered tour guides.

Note: Don't forget your hiking shoes.

Touching a cuddly lion cub in the Lion Park near Lanseria Airport

1. Almost complete cranium of *Australopithecus africanus* ever discovered, belonging to "Mrs Ples" living about 2,6-2,8 million years ago
2. Back view of the "tumulus" at Maropeng, that houses extensive exibitions, focussing on the history of the development of humankind over the past few million years
3. Reproduction of prehistoric Heidelberg Man (*Homo heidelbergensis*), 600.000 years
4. Today's landscape around Hartebeestpoort, once the habitat of Mrs Ples and Little Foot

North West

Parts of the old Transvaal and the Bantustan Bophuthatswana were merged to create the province of Northwest in the rearrangement of provinces in the new South Africa. The typical bushveld changes into grasslands on the high plateau in the east and in the west it runs out into the arid savannah of the Kalahari. The road network is quite well developed with several freeways criss-crossing the region. Although there are no National Parks – in spite of Pilanesberg sometimes being mentioned as such – a number of larger and smaller interesting nature reserves are spread throughout the province. Some of them permit big game hunting in the hunting season and this could reduce the freedom of movement of ecotourists. (Picture below: Early morning in Hartbeespoort)

Borakalalo

The varied game reserve (13 500 ha) lies in the far northeastern corner of the province, only 120 km from Pretoria. Savannah, bushveld, woodland and hills, the Klipvoor Dam and a wonderful riverine forest on the Moretele River offer habitats for 35 mammals and more then 300 bird species. White Rhino, Cape Buffalo, Hippo, Giraffe, Eland, Roan Antelope, Zebra, Waterbuck, Leopard, Caracal, Black-backed Jackal, Wild Cat and Spotted Hyena occur, as do Crocodile. Easy to spot are several types of Kingfisher, Shrike and Cuckoo. Also present are species that are rarely seen around Johannesburg/Pretoria nowadays like Red-billed Hornbill, Marabu Stork, Meyer's Parrot, Martial Eagle, Brown Snake Eagle, Wahlberg's Eagle, African Hawk-Eagle, Vulture and Crimson Boubou. Serious bird watchers can make use of the two birdhides. A complete checklist is available at reception. There are hiking trails in the wooded areas near the river that can be used at one's own risk. Moretele and Phudufudu Camps are equipped with safari tents and facilities of varying standards. There is no electricity; all equipment is run on gas. At the Pitjane Camp near the dam simple sites for caravans and tents are provided

Ecotip: Please take note that animals often flee when you approach them on foot. Move towards them surreptitiously, preferably against the wind, wear inconspicuous clothing and talk – if you must – only in whispers; avoid heavy perfume and glittering jewellery. Don't smoke! Best times for observations (also for photos) are in the early morning and late afternoon till sunset, especially near the water holes. In some reserves the opening and closing times are not enforced quite so strictly as e.g. at the Kruger Park.

Rustenburg Area

De Wildt Cheetah Centre

Coming from Hartebeestpoort Dam a drive of about 6 km brings you to the world famous breeding centre. It concentrates on the preservation of rare mammals, especially Cheetah, Wild Dog and Brown Hyena. In addition they also conduct successful breeding of Suni, Oribi, Serval and Riverine Rabbit which they hand over to other reserves. The so-called King Cheetah also has been bred successfully. Originally it was though to be a subspecies, but the researchers at De Wildt determined unequivocally that it is only a conspicuously patterned variance of the Cheetah (*Acinonyx jabatus*). With prebooking, visitors can enjoy the centre and its animals on a three-hour drive. Overnight accommodation is available in the adjoining De Wildt Cheetah Lodge.

Kgaswane

The mountain reserve is situated in the pretty Magaliesberg range between Gauteng and the Northwest Province, quite close to Rustenburg. Several hiking trails wind around water falls and natural bathing spots and lead to clay pans and mountain crests with panoramic views. The rustic camping sites along the paths are among the best in the country.

This small super-reserve of 4 300 ha provides a habitat for more than 320 bird species including a breeding colony of rare Cape

---

Visiting the Vulture Restaurant

Since carrion eating hyenas have disappeared from the grasslands utilised for farming in South Africa the bone splinters that are essential for the proper bone formation of young vultures are no longer available to them. When huge cattle herds replaced the game on these grasslands it created a big problem for vultures that now only had meat to feed on. The cattle owners preferred to bury or burn dead animals, in order to prevent the spreading of diseases. Just like in other areas, organisations for the protection of wild life laid out feeding places in the Magaliesberg range to the southwest of Pretoria to ensure the survival of the endangered Cape Vulture and increase the population. Since then its numbers have at least stabilised and deformities among the young birds have decreased. This good example prodded some concerned farmers to lay out further feeding places that are known in South Africa as "Vulture Restaurants". They generally provide good observation of vultures and other birds.

Dream of a lifetime is realised

The private breeding and research centre is the realisation of Ann van Dyk's dream to apply herself to the rescue of the endangered Cheetah. In 1971, when it was founded, only around 700 of the fastest land animal in the world had survived in South Africa. After initial setbacks Anne van Dyk succeeded in greatly contributing to an increase in numbers that almost doubled. These successes, and others – through breeding in Namibia – made it possible to remove, for the time being, the speedy hunter from the growing list of endangered animals.

A glimpse at the diversiy of wild life of the North West Province:

1. Warthog (*Phacochoerua aethiopicus*) mother with her litter
2. De Wildt Cheetah Centre, famous for its immense contribution to save the engangered fast cat
3. The nervous Black Spitting Cobra (*Naja nigricollis woodii*) is present in the dry westerly parts of the province, occurs also in Namaqualand
4. Young baboon meets Vervet Monkey
5. A Southern Rock Agama or Bloukopkoggelmander is basking on a tree trunk

Vulture, Martial Eagle and Black Eagle. More than 20 other raptors occur here. Pride and joy of the reserve is its successful breeding of Sable Antelope. Among the 30 types of mammals we find rarities like Oribi, Brown Hyena and Aardwolf. You can obtain a comprehensive list of mammals, birds, shrubs and trees at reception. Birds and mammals are given in English, German, Afrikaans and Setswana. Overnight stay: Tent and caravan sites with ablutions and some simple tent sites along the footpaths.

Pilanesberg National Park

Although officially there are no national parks in the Northwest Province the name of this 500 km² reserve of the erstwhile Bophuthatswana remains. The game park is closely linked to the adjoining Sun City and Lost City. At the centre of the reserve lies, among bushveld and arid savannah, a 1 200 million year old and long extinguished volcanic crater surrounded by green hills. It also has wooded gorges and undulating grassy hills. Project Genesis reintroduced game that once roamed the area. Most animals of the grasslands are again present including Brown Hyena, Wild Dog, Aardwolf, Hippo and Roan Antelope. About 50 Lion and a dozen Cheetah live here, 170 Elephant, 300 White Rhino and about 100 Black Rhino as well as more than 40 of the rare Sable Antelope. The Tbc-free Buffalo herd has grown to almost 100 animals and regularly provides replenishment for other reserves in the province. The numbers and variety (more than 350) of birds is amazing. More than 80 bird species are housed in a huge walk-in aviary and are much easier to photograph there than outside.

Game drives in this amazing world are most rewarding in the early morning or late afternoon. On game drives at night the accompanying ranger is able to point out all sorts of nocturnal animals by means of his powerful search beam, among them owls and nightjars. It is also possible to join ecosafaris during the day or take part in "Green Hunting" – the anaesthetising of rhino, elephant or lion and lending a hand in their loading and transportation to other reserves. In the early morning hot-air balloon flights are offered.

Lichtenburg/Ditsobotla

Game Breeding Centre

The Game Breeding Centre of Lichtenburg measures 4 500 ha and is a jewel. It forms part of the National Botanical Garden of Pretoria. The breeding centre and game reserve is predominantly geared to breeding indigenous wild life for zoos all over the world, especially rare and endangered species, but also concentrates on rare exotic animals. Apart from antelope and stag species from Arabia, China, India and Northern Africa there are wild horses from Mongolia, sturdy wild cattle from India (Gaur), dwarf hippos from West Africa and Red or Forest Buffalo (*Syncerus caffer nanus*) from Central Africa.

The area is well supplied with water and has numerous clay pans whose peat-like soil had been used by the indigenous population as fuel during dry years. At the time of the diamond rush large, chokingly smoking, subterranean peat fires were raging. Parts of

Killer Elephants

In excess of 100 rhinoceroses have been killed by elephants in the last decade, most of them in Pilanesberg, but it also occurred in the game parks in Zululand. The culprits were always young elephant bulls that had grown up as orphaned calves and lacked leaders (of a herd) and came into must at a young age. Their sexually prompted aggressiveness was directed at the cumbersome rhinoceros. These young male elephants were missing the presence of older bulls that would have retarded the sexual maturation of the young bulls. They all came from the Kruger Park, where they had been spared during the annual culling, because they could be relocated without difficulty at the time. After a period of being at a loss, mature elephant bulls were brought into the new areas for elephants. This did the trick to reign in the young Turks and ensure the habitat for inexperienced herds. The transportation of elephants weighing several tons had meanwhile become possible by means of improved loading facilities.

Aggresive elephants

1. Herd of Burchell's Zebra (*Equus burchelli*) at sunset, Pilanesberg
2. Zebra stallion watches a young warthog passing by
3. Alert Caracel *(Felis caracal)* in a tree
4. & 5. Pére David's Deer (*Elaphurus davidianus*) – extinct a couple of hundred years in the wild, is bred to ensure the survival of the species at the Lichtenburg breeding station of the Pretoria Zoo

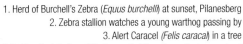

the extended wetland area currently belong to the breeding centre.

The huge bird watching site is one of the biggest and best in the country. 250 different species have been identified in the wetland biotope, the acacia thicket and adjoining grassland. A special attraction is the Vulture Restaurant with an excellent birdhide and a lovely picnic site in the vicinity. At times dozens of White-backed Vulture congregate here, they have even been counted in hundreds. Lappetfaced Vulture are also quite numerous. Hooded Vulture and Cape Vulture are seldom seen.

Madikwe Game Park

This exclusive 60 000 ha game park on the border with Botswana is situated on a great plain with bushveld and grassland. The reserve became well-known for its successful reintroduction of packs of Wild Dog. The 66 species of mammals include the Big Five. As a photographer you should keep in mind that in this reserve big game hunts are conducted, and for that reason the animals are probably shyer than in the Kruger Park. Visitors can participate in guided safaris, daytime or night-time. Day visitors are not admitted.

Tip: During the quieter season in winter you can sometimes get a reduction in price.

Botsalano

The Wildlife Reserve/Sanctuary (5 800 ha) lies approximately 25 km north of Mafikeng towards the border to Botswana (R27). It has the typical landscape of the Kalahari with thorn bushes in red sand, but it also offers some shady woodland as a relief and is situated within a 2 400 million year old volcanic crater, one of the oldest in the world and about twice the age of the one in Pilanesberg. Breeding of White Rhino and some antelope is carried on and the reserve also has many Giraffe, Black Wildebeest, Red Hartebeest, Eland and Gemsbuck (Oryx Antelope), as well as both Springbuck and Impala that occur together nowhere else. The animals are quite shy, probably because here, too, trophy hunting takes place. This actually puts a question mark over the name – "Friendship". On the other hand it is said that up to a thousand Cape Vulture glide over from the abattoirs of Lobatse. The strategically placed water hole is usually well frequented.Overnight accommodation is provided in safari tents or bush camps. A camping site with basic facilities is situated at the entrance.

Barberspan Bird Sanctuary

This more than 4 000 ha wetland has extensive areas of water surrounded by undulating grassland and is of international significance. It lies 17 km to the northwest of Delareyville on the N14 towards Sannieshof, about 300 km from Johannesburg. Over the years it has gained in importance, as it serves as halfway station for migratory birds and as habitat for the relatively large number of water loving birds of which 365 are registered, among them pelicans, flamingos, terns, ibises, herons, cranes, bittern and grebes. Flamingos flock in their thousands, but they do not breed there. All bird species are easy to observe from the strategically placed bird hides.

Several buildings with fully equipped dormitories and showers are available for overnight stays. Bring your own linen and cooking utensils.

Molopo Game Reserve

The 24 000 ha reserve in the southern Kalahari on the border to Botswana is covered with red, wavy dunes and silvery grass and Kalahari thorn bushes. The reserve forms part of a 10 000 km² intra-provincial raptor sanctuary. There are large antelope like Oryx Antelope (Gemsbuck), Eland and Hartebeest as well as Springbuck, Kudu, Impala, Waterbuck, Burchell's Zebra and Giraffe. Predators present are Cheetah, Black-backed Jackal, Caracal, Genet, Wild Cat and Honey Badger. Some visitors report that it is difficult to approach game, and this is probably due to the fact that here, too, there is an extended hunting season. On the other hand, visitors are permitted to undertake day and night excursions on their own. Camping and caravan sites and accommodation in an old farmhouse are quite reasonable; but they are self-catering.

Taung

"The Place of the Lion (Tau)" lies approximately 40 km south of Vryburg in typical bushveld country. You can reach it easily via the R47. Here, again, a direct line was discovered to our earliest ancestors. The "missing link" is a complete child's face with jaws and teeth, about two million years old. Taung forms part of the UNESCO World Heritage Sites, together with Sterkfontein World Heritage Site (The Cradle of Mankind) in Gauteng, which also includes Makapan's Gat in Limpopo Province.

A diversion from the Taung skull and the memorial in the Buxton marble quarry can be enjoyed at the "Blue Pools" – a picturesque valley nearby with hiking trails leading past caves, streams and cool rock pools. The small reserve of Boipelo (150 ha) has roads for Mountain Bikers.

Accommodation: Three-Star Tusk Taung Hotel on the main road, inside the game park, rooms with air-condition, restaurant, casino, swimming pool, floodlit tennis courts, mini-golf and internet.

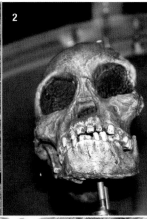

1. White-backed Vultures at the Vulture Restaurant, Lichtenburg Nature Reserve
2. The famous Taung skull is now one of the most important exibits at Maropeng
3. The Taung Heritage Site in the old, disused Buxton quarry where in 1924 the lime encrusted skull of a child was unearthed, belonging to an early hominid, the *Australopithecus africanus*, "southern ape of Africa" The discovery was one of the most significant archaeological discoveries of the time. Since then it has been proclaimed an UNESCO World Heritage site
4. The steep cliffs near the Blue Pools are today a popular spot for abseiling, with picturesque caves and streams at the bottom with a nice picnic spot.
5. Flamingos at Barbers Pan

Hunting without killing

In Botsalano a new type of trophy hunting is being marketed as "EcoHunting". The sportsman shoots his prey with an anaesthetic dart, and if he is successful he is captured with his trophy on a video clip before the victim wakes up. Lions are unfortunately not available.

Free State

The Provincial Parks Board administers 15 game parks and nature reserves scattered throughout the province. Furthermore there are about 30 private game parks and nature reserves, of which the Willem Pretorius Game Park is the largest and most important, followed by the Sandveld Reserve and the Sterkfontein Dam Reserve shown in the picture below.

Bloemfontein, Pearl of the savannah

Mangaung means "Place of the cheetahs" in seSotho. The secretive predatory cat must have been quite numerous on the wide savannah between the Orange and Vaal Rivers when the "fountain of flowers" (Bloemfontein) was chosen as capital of the newly founded Boer Republic, the Orange Free State, in 1854.

Naval Hill, about 1 500m high, affords an excellent view over the city that spreads on all sides into the savannah. It is a favourite place for outings to the little nature reserve where both small Rock Hyrax (Dassies) and large Giraffe are happy to pose for photographers. Springbuck, Burchell's Zebra, Blesbuck and Eland can also be seen. At the lower end lies Hamilton Park with waterfalls and ponds as well as an orchid house with more than 6 000 beautiful orchids, exotic as well as indigenous.

Well worth a visit – especially in spring and early summer – is the Free State National Botanical Garden near Bloemfontein. The vegetation consists predominantly of grassland with scattered trees and typical Karoo plants. There are more than 30 species of mammals, 100 species of birds and 54 reptile species. The attractive medicinal garden has been arranged around traditional Sesotho homesteads. Footpaths are conducive to a prolonged stay.

Sanctuaries for wild animals and plants

The Provincial Parks Board administers 15 game parks and nature reserves scattered throughout the province. Furthermore there are about 30 private game parks and nature reserves, of which the Willem Pretorius Game Park is the largest and most important, followed by the reserves Sandveld and Sterkfontein Dam.

Giant crater at Vredefort

Relics of the biggest meteorite or asteroid hit became the ecological centre of the province. The huge ancient crater can be reached from Parys along the border to Gauteng. In 2005 it was proclaimed the seventh World Natural Heritage Site in South Africa. The cosmic bullet crashed deep into the earth's crust more than 2 000 million years ago, when the supercontinent Gondwana originated. It left a huge crater with a diameter of approximately 250-300 km, whose rims stretched beyond Johannesburg. The enormous, ring-shaped crater wound (astroblem) consists of crushed and deformed basaltic rock that unfolded over the rim. The ricochet of the rocks created a dome that was pushed upwards by the pressure of the molten magma, but later imploded. The projectile from outer space probably had a diameter of 10 km, about the size of Table Mountain. This means it would have developed energy of more than 100 million megaton of TNT on impact, which could have resulted in devastating changes on the planet.

The ecology of the crater area consists of a multitude of habitats, including bushveld and grassland, mountains and gorges. Visitors can undertake small guided safaris through the history of the earth or they can go for hikes. Bicycle tours, wild-water-rafting, abseiling,

A very rare bird

Botha's Lark (*Spizocorys fringillaris*) is a highly endangered endemic resident bird whose numbers are rapidly dwindling due to the destruction of its habitat – certain areas of the Highveld grassland – as a result of agricultural expansion. Only about 1 500-5 000 birds survive in an area of approximately 40 000 km² in southern Mpumalanga and eastern Free State. Only one percent of the total population is protected in nature reserves.

(Photograph: Warwick Tarboton)

Part of the dyke of the Vredefort Dome at Daskop near the centre of the impact *(Photograph: Media Club South Africa, M. Gaylard)*

Vaal River flowing westwards through gaps in the hills surrounding the Vredefort granite dome *(Photograph: Media Club South Africa)*

1. Sentinel (3 165 m) at the northern flank of the Drakensberg Amphitheatre, approached from the Free State side

Free State big cat boom:

2. White male lion with young female on a private Game Reserve, where visitors could walk with white lion pups
3. Lion brothers
4. Visitor with male tiger, the Laohu (old tiger) Valley Reserve in the Free State province is the site of a pioneering international conservation project.

trout fishing, mountain walks or placid paddling to the numerous islands in the adjoining Vaal River are also on offer. Overnight facilities are plentiful.

Seekoeivlei Nature Reserve

This wetland of international significance with Ramsar status lies near Memel in the north eastern part of the province. Buffalo, Roan Antelope and even Hippo inhabit the 5 000 ha nature reserve. Wattled Crane and Blue Crane live here and the endangered Botha's Lark can be seen quite often. In summer the little Eastern Red-footed Kestrel arrive in great numbers after their long flight from Siberia via the Himalayas and India. Memel and Seekoevlei can be reached via Harrismith.

Sterkfontein Dam Nature Reserve

The 17 770 ha reserve developed around the dam whose water is pumped uphill from the Thukela River in KZN and, if necessary, diverted to the Vaal Dam. The dam on the escarpment has one of the longest earth walls in the world. In the reserve that stretches around the dam are several hiking trails that lead through mountain grassland and protea copses into lonely mountain areas. Among the 210 bird species are water birds, raptors and songbirds that have adapted to the mountainous terrain. The Vulture Restaurant, where Cape Vulture sometimes meet up with Bearded Vulture, can be seen from the road leading to the Oliviershoek Pass. Oribi and Black Wildebeest are the less common among the antelopes.

Golden Gate, a mighty sandstone bloc domina and gave the majestic Golden Gate National P its name

The dam is favoured by sailing, water-ski and windsurfing enthusiasts and paragliders.

Accommodation is available in comfortable chalets and on the huge modern caravan and camping site.

Golden Gate Highlands National Park

The National Park of 11 600 ha on the western side of the Drakensberg range has been enlarged by 22 000 ha through the incorporation of the little known Qwa Qwa National Park and also features additional attractions like a Basotho cultural site, a new camp with 18 chalets and a mountain refuge at 2 260 m altitude, as well as several extensive hiking trails and a road for 4x4's. Golden Gate is the only grassland reserve in the country and has 60 grass species and several grassland bird species.

An unusal cross between Arab and Norwegia Fjord Horses are breed at Golden Gate Natior Park and used for riding

Fantastic mountain scenery with massive and colourful sandstone cliffs are the features of this reserve that lies at an altitude of 1 800-2 800 m at the edge of the Maluti Range. The vegetation consists mainly of mountain grassland with some wooded ravines. Among the larger mammals are Eland, Suni and the Black Wildebeest. Black Eagle, Jackal Buzzard and Bald Ibis breed in the reserve. The rare Bearded Vulture can sometimes be seen at the Vulture Restaurant. Tours may be arranged to the nesting sites of the Bald Ibis and to the caves with San rock paintings. Hikes of one or more days are possible. Accommodation is in chalets and simple huts; a hostel is available for youth groups and also a camping site with

Impressive sandstone formations provide the unique character of the area

Rural mountain scene at Golden Gate

facilities. The reserve lies about 360 km south of Johannesburg and can be reached via Harrismith or from the Royal Natal National Park. Winters are quite severe and snowfalls occur. The road from Harrismith runs through the reserve to the town of Clarens that is surrounded by spectacular mountain scenery and known for its arts and crafts. On some farms in the area one can look at San rock art. The Maluti Route starts here.

Maluti Route

This safari by car takes you through the mountain kingdom of Lesotho, the eastern Free State and parts of the Eastern Cape Province, bringing you into contact with SeSotho, Xhosa, English and Afrikaans speaking inhabitants and their traditions. Some rock paintings of the San are to be found in the mountains and caves. Driving down to the coast one crosses the upper reaches of the Orange River near Aliwal North where one can bathe in the hot sulphur springs, and although the once well-known spa is pretty rundown, this is still a pleasure in winter.

Tussen-die-Riviere Game Reserve

This private game reserve at the top end of the Gariep Dam lies "between-the-rivers" Caledon and Orange and is the largest in the province. Visits by ecotourists are limited, since big game hunters come here in autumn and winter. But the area is attractive as it harbours a rich bird life and numerous species of game, the majority of which having been relocated there.

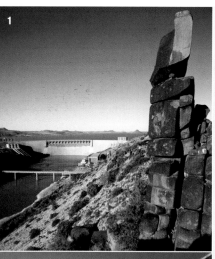

Free State kaleidoscope:
1. The Gariep Dam during a period of severe drought and
2. full to bursting point after heavy rains in the Drakensberg area

Farm scenes:
3. Cartwheeling turkeys
4. Threshing corn in country style
5. Autumn mornig in Clarence
6. Bloemfontein Observatory – magnificent clear night skies attract many visitors

Opposite page:
7. Daybreek at Maselspoort
8. Blue Wildebeest enliven a Free State koppie
9. Sunflower fields near Verkeerde Vlei
10. Basotho homestead near Golden Gate
11. Free State landscape with Inselberg, formed by weathering and erosion, close to the N6 towards Reddersburg. Note: Inselberg is the internationally used term – a very good example of an inselberg is the Platberg (2 350m) at Harrismith

Northern Cape

Habitats in the largest and comparatively sparsely populated province lie mainly in the Great Karoo, Succulent Karoo and the arid grasslands of the Kalahari. There are some important wetlands. The long coastline in the west reflects the cold and nutritious Benguella Current arising in Antarctica. The Succulent Karoo is biologically of great significance because it boasts the greatest diversity of water-retaining plants in the world such as the Kokerboom (as shown below), vygies, and many others found in Namaqualand.

Kalahari Routes

Direct routes to the Kgalagadi Transfrontier Park are from Johannesburg via the R47 Vryburg-Kuruman-Upington and the Kimberley-Route via Griquatown to Upington and from there on the mostly tarred R360 to the entrance at Twee Rivieren.

The road via Kuruman and Hotazel (hot-as-hell) gives you an inkling of the summer heat in the Kalahari. Kuruman, a town of about 10 000 inhabitants, was once upon a time the most famous mission station in Africa. Robert Moffat founded it in 1831 at the source of the Kuruman River, the "Oog van (eye of) Kuruman", which is the largest natural spring in Africa. It was from here that David Livingstone set out on his research explorations. Behind Hotazel the tarred road changes to the typical, bumpy gravel road and follows the Kuruman River along the 385 km to the distant entrance to the reserve at Askam.

Kgalagadi Transfrontier Park

The Kgalagadi Transfrontier Park came about in 1999 by merging the South African Kalahari Gemsbok National Park and the Gemsbok National Park of Botswana. It is the first "Peace Park" in southern Africa and with more than 40 000 km² one of the largest and most unusual reserves in Africa and the most southerly region through which large mammals still migrate in search of food. The South African section comprises almost 9 600 km². It was founded in 1931 to counteract poaching and protect animal species of the Kalahari from extinction. This meant the relocation of the surviving San (Bushmen).

Dry riverbeds are the silent witnesses of the sporadic rainfall. Along the wide sandy beds of the Nossob and Auob the gravel roads lead from one water hole to the next. The two rivers meet at the headquarters of the park at Twee Rivieren. "Big Water" as the San called the Nossob usually flows only once a decade. Here and there a Camel Thorn tree leans over under the weight of gigantic nests of Sociable Weaver birds. Intermittently sparse patches of grass grow. The endless horisons stretch all around, permeated by silence and solitude, heat and dust.

Today the last big game herds of southern Africa are concentrated around the Auob and the Nossob. The more than 40 water holes that were bored here had not been intended for the animals but for the South African army that marched along here in 1915 top fight the German Schutztruppe. Creaking wind pumps bring ground water of low salinity to the surface and this binds many mammals to the river beds.

Animals in arid environment

It is usually Springbuck, Oryx, Blue Wildebeest, Red Hartebeest and Eland that move around among the dunes and briefly visit the water holes. Grey Duiker and Steenbuck like to stick to the dry river beds. Antelope grow about one third larger in the arid areas as compared to other regions. Nevertheless, the Kalahari lions have to catch three times as much prey than their cousins in the Kruger National Park, because they often have to make do with smaller animals; some specialise in hunting Porcupine. There are about 250 lions that concentrate their nightly hunts on the watering holes. Cheetah

Distances in the reserve:

Twee Rivieren – Nossob: 3½ hours	
Twee Rivieren – Mata-Mata: 2½ hours	
Twee Rivieren – Kalahari Tent Camp: 2½ hours	
Twee Rivieren – Grootkolk: 6 hours	
Nossob – Union's End: 3 hours	
Nossob – Mata-Mata (via Kamqua Dune Road): 3½ hours	
Nossob – Bitterpan: 2½ hours	
Nossob – Grootkolk: 2½ hours	
Bitterpan – Mata-Mata: 2 hours	
Mata-Mata – Kalahari Tent Camp: 4 km	

Hot Tips

Avoid scorpion stings by not going barefoot on warm evenings.

For any drive you should have at least 10 litres of water in the car and leave an itinerary behind, so they know where to look for you. In case of a puncture, stay with your car!

It is possible to negotiate up to 40% reductions – depending on the time of year (mostly available during the hot season, October to March).

The canary-yellow flowers of the Koker Boom are often ripped off by baboons to get to the sweet nectar

Namaqualand Aloe

Animals of the Dry Zone:

1. Blue Wildebeest need a lot of water to survive and depend heavily on the artificial water holes in the Kgalagadi National Park

2. The Gemsbuck, probably the mammal most adapted to the dry conditions

3. Sociable Weavers with their huge nests, are widespread in the Kalahari

4. Hartmann's Mountain zebra, likewise very well adapted to dry conditions, southernmost range Northern Namaqualand

hunt by day in open terrain. When the days are short in winter Brown Hyena and Spotted Hyena can sometimes be seen drinking. Some Aardwolf – highly specialised termite-eaters – occur; Leopard and Wild Dog are rare, but the Bat-eared Fox – another termite-eater that will temporarily switch to plant food – goes about digging in the river beds. Cheeky Black-backed Jackal roam around near the roads. It is always a joy to watch Suricate. They live in colonies and quickly become tame.

Best times for watching raptors are between February and April, when extensive rains have stimulated the feeding chain. Martial Eagle, Tawny Eagle, Secretary Bird, White-backed and Lappet-faced Vulture are the most common. Kori Bustard live here and Pygmy Falcon manage to be boarders in the nests of the Sociable Weaver that can sometimes be their prey.

Sandy Roads

The main roads for watching game and birds run along the wide river beds and these sandy roads are kept in good condition so that even smaller sedan cars can drive on them.

The watering places in the dry river beds are ideal spots for observation. In the early morning and late afternoon you might see nocturnal hunters like lions and hyenas. Grazing animals like the brackish water at Rooiputs, Cubitje Quap, Kwang and Kannagauss on the Nossob River. Oryx prefer the saline watering holes of Melkvlei, Jan se Draai, Kaspersdraai and Groot Kolk near Union's End. Large herds of Springbuck can often be seen on the Nossop near Leeudrif and Rooiputs. Some Spotted Hyena live between Rooiputs and Kijkij. The watering places on the Auob are generally not brackish, in spite of their San name "bitter water".

Lion can often be seen at Kamqua and Mata Mata. Raptors visit Rooibrak. The watering hole Dalkeith is known for watching Cheetah and at Craig Lockhart there is a good chance to see Leopard. The solitary, nocturnal Brown Hyena that is adapted to arid zones can often be seen at watering holes in the afternoon. Just like the Kalahari Lion they can go for months without water, getting their moisture from their prey and fruit. Lions like to hunt between Chileka and Kaspersdraai. The ten watering holes north of the Nossob camp are an Eldorado for animal lovers, while bird watchers delight in the numerous Lanner Falcon that visit the reserve in late summer. Cubitje Quap, directly north of the Nossob, is a good spot to observe their breathtaking hunt of Namaqua Sandgrouse and wild doves.

The Fish Eagle, symbol of Africa

Twee Rivieren is the most comfortable of the three traditional tourist camps. It has car rentals, a landing strip for small planes, restaurant, take-away foods, swimming pool and air-conditioned cottages and chalets with 1-2 bedrooms and 24-hour electricity! At night the hooting of the Spotted Eagle-Owl and the African Scops-Owl mingle with the howling of jackals and the giggling chatter of hyenas. When morning dawns, the songbirds take over like Glossy Starling, Pied Barbet, Grey-headed Sparrow, Fork-tailed Drongo, Black Crow, Kalahari Robin, Violet-eared Waxbill as well as Southern Yellow-billed Hornbill, Golden-tailed and Cardinal Woodpecker, Hoopoe and Swallow-tailed Bee-Eater.

Particularly striking among the 170 bird species are the Kori Bustard, raptors and vultures as well as Love Bird and Grey Hornbill. The latter two can be seen on the northern Nossob towards Union's End. During the rainy season (November - March) White Stork and Abdim's Stork and sometimes also Black Stork and Marabou Stork forage in the river beds where they are often joined by Little Stint, Black-winged Stilt, Ruff, Plover and Common Sandpiper.

In the Nossob tourist camp at the upper end of the Nossob Road one becomes especially intimate with the nature of the arid zone. At night the generators provide light for the 3-6 bed cottages and huts with kitchens and showers. The cheaper huts have shared shower facilities. All are provided with fridges and stoves. The Information Centre supplies details about the reserve, but the grey Camel Thorn trees on the sandy camping sites often don't provide enough shade.

1. Fish Eagle breed along the Lower Orange River
2-4. Brown Hyaena – with young (2), dozing (3) and roaming (4)
5. "Gousblomme" in full bloom

Mata-Mata lies on the Auob River among red dunes, 120 km from Twee Rivieren and on the border with Namibia. It is again possible to continue from here into Namibia.

All three tourist camps offer petrol stations, camp and caravan sites and shopping facilities. Annual rainfall is about 200 mm, occurring mainly between January and April.

Three new camps have been established off the beaten track. Kieliekrankie is situated near a dune in the vicinity of Twee Rivieren and boasts a fantastic panorama over the red sands of the Kalahari. Near Urikaruus, in the vicinity of Mata-Mata, Camel Thorn trees frame the view of the Auob. Both camps can be reached with normal sedan cars, but for Gharagab, surrounded by dunes and thorn bush savannah and lying in the most northerly corner of the reserve, a 4x4 is essential. The new camps have comfortable facilities with bathrooms and showers and kitchens equipped with gas fridges, hot water, lights powered by solar energy and grills on the terraces. You need to bring your own firewood and drinking water.

ECOSPOT

Mabuasehube Wilderness Trail

The 150 km long safari road leads through the Kalahari to the Mabuasehube (Red Earth) Reserve that is an extension of the Gemsbok National Park of Botswana. It is ideal for nature lovers who appreciate being alone in pristine nature, and know their way around. The roads can be very dusty and the tent sites in the salt pans are very basic. Visitors are only admitted in groups with at least two 4x4's. All provisions, from petrol/diesel to water must be brought along. Any water – if available – is very brack.

The arid savannah with scattered trees and interspersed with lime salt pans and impressive dune fields resembles the huge Central Kalahari Game Reserve (52 000 km²) in the north. After good summer rains, about March-April, the pans fill up with water and attract large game herds, followed by predators. In the dry season Oryx and Eland use the pans as salt licks.

Safari drives are allowed in one direction only. The route back via the border post McCarthy's Rest poses no problem.

4x4 Safaris: The South African section has the Nossob 4x4 ecotrail. Gemsbuck and Mabuasehube Wilderness Trails are in the Botswana section.

Tswalu Kalahari Nature Reserve

Measuring 1 000 km² this is the biggest and probably the most exclusive private nature reserve between the Limpopo and the Cape of Good Hope. It is positioned in an area of endless solitude and seclusion between the Koranna Mountains and the rim of the Kalahari. Those who love the arid savannah and are looking for peace and quiet will enjoy Tswalu.

The region had been split up into several farms when the Oppenheimer family decided to purchase it some years ago with the intention of reconverting the abused arid savannah to its pristine

TIP

The road network of the province has not been fully developed. Especially the part south of the Orange River should only be tackled with an up-to-date road map or GPS. In some of the older ones paltry side roads are mentioned as "principal highways". There are many dirt roads of varying quality. On the whole, good road maps are easily available in South Africa. Large petrol stations often sell road atlases quite reasonably and these are often more accurate than the sometimes dated enclosures of European travel guides.

Above: Scenes of the Tswalu Kalahari Nature Reserve

136

1. White-backed Vulture landing
2. Both sexes of the Gemsbuck carry horns
3. Horse safari in Tswalu Kalahari Nature Reserve
4. Typical path across Kalahari savannah, Tswalu Kalahari Nature Reserve
5-6. Adaption of Flapp-necked Chameleon to extreme cold (5) and hot (6) weather

condition. The simultaneous development of high class ecotourism was part of the "New Beginning" – its Tswana name.

Professional guides and trackers facilitate real adventures with African wildlife. Stars in this epic are the highly endangered "Desert Rhino" (*Diceros bicornis bicornis*) from the Kaokoland, as well as Kalahari Lion, Cheetah, Spotted- and Brown Hyena, and Wild Dog, but also Sable Antelope, Roan Antelope and Sassaby. Some endangered species are bred here for other reserves. Among the 200 types of birds are 35 raptor species and several others that have adapted to the arid grassland.

San hunters and their predecessors left archaelogical sites with many treasures that have by no means been extensively evaluated. The cultural heritage spans a period of more than 100 000 years and goes back to the end of the Late Stone Age, 10 000 years ago.

Accommodation is luxurious and expensive and caters for a maximum of 30 people.

The tarred and floodlit landing strip can accommodate planes up to the size of Lear and Gulf Stream Jets. There is a daily airshuttle to Johannesburg. Those driving on their own take the tarred road from Kuruman to Hotazel and turn left after 15 km at the signpost to the Kgalagadi Transfrontier Park and then follow the signs to Tswalu.

Waterfall in the Thirstland

The Augrabies Falls are a natural wonder in Southern Africa. They lie in the Augrabies National Park in the arid south west, 120 km west of Upington, on the Orange River. In the 820 km² reserve lives a sustainable population of the Black Rhino from Namibia. A number of antelope and predators also form part of the animal life. The Kokerboom and Euphorbias flourish in this extremely dry region. Dense riverine forests line the river banks.

When good summer rains drench the South African high plateau, up to 400 million litres of water cascade with a deafening roar 56 m from the granite rocks over a breadth of 150 m. The San named the waterfall Augrabies, "the place of big noise". A three-day hike leads through the approximately 20 km ravine with up to 240 m high walls where the water continues on its way to the Atlantic. On short drives or walks you can spot Eland, Klipspringer, Steenbuck and other animals. Excellent bird watching is possible in the early morning and late afternoon. Kori Bustard and Ludwig's Bustard occur and Black Eagle can often be seen in the late afternoon at the viewing point "Echo Corner" at the waterfall. In the ravines Black Stork have their nests. Chalets with air-conditioning and three swimming pools provide comfort. There is a well-kept, shady camping site.

Kimberley

In 1871 a simple cook picked up three diamonds on a hill that was rapidly flattened by diggers rushing in and this lead to the biggest man-made hole in the world – The Big Hole of Kimberley. More than 2,5 tons of diamonds were excavated here by primitive methods by more than 30 000 fortune hunters. The digger's colony was called Kimberley from 1873 onwards and became the world centre for diamonds.

Kimberley's Flamingos

Greater and Lesser Flamingo breed on the Namibian coast (occasionally – with great risks – in Etosha), in Botswana, in Lake Natron in northern Tanzania and now they also breed within sight of the City of Diamonds, Kimberley. So far the ideal breeding site for flamingos of the Rift Valley had been Lake Natron with its warm water and high concentration of magnesium chloride, magnesium sulphate and sodium compounds. But the once innumerable wading birds there are diminishing rapidly. The growing numbers in Kimberley therefore become of increasing importance.

Famous South African diamond

The Cullinan Diamond weighed more than 3 106 carat as a rough diamond and more than 100 cut stones were produced from it. Cullinan I and II are 530 carat and 317 carat and were incorporated in the British crown and sceptre. Alluvial stones that were transported by wind and water can never be as big.

...e of Kuruman, widely
...own as "Die Oog", is not
...nly a tourist atraction, but
...rovides the main town
...n the rim of the Kalahari
...aily with 20 million litres of
...rystal clear water
...lue Wildebeest at dusk
...reater Kudu, Africas most
...ajestic antelope

4-5. Kimberley, internationally
  known for its Big Hole (4) and
  its diamonds (5)
6. Giraffes reintroduced in the
  Kalahari
7. Redbilled Hornbill
8. Engraving of an Elephant,
  chisselled out of a piece of
  rock. More than 400 such
  engravings are spread over a
  small sacred hill at Wildebeest
  Kuil, probably done about
  1000-2000 years ago

All places of interest in the city can be reached on foot or by the historic tram that has been reconstructed and takes the visitor from the imposing City Hall (1899) in romanesque-corinthian style in the city centre to the Kimberley Open Mine Museum and the famous Big Hole with a derrick from 1892 next to it.

The Big Hole

Today you can inspect the Big Hole from an unusual perspective. The glass floor of the new sightseeing platform offers a wide angle view right down into the 800 m deep and 500 m wide pit that is a hollowed-out volcanic funnel (pipe), originally filled with kimberlite containing diamonds and other plutonic rock. A total of 22,5 million tons of gravel were removed between 1869 and 1914 to harvest 2 722 kg of rough diamonds (more than 14,5 million carat) that would form the foundation of De Beers Consolidated Diamond Mines, for a long time the largest diamond empire in the world. After 1914 the ecologically dangerous disfigurement of the surface was discontinued and diamonds were raised more cost effectively by means of underground mining.

Distances: 500 km from Johannesburg, 900 km from Cape Town.

Tip: To visit the Big Hole at sunset is considered to be especially rewarding.

Mokala National Park

South Africa's new National Park is more than a replacement for the deproclaimed Vaalbos National Park, whose title deed reverted to the original owners. Mokala with its 20 000 ha is already substantially bigger and more diverse and it stands to be enlarged to 50 000 ha in the next five years.

From the dolerite hills (Koppieveld) rise small rivers and streams that end in the nearby Riet River. Endless expanses with deep sand and clay pans where Camel Thorn trees grow are typical Kalahari landscapes, while the adjoining Vaalbos bushveld is more Karoo. Both parts form the borderline zone between arid savannah and Nama Karoo.

Camel Thorn trees (a mangling of the Afrikaans name for giraffe "kameelperd" because giraffe like to browse on this thorny acacia – Mokala in Setswana) constitute – together with other acacias – the most important tree species in the western arid zone. Ranging from wispy thorny tree-lets to some 16 m high solid trees, the Camel Thorn is widely distributed over the Northern Cape Province. Its spreading canopy is characteristic. For the inhabitants of the harsh arid savannah it often

proved lifesaving. In the same way it was – and still is – vitally important for the animals that have found refuge in the new park: Mountain Reedbuck, Black and White Rhino, Duiker, Eland, Giraffe, Kudu, Red Hartebeest, Sassaby, Oryx and Roan Antelope, Springbuck, Steenbuck, Blue and Black Wildebeest. A total of 863 animals were relocated from Vaalbos to Mokala within two years.

The new reserve in the Winterhoek area lies 80 km southwest of Kimberley, west of the National Road N12 leading to Cape Town. The annual rainfall is 300-700 mm and falls mainly in summer.

Already on offer or in the pipeline are mountain biking, day hikes, game drives at sunset or by night, guided tours on horseback and excursions to San rock paintings.

Accommodation: Two lodges or on a camping site, some 10 km away. A restaurant and conference facilities, as well as an airstrip for private planes are also there.

Kampfersdam

Huge flocks of flamingos often populate this unexpected bird paradise near Kimberley.

In this wetland biosphere with a small lake (pan) there are often up to 30 000 Greater and Lesser Flamingo. A few thousand regularly nest here and a breeding island in the centre of the pan is being planned. Unfortunately the water – derived from waste water and rain – is polluted with a high concentration of heavy metals that constitutes not only a danger to the flamingos but also to the numerous other water birds that live here. Conservationists are of the opinion that an extension of the reed beds and improved filtering of the waste water could solve the problem.

There are about 180 other bird species like African Spoonbill, Glossy Ibis, Wood Sandpiper, Swift Tern, South African Shelduck, Grey Heron, Curlew, Sacred Ibis, Cape Teal, Cape Shoveller, Avocet, Little Egret, Marsh Sandpiper, Black-winged Stilt, White-winged Tern, White-faced Duck, Little Stint and 4 plover species. Black-chested Prinia, Rufous-eared Warbler and Levaillant's Cisticola live in the riverine thicket.

Kampfersdam lies on the left side of the N12 leading to Johannesburg/Pretoria and can be reached easily on a small field path that runs under the railway bridge.

Opposite is the Dronfield breeding colony of White-backed Vultures. De Beers, who own the farm, put 8 000 ha at the disposal of research. Visits are possible.

1. Greater and Lesser Flamingo at Kampfer's Dam, a wetland and Natural Heritage Site near Kimberley, at present unfortunately contaminated by untreated sewage pumped into the dam, spoiling the breeding ground for the Lesser Flamingo, of which there are now about 50 000, producing annually up to 9 000 chicks on an artificial island
2. Hartmann's Mountain Zebra at Goegap Nature Reserve in Namaqualand
3. Young people enjoy the endloss flower carpets of Namaqualand in springtime
4. The perennial Gazania belongs to the family Asteraceae. They occur in countless hues of varying intensity, like these Botterblom (*Gazania krebsiana* sp.)

Namaqualand

"Garden of the Gods" seems an odd name for the region on the lower end of the Namib Desert that bakes in the summer heat and after a good winter rain turns into a symbol of the Rainbow Nation. Suddenly the bone-dry stony desert erupts with a splendid colourful carpet of short-lived flowers. Hot and dry berg winds can kill this "blooming miracle" overnight, but usually it lasts long enough to allow visitors from all over the world to enjoy this unique wildflower show.

It is, however, very difficult to plan the tour, since everything depends on timely rains. "There are good 'flower years' and bad 'flower years', but there are always some flowers somewhere." So says Colla Swart, doyenne of the local wild flower experts.

The spectacular flower spectacle usually unfolds between August and October, after the last winter rain and consists mainly of Mesembrianthenum and composite flowers of which South Africa has more than 2 000 species.

The flower regions lie about 550 km north of Cape Town on both sides of the (tarred) N7 leading to Windhoek. Springbok, a town with 300 days of sunshine and only 100 mm rain per year, is the centre. Coming from Johannesburg one travels via Kimberley (N12), Griquatown (R64) and Upington.

Goegap Nature Reserve

The reserve measures 15 000 ha and lies 15 km from Springbok. It can be reached on good gravel roads, to be explored by road or on foot. It presents the typical Namaqualand scenery with its plants and animals locked into a relentless battle with aridity. The marvellous wildflower garden with its amazing collection of succulents – more than 500 species – offers a contrasting experience to the mass flowering.

Kamieskroon

Coming to see the wild flowers in this area can be very rewarding, and luckily the little towns of Kamieskroon (67 km south of Springbok), Garies, Bitterfontein and some others are still quite reasonable in their prices. In Leliefontein at the foot of the Kamiesberg Mountains, which is an old mission station with a sundial and Nama village, you can even sleep in a typical "matjieshuis" (reed hut).

Namaqua National Park

The new National Park, 20 km to the northwest of Kamieskroon, is an important feature in the "Garden of the Gods" and one of the prettiest areas in Namaqualand. This 680 km² reserve lies in a mountainous area with several peaks topping 1 500 m. Here you find in a confined space extensive patches with diverse wild flowers. Special protection is afforded to the more than 5 000 different species of succulents, of which more than 2 000 are endemic. The region forms part of the Succulent Karoo and includes the Richtersveld. It is one of the most significant global "hot spots" of biological diversity and is the only arid region that has been enterd in the world

How does this phenomenon in nature come about?

This question is easy to answer: Areas that have lost their ecological equilibrium are taken over by pioneer plants in the form of short-lived annuals. This region is made up of areas of sunbaked fallow fields, overgrazed arid sandy grasslands, desert rims and even spaces next to the road. The location of Namaqualand in the intermediate zone between the winter rainfall areas of the Cape and the arid area with sparse summer rains favours this unexpected flowering season. Within a few days some rain can activate the germination of seeds that have been resting in the ground for years.

Distances inside the reserve:

Sendelingsdrift – Helskloof Entry Gate: 22 km (25 min.)	
Helskloof Gate – Kokerboomkloof: 78,3 k	
Helskloof Gate – Richtersberg: 68,5 km	
Helskloof Gate – De Hoop: 53,7 km	
Richtersberg – De Hoop: 8,1 km (deep sand and sharp rocks)	
Sendelingsdrift – Potjiespram: 9 km	
Sendelingsdrift – De Hoop: 38,2 km	
Sendelingsdrift – Richtersberg – Kokerboomkloof – Helskloof – Sendelingsdrift: 203 km round trip takes approximately 9 hours to complete)	

Lithops sp. at the greenhouse of the Goegap Nature Reserve. They are commonly known as "Living Stones" belonging to the plant family Mesembryanthemaceae. Their succulent leaves are adapted to the surrounding ground and look like pebbles

1.-2. Sea of flowers cover Namaqualand (1) during springtime, as well as parts of the Cape of Good Hope (2)

3. A huge stand of Kokerbome, adapted to the dry region

4. The Buffels River runs only seasonally through the Namaqua National Park

5. Hairy Dewflower (*Drosanthemum hispidum*), internationally also known as Rosea Ice Plant, grows profusely at Monaco's Jardin Exotique in season

6. A male ostrich in Namaqualand

register. Apart from the rare succulents there are also animals like the Cape Mountain Zebra.

The chief ranger of the National Park claims that the flowers do open on overcast days as long as it is warm enough and he cites 17-20° C as minimum temperatures. The best time to film and photograph this miracle of nature is between 10:30 and 16:00. "The sun must be behind you, otherwise the flowers don't face you."

Climate: Summers are hot and dry, average annual rainfall is around 250 mm, ranging from 50 mm in the Richtersveld to 400 mm in the Kamieskroon Mountains, and it falls mainly between June and August. Extended periods of drought are common. Average temperatures are 5-20° C in winter, with occasional night frost and a cold wind on clear days, and 20-35° C in summer.

Horseriding: Excursions of one or more days, also through the Goegap Reserve are available.

Port Nolloth

The little harbour lies 140 km to the northeast of Springbok and became well-known because of diamond divers and smugglers. When they are in season it is sometimes possible to buy freshly caught fish and crayfish. The clean beaches are often littered with kelp. Nearby McDougall's Bay offers interesting accommodation, angling and boat trips.

|Ai-|Ais/Richtersveld Transfrontier National Park

The transfrontier reserve on the lower Orange River was developed in 2003 from the Ai-Ais Hot Springs Game Park (including Fish River Canyon) and the Richtersveld National Park. It protects South Africa's only mountain desert. The incredible diversity of succulents and other desert vegetation in a dramatic landscape is proven to be the richest desert flora in the world with over 360 plant species per square kilometre. The climate is harsh. Water is extremely scarce. Precipitation is low. Mists in the early morning provide the life-saving moisture that also ensures the survival of many insects and mammals. The latter include African Wild Cat, Brown Hyena, Suricate, Aardwolf, Genet, Vervet Monkey, Hartmann's Mountain Zebra, Cape Ground Squirrel, Cape Clawless Otter, Cape Fox, Cape Hare, Rock Hyrax (Dassie), Grey Duiker, Leopard, Bat-eared Fox, Baboon, Grey Rhebuck, Black-backed Jackal, Smith's Red Rock Rabbit, Porcupine, Steenbuck, Striped Polecat, Caracal and three types of mongoose. About 200 bird species are listed. The magic of the flowering season unfolds after good winter rains between June and October.

This habitat of extremes requires tenacity, co-operation and an affinity with nature, and a visitor must be willing to make an effort. During midsummer, day temperatures can climb to over 50 °C and the nights are cool. In winter it can be really cold.

Adventurous roads crisscross the mountain desert. The sparsely marked country roads are mainly for 4x4's and high lying mini busses or pickup vans. It is advisable to travel in convoy. Single cars must report at the park headquarters when departing. Night driving is not permitted.

Well adapted to the dry world:
From the top: Suricate, Springbuck and Bat-eared fox

1. Augrabies Falls, one of the biggest attractions along the Orange River
2. People of the Kalahari
3. Orange River below Upington
4-5. Desolate Richtersveld landscapes
6. Easy prey: Catfish captured in the Orange River bed, at the edge of the Richtersveld

The best routes to the reserve lead from the N7 west of Steinkopf via the diamond towns of Port Nolloth and Alexander Bay to Sendelingsdrift. Permits for entry and overnight stay are available in the office of the reserve. Travelling to overnight accommodation is not permitted after 16h00. There is a ferry service that takes visitors and cars across the Orange River (Transfrontier Route). Diesel and petrol (97 octane) as well as soft drinks can be obtained in Sendelingsdrift during weekdays. Lead-free petrol is available in Alexander Bay.

Guided Hikes

These are offered during the cooler period from 1st of April to 30th September and need to be booked three months in advance. There is a choice of three routes: Vensterval (3 nights); Lelieshoek – Oemsberg (2 nights) and Kodaspiek (1 night).

The starting point for organised hikes is the dramatic Ganakouriep Valley. Up to 9 participants are accommodated. Gas stoves, fridges, hot and cold showers are all provided, but no drinking water. There are not enough trained guides, but groups standing under the leadership of somebody who knows his way around in the area are permitted.

Rest camps

Sendelingsdrift (Reuning Mine): new tourist camp with swimming pool, 10 chalets equipped with airconditioning, fridge, electric stove, shower, veranda with view of the Orange River, camping site for 6 tents, toilets and cold water showers. Potjiespram: site for 18 tents, toilets and cold water showers, ecocourses. De Hoop: site for 12 tents, toilets and cold water showers. Richtersberg-am-Oranje: site for 12 tents, toilets and cold water showers. Kokerboomkloof: site for 8 tents, non-flushing toilets, next tap in Richtersberg (32 km). Tatasberg and Ganakouriep Wilderness Camp: 4x2-bed units each with showers, for self-caterers, 12-Volt electricity for lights (parafine lamps as alternative), fridge, gas stove, hot and cold water, no drinking water.

Distances: Cape Town 875 km, Johannesburg 1 595 km, Durban 1 992 km, Upington 720 km, Springbok 320 km, Port Nolloth 180 km, Alexander Bay 90 km.

Namaqua Adventure Route

This route is intended for 4x4's and has its starting point in Pella. It runs over 640 km along the Orange River to its mouth at Alexander Bay. Pella can be reached from Pofadder. This well-known mission station and small village on the Orange River was founded in 1814. The Catholic Church was built according to pictures from an old German encyclopaedia. Some of the inhabitants live like their forbears, following ecological principles. They cultivate pure dates, pomegranates and grapes.

Accommodation, information and refreshments are offered at the Kultuur Koffie Kroeg of "Ouma Toekoe".

Tip: *Boil drinking water before or, better still, bring your own along.*

TIP FOR EXPLORERS

Tankwa Karoo National Park

The 800 km² research park, miles away from any tourist excursions, lies between the Cedarberg and Roggeveld ranges in the southwestern corner of the Northern Cape Province. It was proclaimed as a National Park in 1986 and is still in the development phase. The name is a Khoi word, meaning "place of the Bushmen". The extremely dry and hot summers of the Karoo proved unsuitable for agriculture. Aborted trials left a desolated countryside in their wake. It will take some time before the Succulent Karoo with its typical landscape, animals, birds, insects and many other forms of life will have returned to its previous biological diversity.

Meanwhile the brilliant and colourful flower carpets bring their own attraction. The list of mammals is also impressive with African Wild Cat, Aardvark, Suricate, Aardwolf, Rock Hyrax (Dassie), Honey Badger, Cape Fox, Cape Hare, Karoo Bush Rat, Klipspringer, Kudu, Leopard, Bat-eared Fox, Black-backed Jackal, Springbuck, Porcupine, Steenbuck and Striped Polecat. Bird watching is especially rewarding. See www.capebirdingroute.org for details.

The Horned Adder, indigenous to the Kalahari

1. Kgalagadi Springbuck still congegrate in big herds

2. Ground Squirrell use their tails to shade themselves from the harsh sun

3. Even White Rhino are kept in some private game reservers of the Kalahari

4. Barn Owl chicks hatched in a barn in the middle of the Kalahari

5. Umbrella Thorn tree

6. Red Hartebeest too survive in this harsh world

7. Two Giraffe at sunset

Ecoadvisor

Please note: No guarantee as to accuracy and completeness can be given with regard to the information and suggestions supplied, and no liability is accepted for possible damages incurred.

General Information

Department of Environmental Affairs and Tourism, Marine and Coastal Management, Private Bag 8012, Cape Town. Tel: 021 4023911, Fax: 021 402 3364.

Botanical Gardens

Durban Botanical Gardens: The oldest (est.1884) and one of the most beautiful in South Africa. Tel. 031 201 1303.

Free State National Botanical Garden: Rayton Rd, 10 km north of Bloemfontein. Tel: 051 436 3530, e-mail: admin@fsnbg.co.za.

Harold Porter Botanical Gardens: Tel: 028 272 9333, e-mail: haroldporter@sanbi.org, web: www.sanbi.org.

Karoo National Botanical Gardens: The only Succulent Garden in Africa and the whole of the southern hemisphere. PO Box 152, Worcester 6850. Tel: 023 347 0785, e-mail: karoodesert@sanbi. org.

Kirstenbosch Botanical Gardens, Cape Town: Conservatory, guided tours (incl. groups) daily. Reservations: Tel: 021 799 8783.

Lowveld Botanical Gardens, Nelspruit: Tel: 013 752 5531, e-mail: admin@glow.co.za, curator@glow.co.za, web: www.nbi.ac.za.

Pretoria National Botanical Gardens: Tel: 012 420 2629, e-mail: upbotgar@scientia.up.ac.za.

Tokai Arboretum: Walking and mountain biking in South Africa's oldest tree park, National Monument. Contact: Safcol, Tokai/Cape Town. Tel: 021 712 7471.

Walter Sisulu National Botanical Gardens, Roodepoort: PO Box 2194, Wilropark 1731. Tel: 011 958 1750, e-mail: SisuluGarden@ sanbi.org

Botanical Society of South Africa: Information, books on flowers of the region, become a member. Head Office, Kirstenbosch, Claremont 7735. Tel: 021 797 2090, e-mail: info@ botanicalsociety.org.za.

Embassies, Consulates

Consulate General of France: PRETORIA – 250 Melk Street/cnr. Middel Street, Nieuw Muckleneuk, Pretoria. Tel: 012 425 1600. Embassy web: www.ambafrance-rsa.org. JOHANNESBURG – Standard Bank Building, 191 Jan Smuts Ave, Rosebank. Tel: 011 778 5600, web: www.consulfrance-jhb.org. CAPE TOWN – 78 Queen Victoria Street, Gardens. Tel: 021 674 4068, web: www. consulfrance-lecap.org

German Embassy: PRETORIA – 180 Blackwood Street, Arcadia, 0083. Tel: 012 427 8900, email: germanembassypretoria@ gonet.co.za. CAPE TOWN – Consulate General, Safmarine House, 19th Floor, 22 Riebeek Street. Tel: 021 405 3000, e-mail: info@ germanconsulatecapetown.co.za

High Commission of the United Kingdom of Great Britain: PRETORIA – "Her Britannic Majesty's High Commission", 255 Hill Street, Arcadia, Pretoria. Tel: 012 421 7800, e-mail: pta.passportenquiries@fco.gov.uk. CAPE TOWN – 15th Floor, Southern Life Centre, 8 Riebeek Street. Tel: 021 405 2400, e-mail:Consular.SectionCT@fco.gov.uk

Embassy of the United States of America: PRETORIA – 877 Pretorius Street, Arcadia 0083, Pretoria. Tel: 012 431 4000, web: http://southafrica.usembassy.gov/. JOHANNESBURG – Consulate General, 1 Sandton Drive, Sandhurst, Tel: 011 290-3000, e-mail: consularjohannesburg@state.gov. CAPE TOWN – 2 Reddam Ave, Westlake. Tel: 021 702-7300, e-mail: consularcapetown@state.gov

High Commission of Commonwealth of Australia: 292 Orient Street/cnr. Schoeman Street, Arcadia, Pretoria. Tel: 012 423 6000, web: http://www.australia.co.za/

Cultural Villages

Cultural Villages are usually simple open-air museums established by the local population and/or form part of nature reserves and private lodges. They portray the culture and customs of various tribes and include performances such as dances, arts and crafts and traditional medicine.

Ebutsini Cultural Village: Design and structure of a typical Swazi village near the border at Oshoek. Guests can stay overnight in 10 Swazi huts arranged in a kraal and fitted out with all modern conveniences and experience traditional dances around the camp fire. Tel: 011 463 3779, e-mail: info@ebutsini.co.za; reservations@pinnaclecollection.com

Ecabazini Zulu Cultural Homestead: Authentic Zulu homestead near the Albert Falls Dam; introduces Zulu culture, traditional farming methods, medicinal plants, Nguni cattle, traditional dances and food; overnight accommodation. Can be reached via the R33, 30 km north of Pietermaritzburg. Tel: 033 342 1928, web: www.ecabazini.co.za, e-mail: ecabazini@futurenet.co.za

Gaabo Motho (near Hebron): Blend of customs of the Tswana, Ndebele, Venda, Zulu and Mokhukhu; survival practices, midwifery and traditional healers. Accommodation in traditional round huts or modern lodgings. Tel: 012 563 0102, e-mail:gaabomotho@yebo.co.za.

Kghodwana Cultural Village: The "Royal Kraal of King Mayitjha" – Mayitjha II was instrumental in establishing this Ndebele Cultural Village and museum in Kwamhlanga, 75 km north of Pretoria on the R573 to Marble Hall. Tel: 013 930 7046, Cell: 083 673 8955 (GPS East: 28.7314; GPS South: -25.5557)

Lesedi Cultural Village: Tel: 012 2051394; 087 940 9933, e-mail: enquiries@lesedi.com, web: www.lesedi.com. (GPS South 25.50.263; East 27.53.064)

Ndebele Royal Kraal: Private Bag X4030, Kwamhlanga 1022. Tel: 013 930 7046. (GPS East: 28.9964; GPS South: -25.0974)

Ndebele Cultural Villages: Botshabelo, (12 km west of Middelburg in the province of Mpumalanga). Address: Klipgat, North West Province (Near Mabopane and Shoshanguve). Office tel: 013 245 9003/9900. E-mail: info@ndebelevillage.co.za

Mapoch Ndebele Village (near Pretoria): Tel: 084 753 8439/ 072 746 5666.

Shangana: Shangaan culture; between southern Kruger Park and Blyde River Canyon. Tel: 013 737 7000/6970, e-mail: reservations@shangana.co.za.

Sudwala Cultural Village: Impressions of tribal life in this area. Tel: 013 733 3037.

Air travel

Inland flights: BA/Comair, Tel: 086 001 1747 web: comair.co.za; **Kulula,** Tel: 086 158 5852 web: kulula.com; **Mango,** Tel: 0861 1MANGO / 086 116 2646, web: flymango.com; **SAA,** Tel. 011 978 1111, web: flysaa.com; **1Time,** Tel: 086 134 5345, web: 1time.com.
Connections to the Kruger Park: Eastgate Airport, Hoedspruit, Tel: 015 793 3681, Kruger Mpumalanga International Airport, Tel: 013-7537500, Phalaborwa Airport, Tel: 015 781 5404, Polokwane Airport, Tel: 015 288 0122.

Galleries & museums (listed in alphabetical order)

Albany Museum, Grahamstown: Tel: 046 622 2312, e-mail: L.Webley@ru.ac.za, web: www.ru.ac.za/albany-museum.
Amathole Museum, King Williams Town: Tel: 043 642 4506, e-mail: museum@amatholeorg.za, web: www.amathole.org.za.
Apartheid Museum, Gold Reef City, Johannesburg: Tel: 011 496 1822.
Bo-Kaap Museum: 71 Wale Street, Cape Town 8000. Tel: 021 481 3939, e-mail: info@iziko.org.za.
Cullinan Dianondmine: Guided tours. Tel: 012 734 0081.
Durban Art Gallery: Second floor, City Hall, Smith Street, Durban. Web: www.durban.gov.za.
Durban Natural Science Museum: 1st floor, City Hall, PO Box 4085, Durban 4000. Tel: 031 311 2256.
East London Museum: Tel: 043 743 0686.
Goodman Gallery Johannesburg: PO Box 411137,Craighall 2024. Tel: 011 788 1113,.
Johannesburg Art Gallery: Klein and King George Streets, Joubert Park. Tel: 011 725 3130, wb: www.joburg.org.za.
Killie Campbell Museum, Durban: Superior collection of Africana. Tel: 031 207 3432.
King George VI Art Gallery: Notable historic art of the East Cape Region. Park Drive, Port Elizabeth, Tel: 041 586 1030.
Lichtenburg/Ditsobotla Art Gallery: Lichtenburg Publicity Association. Tel: 018 632 3051, e-mail: info@lichtenburg.co.za.
Museum Africa: Exhibition of works of the Johannesburg Labour Movement in culture, music and politics. Furthermore the Bensusan Museum of Photography and exhibits of South African rock art as well as a geological collection. Mary Fitzgerald Square, 121 Bree Street, Newtown 2113. Tel: 011 833 5624.
National Cultural History Museum: Visagie Street, Pretoria. Tel: 012 324 6082.
Nelson Mandela Metropolitan Art Museum: 1 Park Drive, Port Elizabeth 6001. Tel: 041 586 1030, e-mail: artmuseum@ artmuseum.co.za.
Nelson Mandela Museum, Mthata (Umtata): Tel: 047 532 5110.
Pierneef Museum, Pretoria/Tshwane: Tel: 012 323 1419.
Pretoria Art Museum: Cnr. Schoeman and Wessels Street, Arcadia Park, PO Box 40925, Arcadia 0007. Tel: 012 344 1807/8, e-mail: art.museum@tshwane.gov.za.
Sammy Marks Museum, Pretoria: Tel: 012 802 1150, restaurant: 012 802 1485.
South African Museum: 25 Queen Victoria Street, Cape Town. Tel: 021 481 3800.
South African National Gallery, Cape Town: Government Avenue, Company's Garden, PO Box 61, Cape Town 8000. Tel: 021 467 4660, e-mail: info@iziko.org.za.
Tatham Art Gallery: Opposite City Hall, PO Box 321, Pietermaritzburg 3200. Tel: 033 392 2801, web: www.tatham.org.za.
Transvaal Museum of Natural History: Paul Kruger Street, Pretoria. PO Box 413, Pretoria 0001. Tel: 012 322 7632.

UNISA Art Gallery: 5th floor, Theo Van Wyk Building, B-Block, University of South Africa Main Campus. Tel: 012 429 6255, e-mail: randam@unisa.ac.za, web: www.unisa.ac.za.

Health

Diarrhoea and Cholera: Most cases of diarrhoea, and especially cholera, are preventable by careful attention to hygiene with regard to food and drinking water. Basic rules are: Drink only safe water (tap water in the towns and cities is fine). When in doubt use only filtered water, disinfected water (chlorine tablets) or boiled water. When camping in the bush use drinking water also to brush teeth or rinse dishes.
First Aid Equipment: Well-equipped First Aid Boxes can be obtained from the Automobile Association of South Africa (AA). AA-shops: Tel: 083 84322, or 011 799 1001; web: www.aa.co.za.
HIV/AIDS: South Africa has a high (and rising) rate of infection with the immune deficiency disease. More than 20 % of the adult population are probably infected with HIV. Sex, drug abuse (contaminated needles) and to a lesser degree blood transfusions, constitute a high risk. Use of condoms is advisable at all times, but especially with casual sex.
Vaccinations: Tetanus, Diphtheria, as well as Poliomyelitis (Infantile Paralysis) and Hepatitis A are recommended for extensive stays of 4 weeks or more, and specially when visiting high risk areas or engaging in high risk actions Hepatitis B, Rabies and Typhus should be included.

Malaria: Seasonally there is a high risk in the eastern parts of the country (northeastern KZN, Mpumalanga, Limpopo, including the Kruger Park) and Kgalagadi National Park. Transmission is by the blood sucking female Anopheles-mosquito that is active at night. If not treated in time it can be deadly, especially the dangerous Malaria tropica strain. It may be weeks or even months before the disease manifests itself. Fever and other symptoms therefore warrant a visit to the doctor even if a long time has passed since the visit. Malaria prophylactics and mosquito nets are urgently recommended for all areas at risk.
Medical Treatment: Private hospitals in the large cities maintain European standards, while the state hospitals are overcrowded and suffer from budget cuts and staff shortages. Health care in the rural areas is substantially inferior to that in the larger cities and towns.

Bilharzia: This chronic infection is caused by blood flukes that are transmitted by freshwater snails that act as intermediate hosts. Bilharzia is not common in South Africa, but one should avoid skin contact with stagnant and slow flowing water, especially in KwaZulu-Natal and in the Lowveld (Kruger Park). There is no prophylaxis. If treatment is begun in time it usually is effective. Symptoms are pain in the bladder, bloody urine or dysentery-like complaints.
Sun protection: High priority, especially in summer (please take note of warnings in South African media). Use SPF35 or higher.

Telephoning

International codes: Great Britain: 0044, United States of America: 001, Australia: 0061, New Zealand: 0064. *Remember to omit the zero before the local code overseas.*
Information: Inland: Tel: 1023, International: 0903. Cellphones: known as cellphones in South Africa and can be used in South Africa with SIM-Cards from Europe (except in isolated areas). For phoning inside the country (and for security reasons) a

South African pre-paid SIM-Card should be purchased to obtain "air time". Telephone calls overseas are cheaper when using a telephone card for the landline.

N.B.: In the information supplied by us, South African telephone numbers are given as they are dialled inland.

Nature conservation regulations

Picking and digging out of protected plants (e.g. orchids) and catching of wild animals is strictly controlled by regulations pertaining to nature conservation and protection of species and any transgressions can lead to heavy fines and imprisonment of between 2 and 10 years. This also applies to the export of plants and animals without obtaining the necessary permits. Even the feeding of baboons and other wild life can bring on heavy fines.

Climate and travelling times

Positioned on both sides of the 30th southern degree of latitude the climate in South Africa in summer is markedly under the influence of the subtropical high-pressure zone that forms a belt of rain shadow. The southeastern trade winds and high pressure zones of the Atlantic and Indian Ocean react with each other and result in the summer weather that is typical for this region: Long, sunny days interrupted by impressive cloud formation and heavy rain that usually takes the form of thunderstorms in the inland (Highveld). Altitude and oceans have an influence on the pretty temperate climate, but with marked regional variations. For example the average annual rainfall varies from 464 mm in the Drakensberg, 800 mm in the Kleinberg and more than 2 000 mm in the alpine zone.

In winter the nights inland are clear and frosty and the days mild and sunny. The subtropical coastal areas of KZN experience neither frost nor hail. Snow is on the whole restricted to the mountain peaks and the high-lying areas of the Cape and the Drakensberg in the south and southeast. Constantly changing parameters make short-term weather prognosis quite difficult, but there do exist some typical weather patterns for summer and winter that can serve as a guideline for visitors. Of course, no binding predictions can be made as to the recurring periods of droughts, floods or unseasonable cold spells.

South African weather service: www.weatherservice.co.za

Seasons

South Africa being in the Southern Hemisphere means the seasons are opposite to those in Europe and North America. The largest part of the subcontinent lies in the summer rainfall area and experiences irregular rainfall. The rainy season stretches from October to April. The west has an arid semidesert climate and the southwestern Cape has a Mediterranean climate with rainstorms in winter. The occasional summer rain is usually in the form of a thunderstorm. Strong southeasterly winds hit the Cape in summer and the "Cape doctor" (as these winds are called) blow away polluted air and makes for the bright blue skies, as well as providing the famous "table cloth" (clouds) spreading over Table Mountain.

Always "in season"

South Africa can be visited right throughout the year. Observation of wild animals is especially rewarding in the drier winter months between April and October, because during this period the game must seek out the waterholes, and the vegetation is less dense and affords better view. Furthermore the risk of malaria is substantially reduced in the affected regions.

Tip: The long school holidays in South Africa are in July and December – so that is the time when holiday resorts on the coast, nature reserves and game parks are crowded. Visitors travelling during the hot summer time can find some respite in the higher regions of the Drakensberg Mountain and along the Cape peninsula where the climate is more temperate.

Safety

South Africa suffers from a high crime rate. While there are spacious and well-kept residential areas the majority of the non-white population still live in crowded "townships", often in slum-like houses and huts. Not only these 'townships', but also the inner cities of Johannesburg, Pretoria, Cape Town, Durban and other metropoles experience high crime rates. These areas should be avoided outside of business times and on Sundays and public holidays. Even during daytime vigilance needs to be exercised at all times. Tourist visits to the cities and "townships" should always be in organised form and with a knowledgeable guide.

Avoid travelling on suburban trains or so-called minibus-taxis and especially hitchhiking. When travelling by car, precautions regarding the danger of hijacking and so-called "smash-and-grab" attacks include keeping the car windows closed (except for a very narrow opening at the top) and the doors locked from inside. Don't leave handbags, cameras and clothes prominently in sight inside the car. Avoid displaying or wearing cameras, jewellery and other valuable goods. Tourists are prime targets for thieves on the streets, and since the latter are usually ready to use force it is advisable not to put up a fight.

When driving overland you should stick to main roads arteries wherever possible and avoid driving at night. A breakdown of one's car can constitute a serious risk, especially when it is dark. Avoid isolated view points or picnic sites.

The SA Police Service issues a brochure titled "Visitor Safety Tips" Ask for one at a tourism office.

National Tourism Information and Safety Line: 083 123 2345
Emergency number (from mobile phones): 112
Police emergency number: 10111; **Ambulance:** 1022

Road safety: Most countries drive on the right. Please remember, especially when crossing roads that in South Africa we drive on the LEFT. South African drivers are mostly undisciplined, so please drive defensively. Diesoline in South Africa is of good quality, so fill up before you cross the border.

Beaches: Swim at beaches where life savers are on duty and obey them. In KwaZulu-Natal swim only at beaches that have shark nets.

For beach safety in Cape Town – Metro Police: Tel: 086 076 5423, National Sea Rescue Institute: Tel: 021 449 3500.

Durban: Beach Patrol (safety & security service): Tel: 031 368 4453. Mountain Rescue: Tel: 031 307 7744, Sea Rescue: Tel: 031 361 8567.

NOTE: Fires kill many animals, young birds, reptiles and insects. Fines and jail terms for starting bush fires are severe, as are the fines for picking wild flowers.

Observatories: Boyden Observatory, Bloemfontein. Contact

Dr. Matie Hoffman, Tel: 051 401 2924. Southern African Large Telescope (SALT): International observatory near Sutherland, ± 400 km from Cape Town. Tel: 021 460 9350.

Shopping: In and around the larger cities the range of products on offer is very good, but in the rural areas this high standard is not present and foreign newspapers and magazines are rarely available there. **VAT:** Tourists can reclaim Value Added Tax at the airports when they leave. Keep receipts for purchases that you can show physically ie not haircuts or movie tickets.

Animals on land and in the sea

Ocean and Coast:
Bayworld Oceanarium and Snake Park: Port Elizabeth. Tel: 041 584 0650, web: www.bayworld.co.za

uShaka Sea World: Durban. Giant aquariums with sea creatures occurring along the coast. Tel: 086 110 2479, web: www.ushakamarineworld.co.za

Whales, Dolphins and Great Whites: KZN Coast: Activities in the sea increase with the "sardine run" when the shoals of sardines arrive in June-July. Information: Tel: 082 284 9495. Ocean Safaris, Durban: Whales, dolphins, shark nets, scuba diving. Cell: 084 565 5328, e-mail: indo@airandoceansafaris. co.za, web: www.airandoceansafaris.co.za. **Eastern Cape:** Whale watching from East London, Port Alfred and Kenton Beaches, Port Elizabeth, Jeffrey's Bay, St. Francis Bay, Tsitsikamma National Park, Wild Coast. Ocean Blue Whale Watching: Plettenberg Bay beach. Whales, seabirds, sharks, seals. Tel: 044 533 5083, e-mail: info@oceanadventures.co.za, web: www.adventures.co.za. Ocean Safaris: Plettenberg Bay and Knysna. Tel: 044 533 4963, e-mail: info@oceansafaris.co.za, knysna@oceansafaris.co.za. **Western Cape:** Southern Right Charters, Hermanus: Tel: 082 353 0550, e-mail: seascapes@hermanus.co.za, web: www. southernrightcharters.co.za or visit the Whale Shack in the New Harbour. **Whale calves in San Sebastian Bay:** Witsand Tourism. Tel: 028 537 1010, web: www.witsandtourism.co.za.

Shark Africa, Mossel Bay: Great Whites. Cage diving. Tel: 044 691 3796, e-mail: sharkafrica@mweb.co.za, web: www.sharkafrica. co.za. Hermanus: Cell: 083 746 8985

Bird Parks and demonstrations of birds in flight
Bird of Prey Centre: Box 152, Lynedoch 7603. Tel: 021 858 1826, e-mail: eagles@telkomsa.net, web: www.eagle-encounters. co.za. **Bird Island Nature Reserve:** Lambert's Bay, PO Box 200, Vanrhynsdorp 8170. Tel: 072 133 1440. **Falcon Ridge Bird of Prey Centre:** Drakensberg, Champagne Valley. Cell: 082 774 6398. **Demonstrations of Raptors:** Thousand Hills. Tel: 031 777 1871, Cell (Shannon): 082 925 3023. **Lammergeier Hide, Giant's Castle:** Observation of Bearded Vultures and other raptors between May and September. Reservation preferably a year in advance. Reception: Tel: 036 353 3718.
Polokwane Bird Sanctuary & Moletšie Bird Sanctuary: Tel: 015 290 2177. **Umgeni River Bird Park, Durban:** Flight demonstrations daily. Tel: 031 579 4600. **Uvongo Bird Park:** Indigenous and exotic birds. Tel: 039 317 4086. **World of Birds Wildlife Sanctuary:** Valley Road, Hout Bay 7806. Tel: 021 790 2730, web: www.worldofbirds.org.za.
Zululand Birding Route: More than 600 bird species. Tel: 035 753 5644. **Hides and walkways among the tree tops in the Dlinza Forest near Eshowe:** Tel: 035 474 4029, e-mail: boardwalk@zbr.co.za, web: www.zbr.co.za/boardwalk

Animal Parks
Cango Wildlife Ranch, Oudtshoorn: Tel: 044 2725 593, e-mail: cango@kingsley.co.za, web: www.cango.co.za. **Cheetah Centres: De Wildt Cheetah Centre:** Northwest. PO Box 16, De Wildt, 0251. Tel: 012 5041921, e-mail: cheetah@dewildt.org.za. **Cheetah Outreach Programme:** Spier, near Stellenbosch. Lynedoch Rd (R310), Box 116, Lynedoch 7603. Cell: 082 491 0231, e-mail: Cheetah@intekom.co.za, web: www.cheetah.co.za. **Lion Park Johannesburg:** More than 80 lions. PO Box 2140, Fourways 2055. Tel: 011 691 9905, e-mail: lionpark@cknet.co.za, web: www.lion-park.com. **Rhino and Lion Park:** Tel: 011 957 0106. **Hartebeespoort Dam:** Snake Park and Cheetah Centre. On the slopes of the Magaliesberg Mountains. Tel: 012 253 0266. **Meerkat Magic, Oudtshoorn:** Tel: 082 413 6895, e-mail: gmmcilrath@mweb.co.za, web: www.meerkatMagic.com. **Ostrich Farms: High Gate:** 10 km outside Oudtshoorn. Tel: 044 272 7115/6, e-mail: hosf@mweb.co.za, web: www. highgate.co.za. **Safari Show Farm:** Oudtshoorn, with "Ostrich Palace", National Monument. Tel: 044 272 7311/2, e-mail: safariostrich@mweb.co.za, web: www.safariostrich.co.za. **Wildlife Rehabilitation Centre Moholoholo:** Box 1476, Hoedspruit 1380. Tel: 015 795 5236. **Game Breeding:** Lichtenburg Game Breeding Centre: Tel: 018 632 2818, e-mail: andre@zoo.co.za. **Mokopane Game Breeding Centre:** Tel: 015 491 4314, e-mail: mark@zoo. ac.za. **Zoos:** Bloemfontein Zoo: Tel: 051 405 8483. **National Zoo, Pretoria:** Tel: 012 328 3265. **Johannesburg Zoo:** Tel: 011 646 2000.

Reptiles
Crocodile Centre, St. Lucia: Crocodiles, South African reptiles, daily guided tours. P/Bag X03, St Lucia, 3936. Tel: 035 590 1386. **Crocworld, Scottburgh:** Feeding daily at 11h00 and 15h00. Tel: 039 976 1103, e-mail: crocworld@cbl.co.za, web: www. crocworld.co.za. **Crocodile Creek, Tongaat:** Tel. 032 944 3845. **Sea Turtles, Kosi Bay:** Excursions in December and January. PO Box 555, KwaNgwanase 3973. Tel: 035 592 0234. **Wildlife Rehabilitation Centre, Moholoholo:** Box 1476, Hoedspruit 1380. Tel: 015 795 5236. **Pure Venom Reptile Farm:** Izotsha (KZN): Largest collection of indigenous and exotic reptiles in Africa. Tel: 039 685 0704, e-mail: info@purevenom.com, web: www. purevenom.com. **Fitzsimmons Snake Park:** Durban. Tel: 031 337 6456. **Khamai Reptile Park:** Box 175, Hoedspruit 1380. Tel. 015 795 5203, e-mail: reptile@yebo.co.za.

Sport and Recreation

Rugby: South African Rugby Museum, Cape Town. Tel: 021 659 6768, e-mail: john@sarugby.co.za.
Cricket: E-mail: info@cricket.co.za, web: www.cricket.co.za.
Soccer: KICK OFF, South African Internet Magazine: http://www. kickoff.com. Premier Soccer League, Johannesburg: PO Box 15740, Doornfontein 2028. Tel: 011 482 9111, web: ww.psl.co.za. The national league presently consists of "Premier Division" and "First Division".
On the Ocean: Harbour tours and ocean excursions: Durban, Wilson's Wharf. Tel: 031 337 7751, web: www.isleofcapri.co.za. **Pelagic Excursions from Simon's Town, Hout Bay:** Avian Leisure. Tel: 021 786 1414, Cell: 083 272 2455, e-mail: avianleisure@ netpoint.co.za, web: www.avianleisure.com. **Seal Island Trips, Hout Bay:** Boats with glass floors. Circe Launches, PO Box 26290, Hout Bay 7872. Tel: 021 790 1040, e-mail: circe@softcract.co.za, web: www.circelaunches.co.za. Drumbeat: Tel: 021 790 4859.

Canoeing: North Coast KZN, DumaManz: Tel: 033 212 2055, Infinity Marine: Tel: 032 946 0918.

Bungee Jumping

Bloukrans Bridge: Reservation: Tel: 042 281 1458, Cell: 083 231 3528. **Graskop:** Tel: 013 767 1621. **Gouritz Bridge:** (40 km east of Plettenberg Bay) Tel: 044 697 7001, Cell: 083 414 2380. **Oribi Gorge:** Tel: 039 687 0253, e-mail: oribigorge@worldonline.co.za, web: www.oribigorge.co.za.

Canopy Tours

Karkloof: Near Howick (KZN). Tel: 033 330 3415, e-mail: info@karkloofcanopytour.co.za, web: www.karkloofcanopytour.co.za. **Magaliesberg:** In a ravine. Tel: 014 535 0150, e-mail: info@magaliescanopytour.c.za, web: www.magaliescanopytour.co.za. **Tsitsikamma:** Among the tree tops in the Tsitsikamma Forest. Tel: 042 281 1836, e-mail: info@treetoptour.com, web: www.treetoptour.com.

Steam trains

Banana Express: Narrow gauge railway, inland to Izotsha and back. Inchanga Choo Choo: Tel: 031 303 3003, e-mail: robmac2005@telkomsa.net, web: www.umgenisteamrailway.co.za. **Outeniqua Choo-Choo:** Outeniqua Transport Museum, 2 Mission Street, George. Tel: 044 801 8288.

Extreme sports

Adventure-Kloofing: Climbing in gorges.
CAPE TOWN: 24 Crown Street, 7925 Cape Town, South Africa, PO Box 2415, 7740 Clareinch. Tel: 021 447 4985, e-mail info@frixion.co.za. GEORGE: Robert Peschel, P.O. Box 2068, George 6530, e-mail: robert@etime.co.za. GRABOUW: Suicide Gorge, Grabouw 7160, e-mail: hcassels@capenature.co.za. MONTAGU: Nuy River Gorge Kloofing. Jürgen Wohlfarter, PO Box 501, Montagu 6720, e-mail: info@simonskloof.com.

Flying

Helicopter and Marine Service, Cape Town: Waterfront. Tel: 021 418 0200, e-mail: gary@helibas.com. **Capri Tours and Helicopters, Tsitsikamma:** Cell: 082 749 9042, web: www.caprihelicopters.co.za. **Helicopter Experiences, Air Safaris:** Durban. Cell: 084 257 0835, e-mail: info@airandoceansafaris.co.za, web: www.airandoceansafaris.co.za. **Gliding:** Bloemfontein Gliding Club: web: www.bgc.org.za. **Gariep Dam Aviation Club:** Xhariep Dam Nature Reserve: e-mail: peter@gariepgliding.com.

Golf

Cathedral Peak Golf Course: The golf course belonging to the hotel in the majestic Drakensberg Mountains is considered a challenge. Tel: 036 488 1888, web: www.sa-venues.com/kzn/cathedral_peak.htm. **Durban Country Club:** On the waterfront. Tel: 031 309 1373. **George:** Fancourt Country Club Estate. Tel: 044 804 0030, web: www.fancourt.com. **Hans Merensky Country Club, Phalaborwa:** Borders on the Kruger Park. Club Road, Phalaborwa. Tel: 015 781 3931, PO Box 4, Phalaborwa 1390. e-mail: gitw@hansmerensky.com. **Knysna Golf Club:** Beautiful scenery, positioned below sea level. Tel: 044 384 1150, web: www.knysnagolfclub.com. **Mossel Bay Golf Club:** On the waterfront. Tel: 044 691 2379, web: www.mosselbaygolfclub.co.za. **Oudtshoorn Golf Club:** Surrounded by three mountain ranges. Tel: 044 272 4201. **Plettenberg Bay, Goose Valley:** Breathtaking scenery on the Keurbooms Lagoon. Tel: 044 533 5082, web: www.goosevalleygolfclub.com. **Royal Port Alfred:** A favourite of tourists. Tel: 046 624 4388. **Selborn Country Club:** Pennington, between the sea and the sugar cane fields. Cell: 039 975 3564.

Skukuza Golf Course: This unusual golf course in the Kruger Park is suitable for golfers of any handicap and adjoins the Skukuza Tourist Camp. Visits of wild animals of all descriptions can never be ruled out. Before you can start a game an indemnity form has to be signed. Info and reservation: Tel: 013 735 5543, e-mail: skukuzagolf@sanparks.org. **Wild Coast Sun Country Club:** The marvellous golf course situated on the border of KZN is part of the Wild Coast Sun Hotel and Casino. A "golf academy" forms part of it where single players or groups can be coached by professionals. Tel: 039 305 2799.

Hotair-Ballooning

Hartebeestpoortdam: Bill Harrop hot-air balloons: Tel: 011 705 3201, Cell: 080 Balloon (705 3201), e-mail: bill@balloon.co.za, web: www.balloon.co.za. **Little Karoo:** Kleinplaas/Oudtshoorn. Cell: 082 784 8539, e-mail: charl@balloondrifters.co.za, web: www.balloondrifters.co.za.

Water sport

Scuba diving, Cape: The Maori wreck near Hout Bay, the Atlantic coast near Oudekraal and Miller's Point on False Bay are great favourites. Web: www.scubashack.co.za; www.africasharkdivesafaris.com; **Diving Adventure, Durban:** Aliwal Shoal and Sodwana. Aliwal Shoal: Tel: 031 561 5178, Tel: 0860 3482 4378. Diving and Training: Amatikulu Dive Tours: Tel: 039 973 2534. Dive School-Meridian Dive Centre: Tel: 039 973 2813. Aliwal Dive Charters (South Coast): Tel: 039 973 2233. **Surfing:** South Africa's highest and roughest waves can be experienced at the "Dungeons", close to Long Beach in Noordhoek. Other favourite spots are between Strand and Betty's Bay. Tel: 021 851 4022, e-mail: helderberg@tourismcapetown.co.za. **Windsurfing:** Blaauwberg Strand on the west coast. Tel: 021 556 7679, web: www.windfinder.com

Horse riding

Drakensberg Excursions: Appaloosa, Sans Souci Farm, Kamberg Valley. Tel: 033 267 7227, e-mail: trisha@bergtrails.co.za. **Other trails:** Spioenkop, Rugged Glen, Sani Pass (also Horse-Trekking). **Durban beach:** Horseback Beach Adventure: Tel: 031 467 0752. Wellesley Stables: Tel: 031 568 1881. **Hout Bay:** Beach, dunes, forests. **Cape Town Tourism:** Tel: 021 790 1264/ 021 790 0456. **Maputaland Horse Safaris:** Day rides or safaris of 3-8 days, base camp in the wild. Tel: 083 556 6609, e-mail: safarismail@maputaland.net, web: www.maputaland.net. **Noordhoek (Cape Town):** Kakapo Horsetrail, The Dunes. Tel: 021 789 1723, e-mail: thedunes@telkomsa.net. **Springbok:** Short outride and riding safaris lasting several days, also through the Goegap Reserve: Tel: 027 712 3337, e-mail: namaquahorsetrails@telkomsa.net. **Wild Coast Riding and Hiking Trails:** Tel: 039 305 6455, e-mail: reservations@wild-coast.co.za. Amadiba Adventures: Opposite Wild Coast Sun entrance: Riding and hiking along the Wild Coast (1-6 days). Local initiative: Tel: 039 305 6455, e-mail: amadiba@euwildcoast.za.org.

Elephant rides

Elephant Experience: Knysna. Tel: 044 532 7732, e-mail: kep@pixie.co.za, web: www.knysnaelephantpark.co.za. **Elephant Sanctuary:** Hartebeespoort. Tel: 012 258 0423, e-mail: elephantsanctuary@mweb.co.za. **Elephant Sanctuary (near Plettenberg Bay):** Close encounter with elephants, rides. Tel: 044 534 8145, e-mail: crags@elephantsanctuary.co.za. **Hoedspruit Research and Breeding Centre:** Camp Jabulani. Tel: 015 793 1265, e-mail: reservations@campjabulani.org.za, web: www.campjabulani.com.
Pilanesberg Elephant Back Safaris: Cell: 083 382 5905,

e-mail: elephantpark@xsinet.co.za, web: www.gametrac.co.za. **Shamwari:** Tel: 044 533 9006.

Dripstone caves
Oudtshoorn: Cango Caves – about 30 km from Oudtshoorn. Tel: 044 272 7410, e-mail: reservations@cangocaves.co.za, web: www.cangocaves.co.za. **Sudwala Caves:** Box 48, Schagen 1207. Tel: 013 733 4152.

Wild Water Rafting
River Rafting and Canoeing weblinks: www.sa-venues.com/activities/white-water-rafting; www.uncoverthecape.co.za/extreme/river-rafting/index.htm; www.drakensberg-tourism.com/white-water-rafting.html; http://home.intekom.com/ecotravel/index.htm; www.places.co.za/html/white_water_rafting.html; www.southafrica.info/travel/adventure/adventure.htm.
Olifants River: Hoedspruit, Tel: 015 795 5250, Cell: 082 572 2223, e-mail: catfishmweb.co.za.

HIKING AND TREKKING
Kruger Park
Wilderness Trails: Up to eight participants in the age group 12-60 years can take part. Adequate fitness level is a precondition. An experienced ranger is the guide in the wilderness. Three overnight stays are envisaged. Note: Wear clothing in neutral colours, including anorak; hat and sun lotion essential, torch and strong, comfortable hiking shoes. Info and reservation in the relevant camps. **Metsi-metsi Trail:** Skukuza. Tel: 013 735 4000; **Napi Trail:** Pretoriuskop. Tel: 013 735 5128; **Nyalaland Trail:** Punda Maria. Tel: 013 735 5128; **Olifants Trail:** Letaba. Tel: 013 735 6636; **Sweni Trail:** Satara. Tel: 013 735 6306; **Wolhuter Trail and Bushman Trail:** Berg-en-Dal. Tel: 013 735 6106; **Lebombo Ecotrail:** Accompanied by professional guides. During the dry season this tour can only be undertaken by 4x4 vehicles. It commences at the Crocodile Bridge on Sundays and ends in Pafuri in the north on Thursdays. For cross-country drivers there are also four ecotours on offer (4x4's) each take four hours: Northern Plains Trail-Shingwedzi, Nonokani Trail-Phalaborwa Gate, Mananga Trail-Satara, Madlabantu Trail-Pretoriuskop. Longer routes for 4x4's run through various parts of the Kruger Park. Info and reservation: Tel: 012 428 9111 or Hester van der Berg: Tel: 012 426 5117.

Cape of Good Hope
Hiking tours lasting several days are on available between Table Mountain and Cape Point: Cape of Good Hope Hiking Trail, five-day Hoerikwaggo Trail and six-day mountain hike for experienced hikers who can manage on their own, partly through rough terrain, but also three-day luxury excursions with mountain guide, carriers, meals served and comfortable overnight accommodation. Table Mountain National Park. Tel: 021 780 9526.

Mountain climbing
Mountain Climbing Club of South Africa: web: www.mcsa.org.za. Cape Mountain Club (Mon - Fr: 10h00 -14h00), Tel: 021 45 3412. **Drakensberg Mountains, Cape Folded Mountain Ranges.** Climbing or kloofing: Mountain Club of SA. Cell: 082 990 5877. Eduventures: Cell: 083 264 5285.

Drakensberge and Zululand
Queen's Causeway and Cascades: An easy walk in the Royal Natal National Park that Princess Elizabeth and her sister Margaret Rose undertook during their visit to south Africa in 1947. Somewhat more strenuous is the excursions through the Vemvaan Valley to Policeman's Helmet that was carved out by erosion and offers breathtaking views. The day tour to the Thukela

Gorge is considered one of the most attractive day excursions in the Drakensberg Mountains. Hikes lasting several days lead to the rock paintings by the San in the Didima Gorge and can be started from the Monk's Cowl Mountain Reserve. One can hire a good mountain guide for this tour. The Giant's Cup Trail lasts five days and covers the areas from the Sani Pass to Bushman's Nek. It must be booked in advance and has acceptable overnight accommodation. **iMfolozi Wilderness Trails, Zululand:** The mother of all wilderness hikes. Enzemvelo KZN Wildlife, PO Box 1306, Cascades 3202. Tel: 033 845 1067.

Wanderlust
For short hikes you need only motivation and a love of nature, a walking stick and sturdy shoes. For longer hikes with real interaction with your environment or "trekking", you need to be well prepared and observe the pertaining regulations (displayed in tourist centres). Even the pleasant Drakensberg Mountains should not be underestimated. Climbing in the Escarpment could require climbing iron, oxygen cylinder and climbing rope.

Addo Elephant National Park: Spekboom Trail (3-4 hours), 2 trails in the Zuurberg Mountains, either one-hour or five-hours. Tel: 042 233 8600.
Augrabies Falls: Klipspringer Trail, 2 days, overnight accommodation. Tel: 011 656 0606.
Mossel Bay: Oyster Catcher Trail Tel. 044 6991204, e-mail forban@mweb.co.za.
West Coast National Park: Strandveld Eco Trail starts from Geelbek Homestead. (2 -3 days). Postberg Flower Trail is only on offer during the flower season in spring, reservation in the reserve. Tel. 022 772 2144.
Hikes of one or more days in the Eastern Cape: (pre-book): Amadiba Adventures, Wild Coast, 50 km, Tel. 039-3056455, Amatola Hiking, King William's Town, 19 km,Tel: 043-6424148, Dolphin Trail, Tsitsikamma, 17 km, Tel. 042-281- 1607,Ecowa Trail, Elliot, 47 km, Tel. 045-9311011, Kariega Trail Kenton-On-Sea, 8-10 km, Tel. 0413630263, Lammergeier Trail, Lady Grey, 15 km, Tel. 051-6031114, Mkambati, 15 km, Tel 0397273273, Strandloper Trail, Kei Mouth, 57 km, Tel. 043-8411046, Transkaroo Hiking Trail, Middelburg, 40km Tel. 049-8431506, Tyume Indigenous Forest, Hogsback, 22 km, Tel: 043-6424148.

MOUNTAIN BIKING
De Hoop Nature Reserve: High level of competence required. 2-3 days, various routes from farmhouse (base). Tel: 028 542 1126.
Deer Park, Cape Town: Info: Parks and Forests. Tel: 021 782 2849. Citrusdal: 11 scenic rides, best time July-October. Tel: 022 921 3210. **Cederberg, Maltese-Cross:** 16 km. Difficult terrain, overnight stay, tent site. Tel: 027 482 2825. **Knysna:** Rides through indigenous forest. Tel: 044 382 2010, e-mail: info@deepsoutheco. com. Joyrides: Tel: 044 272 3436, e-mail: backpackers@isat. co.za. **Mountain Zebra Park:** 37 km good gravel roads. Tel: 048 881 2427. **La Motte Plantation, Franschoek:** Easy to difficult, through wooded areas. April-November.
Plan own routes. SAFCOL, Tel: 021 876 2061. **In die Diepte, Graskop:** 17 km. Overnight stay in huts. Mondi Forests. Tel: 013 768 1027. Mariepskop Forestry Area, Mariepskop near Graskop: 20 km. Tent site along the Blyde River or stay in a chalet. Tel: 015 793 2581.
Grootvadersbosch, Heidelberg: 25-28 km. Road with hurdles. Tel: 014 717 5812, e-mail: info@waterberg, web: www.stamvrugtrails. co.za. **Leliefontein, Kamieskroon:** 20 km. Easy flower route.

Namaqualand District Council. Cell: 0251 22011. **Langebaan/ Saldanha Bay:** Several ecoroutes of 10-25 km. Also with guides. Tel: 022 772 1793, e-mail: alan@live2ride.co.za, web: www. live2ride.co.za. **Goegap Nature Reserve, Springbok:** 20 km. Ride through reserve. Tel: 027 718 9906/ 0251 21880. **Storms River:** Ride through Tsitsikamma State Forest. 22 km. Ride through the old Storms River Pass. Tel: 042 541 1557. **Cathedral Peak:** 70 km ecoroute through Drakensberg Mountains. Tel: 033 147 1981, **Dragon's Peak:** Several routes from hotel or camping site as base. Dragon Peak's Holiday Resort. Tel: 036 468 1031.

Tip: Good advice supplied by Durban Mountain Bike Club. Cell: 082 454 8561 (Cliff Gore). Also see web: mtbroutes.co.za

---

Bicycle Safaris
Safaris on bicycles in reserves are apparently catching on only slowly. Cape Nature Conservation sets the example and has introduced well signposted cycle tracks in many of its reserves. Table Mountain National Park also boasts several signposted cycle tracks. In the Kruger Park you may only cycle when accompanied by rangers.

Infos, reservation
WESTERN CAPE
Cape Town
Cape Mountain Rescue: Tel: 021 948 9900. **NSRI:** Tel: 021 449 3500. **Tourist Safety Unit:** Tel: 021 421 5116. **Cape Mountain Club:** Safety information and addresses. Tel: 021 405 3412. **Cape Town Tourism Information Office:** Tel: 021 405 4500, fax: 021 405 4524, e-mail: info@tourcapetown.com. **Namaqua National Park:** Information on the flower season can be obtained from the "Flower Hotline" in Cape Town: Tel: 021 418 3705. **Groot Constantia:** Tel: 021 794 5128. **Table Mountain Cable Way:** Tel: 021 424 8181. Cape Town and Western Cape Tourism: Web: www.tourismcapetown.co.za. **Two Oceans Aquarium:** Dock Road, V & A Waterfront. Tel: 021 418 3823, e-mail: aquarium@ aquarium.co.za. **V&A Waterfront:** Tel: 021 408 7600, fax: 021 408 7605, e-mail: info@waterfront.co.za, web: www.capetown-waterfront.co.za. **Kirstenbosch National Botanical Garden:** Rhodes Drive, Cape Town 6970. Tel: 021 799 8783, fax: 021 761 5626, e-mail: kirstenbosch@tourismcapetown.co.za. **Wineland Tourism:** Tel: 021 872 0686. Wine Routes on horseback and on foot: Information: **Cape Town Tourism:** Burg Street, Cape Town. Tel: 021 487 6800. **West Coast Tourism:** Tel: 022 433 8505, web: www.capewestcoast.org. **Bird Island:** Booking is not essential. Information: The Manager, Bird Island Nature Reserve, PO Box 200, Vanrhynsdorp 8170, Cell: 072 133 1440 or at the Visitor's Centre Guano Museum.

Robben Island
Tickets for boat trip and guided tour in the museum and visitor's centre on Canal Walk at the Clock Tower, V&A Waterfront, or Nelson Mandela Gateway. Tel: 021 413 4200, e-mail: ereservations@robben-island.org.za. Trips by helicopter: Civair, PO Box 120 Newlands, 7725. Tel: 021 419 5182.

Rest of the province: Hermanus: Tourism Bureau, cnr. Mitchell/ Lord Roberts Street. Tel: 028 312 2629, e-mail: infoburo@ hermanus.co.za, web: www.hermanus.co.za/info. **Heidelberg Tourism:** Gateway to the Garden Route. Tel: 028 722 2700, web: www.tourismheidelberg.co.za. **Mossel Bay Tourism:** Tel: 044 691 2202, e-mail: mbtb@mweb.co.za, web: wwwvisitmosselbay. co.za. **Dias Museum:** Tel: 044 691 1067, e-mail: info@diasmuseum.

co.za, web: www.diasmuseum.co,za. **Hout Bay:** Houtbay Tourism Office. Tel: 021 790 1264, e-mail: houtbay@tourismcapetown. co.za, web: www.houtbay.org. **Overberg Area:** Overberg Tourism. Tel: 028 214 1466, e-mail: info@capeoverberg.org, web: www. tourismcapeoverberg.co.za. **Knysna:** Houseboats. Tel: 044 386 0007, e-mail: info@houseboats.co.za, web: www.houseboats. co.za. Springtide Sailing Charter: Cell: 082 470 6022, e-mail: info@springtide.co.za, web: www.springtide.co.za. Knysna Tourism: Tel: 044 382 5510. **Plettenberg Bay Tourism:** Tel: 044 533 4065. **Lambert's Bay Tourism:** 5 Medical Centre, Main Road, Lambert's Bay 8130. Tel: 027 432 1000, e-mail: lambertsinfo@ mweb.co.za.

Eastern Cape
Apple Express narrow-gauge steam train: Tel: 041 507 2333. **Buffalo City Tourism:** East London. Tel: 043 722 6015. **Gariep Tourism:** Tel: 051 654 4140. **Cape St. Francis Tourism:** Tel: 042 294 0076, web: www.stfrancistourism.co.za. **Eastern Cape Tourism Board:** Tel: 043 701 9600, web: www.ectourism.co.za. **East London:** Adventure Village. Tel: 043 734 3055. **Graaff-Reinet Tourism:** Tel: 049 892 4248, e-mail: info@graaff-reinet. co.za, web: www.graaf-reinet.co.za. **Jeffreys BayTourism:** Tel: 042 293 2923, e-mail: jbaytourism@telkomsa.net, web: www. jeffreysbaytourism.org. **Nelson Mandela Bay (Port Elizabeth) Tourism:** Tel: 041 585 8884. **Rhodes:** Tel: 045 974 9277, e-mail: edh@lbrand.com. **Wild Coast Holiday Association:** Tel: 043 743 6181, e-mail: meross@iafrica.com. **Wild Coast Tourism:** Umtata. Tel: 047 531 5290.

KwaZulu-Natal
Durban: Tourist Junction, 160 Pine Street. Tel: 031 304 4934, e-mail: funinsun@iafrica.com, web: www.durbanexperience.co.za. **Tourism KwaZulu-Natal:** Durban. Tel: 031 366 7500, web: www. zulu.org. **Elephant Coast Tourism:** Tel: 035 562 0353. **Zululand Tourism:** Tel: 035 870 0812. **Midlands Meander:** Howick. Tel: 033 330 8195, e-mail: info@midlandsmeander.co.za, web: www. midlandsmeander.co.za. **Pietermaritzburg Tourism:** Tel: 033 345 1348. **Sani Pass Landrover Trips:** From Underberg Hotel (Passport). Tel: 033 701 1628, e-mail: info@majoradventures. com. web: www.majoradventures.com. **Sharks Board:** Tel: 031 566 0400. **Valley of a Thousand Hills:** 40 km north of Durban. Thousand Hills Experience. Tel: 031 765 1516/031 774 1874. **Zulu Village:** Tel: 031 777 7167. **Safaripark pheZulu:** Tel: 031 777 1000, e-mail: info@phezulusafaripark.co.za, web: www. phezulusafaripark.co.za. **Victoria Street Indian Market:** Durban. Tel: 031 306 4021. **South Coast:** Amanzimtoti Visitors Bureau Tel: 031-903 7498, web: www.amanzimtoti.org.za. South Coast Information: Tel: 039 315 5168, e-mail: sctourism@venturenet. co.za, web:www.southcoast.kzn.org.za. **Umdoni Coast Tourism:** Tel. 039-976 1364. **Hibiscus Coast Tourism:** Tel. 039-312 2322.

FREE STATE
Free State Tourism: Tel: 051 403 3606. Bloemfontein Tourism: Hoffman Square, PO Box 639, Bloemfontein 9300. Tel: 051 405 8489, e-mail: information@bloemfontein.co.za, web: www.linx. co.za/Bloemfontein. **Free State Tourism:** Bojanala Building, 34 Markgraaf Street, Bloemfontein; Private Bag X20801, Bloemfontein 9300. Tel: 051 403 3719. Bagamoga Lion Farm: Approximately 30 km from Bloemfontein, near the holiday resort Maselspoort. Chalets, house up to 4 persons. Tel: 051 861 1057, e-ail: shaba@connix.co.za. National Museum, Bloemfontein: 36 Aliwal Street. Tel: 051 447 609, email: ornito@nasmus.co.za.

Vredefort Dome: Tourism and Information Development Centre: Box 912, Potchefstroom 2520. Tel: 018 293 1611, e-mail: tidcpotch@mweb.co.za. Otter's Haunt/Parys: Tel: 056 818 1814, e-mail: info@otters.co.za. Vredefort Tourism Bureau, Vredefort Library, Vredefort: Tel: 016 976 0765.

MPUMALANGA

Barberton: Information Bureau. Tel: 013 712 2121. Chrissiesmeer: Birding and stargazing (Aretha Strydom). Tel: 017 847 2034, Cell: 082 821 3081. Field Flower Days: Hester. Cell: 073 194 6801. Frogging: Anne Steinberg. Tel: 017 847 0051/082 804 1771. Overnight accommodation on farms: Tel: 017 847 0051/082 804 1771, e-mail: info@florence.co.za. Dullstroom: Information: Tel: 013 254 0254. Accommodation: Main Road, Box 45. Tel: 013 254 0020. Dullstroom Inn Family Hotel: Tel: 013 254 0071. Graskop: Information Centre: Tel: 013 767 1321. Tsisini Silk Farm: Visits: Tel: 013 767 1665. Nelspruit: Lowveld Information: Tel: 013 755 1988. Pilgrim's Rest: Information Centre: Tel: 013 768 1211. Gold Panning, Box 39, Pilgrim's Rest 1290. Tel: 013 768 1296.

Limpopo

African Ivory Route: Tel: 015 295 3025/015 291 3717. Reservations: Tel: 015 295 2829, e-mail: infoair@mweb.co.za, web: www.africanivoryroute.co.za.

Gauteng

Gauteng Tourism Authority, Johannesburg: Corner of Henry Nxumalo and Jeppe Streets. Tel: 011 639 1600, e-mail: tourism@gauteng.net, web: www.visitgauteng.net/www.gauteng.net/; www.joburg.org.za; www.soweto.co.za. Johannesburg Publicity Association: Tel: 011 294 961/4. Pretoria Tourism: Tel: 012 337 4430. Maropeng: Where and What: Interpretation Centre, Cave Tours only with registered tour guides. Tel: 011 956 6342. Wonder Caves with impressive dripstones: Tel: 011 957 0106/9. Lion and Rhino Nature Reserve: Tel: 011 957 0044. Cradle Restaurant: Tel: 011 659 1622. E-mail: enquiries@thecradle.co.za. Accommodation: Cradle Forest Camp with chalets, caravan- and camping sites in the near Drakensberg Lover's Rock family resort: Tel: 014 572 3789. Don't forget your hiking shoes. General Tourist Information: Johannesburg Publicity Association: c/n Market & Kruis Street, Tel: 011 294 961/4.

Northwest

Magalies Meander: Arts and Crafts Route: Tel: 012 318 9559. Taung: Accommodation: Three-Stars Tusk Taung Hotel on the Main Street, inside the Wilderness Reserve. Rooms with air-conditioning, restaurant, casino, pool, floodlit tennis courts, mini golf, internet. Tusk Taung Casino Hotel, Box 201, Taung Station 8580. Tel: 053 994 1820, e-mail: taung@tusk-resorts.co.za. Cradle of Humanity, Sterkfontein: Tour of caves with registered tour guides. Tel: 011 956 6342. Maropeng Interpretation Centre: Tel: 014 577 9000, web: www.discover-yourself.co.za.

Northern Cape

Northern Cape Tourism Authority: Tel: 053 833 1434, web: www.northerncape.org.za. Kimberley: Big Hole and Kimberley Mine Museum. Tel: 053 833 1557; Duggan Cronin Photo Gallery. Tel: 053 842 0099; McGregor Museum. Tel: 053 842 0099; Sol Plaatje House. Tel: 053 833 2526; Duggan-Cronin Ethnographic Gallery, Alexander McGregor Memorial Museum, Sol Plaatje

Museum. Tel: 053 833 2526. Kuruman: Tourism Information, Private Bag X1522, Kuruman 8460. Tel: 053 712 1095/6/7, e-mail: kurmun@gasegonyana.gov.za, web: www.kurumankalahari. co.za; Moffat Mission, PO Box 34, Kuruman 8460. Tel: 053 712 1352/2645, e-mail: inquiries@kuruman-mission.org.za, web: www.kuruman-mission.org.za. Namaqua Adventure Route: Overnight accommodation. Information, refreshments: "Kultuur Koffie Kroeg van Ouma Toekoe", Christine Jannetjies, PO Box 187, Pella 8891. Tel: (Messages) 054 923 730. Namaqualand flower season: Information: Cape Town "Flower Hotline". Tel: 021 418 3705. Suggestions on flowers and overnight accommodation: Springbok Tourist Centre (Nama Khoi Municipality): Tel: 027 712 1880. Kamieskroon: Hotel and Camping. Tel: 027 672 1776. Flower Photo Workshop. Tel: 027 672 1614, e-mail: kamieshotel@kingsley.co.za.

Eco Spots

National Parks

Reservations for all National Parks are accepted by the SAN Parks Head Office in Pretoria. SAN Parks, PO Box 787, Pretoria 0001. Tel: 012 428 9111 (Mon-Fri), fax: 012-343 0905, e-mail: reservations@sanparks.org, **web: www.sanparks.org**

IAi-IAis/Richtersveld Transfrontier National Park: Tel: 027 831 1506, fax: 027-831 175, e-mail: willeml@sanparks.org.
Addo Elephant National Park: Gorah Elephant Private Camp. Tel: 044 532 7818. Also top class River Bend Country Lodge with all facilities and activities and a "Vitality Studio". Tel: 042 233 8000, fax: 042 233 8028, e-mail: reservations@riverbend.za.com, web: www.riverbend.za.com.
Mountain Zebra Nationalpark: Cottages, restorated Victorian style manor house, well-equipped caravan and tent sites, petrol station, restaurant and pool. Tel: 048 881 2427/048 881 3434, fax: 048 881 3943, e-mail: johandk@sanparks.org.
Camdeboo National Park: Short and long hikes, with or without overnight stay. Info and reservation direct: Tel: 049 892 3453.
Golden Gate Highlands National Park: Tel: 058 255 0012. Fossil search: Tel: 058 256 1314.
Kgalagai Transfrontier National Park: 4x4 safaris, South African section: Nossob 4x4 ecotrail: Tel: 054 561 2000. Gemsbok and Mabuasehube Wilderness Trails, Botswana Section: The Parks and Reserves Reservations Office in Gaborone, PO Box 131, Gaborone, Botswana. Tel: 00926 318 0774, fax: 00926 318 0775, e-mail: dwnpbots@global.bw.
Marakele National Park: Tel: 014 777 1745, fax: 014 777 1866.
Mokala National Park: Lodges or camping sites, restaurant, conference facilities, airstrip for private planes. Info and reservations: Tel: 053 204 0158/164/168, fax: 053 204 0176.
Namaqua Nationalpark: Near Kamieskroon. Tel: 027 672 1948, fax: 027-672 1015.
Karoo National Park: Accommodation in chalets and family cottages in Cape Dutch style, pool. Reservations direct line: Tel: 023 415 2828/ 9, fax: 023 4151671. Entrance gate remains open till 22h00 for late arrivals.
Kruger National Park: Tel: 0861 KRUGER or 021 468 7255. Tourist Camps (predominantly camping and caravan sites, shops, petrol station). *Southern part:* Berg-en-Dal (including Malelane), Crocodile Bridge, Lower Sabie, Pretoriuskop, Skukuza; *Central part:* Olifants, Orpen (including Maroela and Tambotie), Satara (including Balule); *Northern part:* Letaba, Mopani, Punda Maria,

Shingwedzi, Tsendze (rustic). *Bushveld Camps:* Bateleur, Biyamiti, Shimuwini, Sirheni, Talamati. *Bush Lodges:* Boulders, Roodewal. *Luxury Lodges:* Imbali Safari Lodges, Jock Safari Lodge, Lukimbi Safari Lodge, Rhino Walking Safaris, Shishangeni Private Lodge, Singita Lebombo Private Game Lodge, Tinga Private Game Lodge, Pafuri Camp. *Night Hides:* Sable, Shipandani.

Table Mountain National Park: (TMNP): Tel: 021 701 8692, e-mail: tablemountain@sanparks.org. **General information:** Tel: 021 701 8692. Head Office: Westlake, PO Box 37, Constantia 7848. Buffelsfontein Visitor's Centre: Tel: 021 780 9204. Boulders Penguin Colony: Tel: 021 786 2392. Cape Point: Plateau Road, Simon's Town,7975. Tel: 021 780 9010, fax: 021 780 9203, e-mail: capepoint@concor.co.za, web: www.capepoint.co.za.

Silver Mine Nature Reserve (forms part of TNNP): Camping site and accommodation for participants of the Hoerikwaggo Trail that lasts several days. Info at Sunbird Education and Resource Centre: Tel: 021 715 0011, e-mail: tablemountain@sanparks.org, web: www.tmnp.co.za.

West Coast National Park: Accommodation in beach cottages, house boats (some double-storied), dormitories and on camping sites. Tel: 022 772 2144. Information regarding house boats: web: www.houseboats.cjb.net. Hotels, chalets and B&B in Langebaan, near the entrance to the reserve.

Other National Parks: Augrabies National Park, Bontebok National Park, Cape Agulhas National Park, Knysna National Lake Area, Mapungubwe National Park, Tankwa Karoo National Park, Tsitsikamma Coastal National Park, Wilderness National Park.

PROVINCIAL- AND PRIVATE RESERVES

Western Cape Province
Cape Nature Conservation: Info: Tel: 021 426 0723, e-mail: capenature@tourismcapetown.co.za. Reservations: Tel: 021 659 3400, e-mail: reservations@capenature.co.za. **Cederberg Wilderness Area:** Tel: 027 482 2403. Clanwilliam Tourism Bureau, Main Road, PO.Box 5, Clanwilliam 8135. Tel: 027 482 2024, fax: 027 482 2361, e-mail: cederberg@lando.co.za. **De Hoop Nature Reserve and Marine Protected Area:** Longstreet, Bredasdorp 7280. Tel: 028 425 5020, fax: 028 425 5030, e-mail: bredasdorp@capenature.co.za, web: www.dehoopcapenature.com.
Fernkloof Nature Reserve: Voëlklip, Hermanus 7200. Tel: 028 313 8100.
Grootvadersbosch: Indigenous forest and wilderness. PO Box 109, Heidelberg 6665. Tel: 028 722 2412, fax: 028 722 2838, e-mail: bredasdorp@capenature.co.za, web: www.capenature.co.za.
Kogelberg Nature Reserve: The Administration Manager, Kogelberg Nature Reserve, Private Bag X1, Kleinmond 7195. Tel: 028 271 5138, fax: 028 272 9425, e-mail: mearl@kogelbergbiosphere.co.za.
Highlands Overnight Trail: Tel: 021 483 2949/51, fax: 021 483 3500, e-mail: hothol@cnc.org.za. Booking essential.
Rocher Pan Marine and Nature Reserve: PO Box 170, Velddrif 7365, e-mail: velddriftoerisme@telkomsa.net.
Swartberg Nature Reserve: Queen Hotel Complex, Oudtshoorn 6620. Tel: 044 802 5310, fax: 044 802 5313, e-mail: george@cnc.org.za.

Wildflower Reserves: *Koeberg Nature Reserve*: Melkbosstrand, Kapstadt. Tel: 021 553 2466.
Oudepost Wild Flower Reserve: Off the R307 near Darling. Tel: 022 492 3361.

Postberg Flower Reserve: Exit R27 near Langebaan. Tel: 022 772 2144.
Ramskop Nature Reserve, Clanwilliam: Tel: 027 482 8000.
Rondeberg Private Nature Reserve: Exit R27 near Langebaan, Darling. Tel: 022 492 3099.
SAS Saldanha Nature Reserve: Defence Base in Saldanha. Tel: 022 702 3523.

Other Nature Reserves: Groot Winterhoek Wildnerness Area, Limietberg Nature Reserve, Jonkershoek Nature Reserve, Assegaaibosch Nature Reserve, Reserve, Hottentots Holland Nature Reserve, Walker Bay Nature Reserve, Salmonsdam Nature Reserve, De Mond Nature Reserve, Vrolijkheid Nature Reserve, Marloth Nature Reserve, Grootvadersbosch Nature Reserve, Boesmansbos Wilderness Area, Anysberg Nature Reserve, Gamkaberg Nature Reserve, Swartberg Nature Reserve, Outeniqua Nature Reserve, Goukamma Nature Reserve, Kammanassie Nature Reserve, Keurbooms River Nature Reserve, Robberg Nature Reserve.

Eastern Cape Province
Eastern Cape Tourism Board: Cnr. Longfellow and Aquarium Streets, Quigney, East London, PO Box 18373, Quigney, East London 5211. Tel: 043 701 9600, fax: 043 701 9649, e-mail: info@ectourism.co.za.
Mthatha: Reservation Office: Tel: 047 531 5290, fax: 047 531 5291.

Private Nature Reserves: Amakhala: PO Box 10, Patterson, 6130. Tel: 042 235 1608, fax: 042 235 1041, e-mail: centralres@telkomsa.net.
Baviaanskloof: Tel: 040 635 2115, fax: 040 639 2171, e-mail: info@ecparksboard.co.za, web: www.ecparksboard.co.za.
Cape Recife Coastal Reserve: Municipal Parks & Recreation Department. Tel.: 041 585 9711. Bird & Ecotours provides guided tours and information. Tel: 041 466 5698, e-mail: apmartin@global.co.za.
Hluleka Nature Reserve: Wild Coast, lagoon, indigenous forest. Tel: 040 635 2115.
Kariega: Kenton-On-Sea. Tel: 046 636 7904, fax: 046 636 2288.
Mkambati: Lodge with 5 double rooms, pool and sea view. Self-catering in simple roundhuts and cottages. Tenting is also possible. Tel: 047 131 2712, fax: 047 131 2713. Keval Travel: Tel: 039 306 9000.
Shamwari: Tel: 042 203 1111, fax: 042 235 1224. **Tiffendell Ski Resort:** Tel: 045 974 9006, e-mail: resort@snow.co.za. **Van Stadens Wild Flower Reserve:** Tel: 041 955 649..

KwaZulu-Natal
Natal Sharks Board, Durban: Tel: 031 566 0400, fax: 031 566 0499, Private Bag 2, Umhlanga 4320. **Butterfly Farm:** Old South Coast Road, Ramsgate. Tel: 039 314 9307. **Tala Private Game Park:** 70 km northwest of Durban. Tel: 031 781 8000. **Tembe Elephant Park (privatised):** Tel: 031 267 0144, fax: 031 266 8718, e-mail: info@tembe.co.za. **Umtamvuna Nature Reserve:** Tel: 039 311 1932. Botanical Paradise with several foot paths, nesting sites of Cape Vultures. **Lammergeier Hide:** Contact the camp manager. Tel: 036 353 3718, fax: 036-353 3775.
The following reserves in the province are administered by Ezemvelo KZN Wildlife:
Drakensberg (uKhahlamba-Drakensberg): Cathedral Peak Area, Champagne Valley, Monk's Cowl Mountain Reserve, Cobham Mountain Reserve, Didima Camp, Giant's Castle Game Reserve,

Kamberg Mountain Reserve, Royal Natal National Park, Sani Pass. South-Eastern Region: Greater St. Lucia Wetland Park, Hluhluwe-Imfolozi Park, Ithala Nature Reserve, Mkhuze-Game Park, Ndumo Game Park, Pongolapoort Nature Reserve, Sodwana, Rocktail and Kosi Bay. **All enquiries and reservations can be sent to:** Ezemvelo KZN Wildlife Central Reservations: PO Box 13069, Cascades 3202, Pietermaritzburg. Tel: 033 845 1000, fax: 033 845 1001, email: webmail@kznwildlife.com; **web: www.kznwildlife.com**

Free State

Nature & Environmental Conservation: Bloemfontein Tourist Centre, 60 Park Road. Tel: 051 447 1362, fax: 051 447 1363.
Maluti Tourism Route: Tel: 051 924 5131.

Nature Reserves administered by the province: Arizona Game Lodge, Bokpoort Ranch, Caledon, Erfenis Dam, Fiko Patso, Golden Gate, Kalkfontein Dam, Koppies Dam, Qwa-Qwa Park, Rustfontein Dam, Sandveld, Seekoeivlei, Soetdoring, Sterkfontein Dam, Thaba N'chu, Tussen-die-Riviere, Willem Pretorius, Witsieshoek, Xhariep Dam.

Mpumalanga

Nature Conservation: Mpumalanga Parks Board: Halls Gateway, Private Bag X11338, Nelspruit 1200. Tel: 013 759 5300, fax: 013-755 4014.

Nature Reserves administered by the province: Barberton Nature Reserve, Blyde River Canyon Nature Reserve, Gustav Klingbiel Nature Reserve, Loskop Dam Nature Reserve, Mabusa Nature Reserve, Mahushe Shongwe Reserve, Mdala Game Reserve, Mkhombo Nature Reserve, Mthethomusha Game Reserve, Nooitgedacht Dam Nature Reserve, Ohrigstad Dam Nature Reserve, Skosana Nature Reserve, Songimvelo Game Reserve, Verloren Valei Nature Reserve.
Private Reserves: Mala Mala Reserve (30 000 ha), P.O. Box 2575, 2125 Randburg, RSA. Londolozi (18 000 ha), PO Box 1211, 2157 Sunninghill Park, RSA. Mount Sheba Hotel Nature Reserve: Box 100, Pilgrim's Rest 1290, Tel: 013 76 8124. Sabi Sabi: Tel: 011 447 7172, fax: 011 442 0728, PO Box 52665, Saxonwold, 2132, e-mail: res@sabisabi.com.

Limpopo

Limpopo Tourism and Parks Board: PO Box 2814, Polokwane 0700. Tel: 086 073 0730 / 015 290 7300. Reservations: Tel: 015 290 7355, fax: 015 290 7370, e-mail: info@golimpopo.com, web: www.golimpopo.com.

Nature Reserves administered by the province: Atherstone, D'Nyala, Blouberg, Doorndraai, Grootbosch Nature Reserve, Hans Merensky, Lekgalameetse (Wolkberg region), Letaba Ranch (adjoining Kruger Park), Makuya (adjoining Kruger Park), Mutale Ivory Route Camp, Man'Ombe, Manavhela Ben Lavin, Manyeleti (adjoining Kruger Park), Masebe, Mokolo Dam, Musina, Nwanedi, Nylsvley, Percy Fyfe, Rust de Winter, Rain Queen Modjadji and Modjadji Cycad Nature Reserve, Schuinsdraai (large number of crocodiles), Wolkberg Wilderness Area.

Nylsvley: Friends of Nylsvley (Marion Dunkeld-Mengel). Tel: 012 667 2183. PO Box 80, Irene, 0062, e-mail: friendsnylsvley@mweb.co.za, web: www.nylsvley.co.za. Nylsvley Nature Reserve: Box 508, Mookgophong. Tel: 014 743 1074. Reserve, shady camp site, also for groups. Bookings for accommodation through Limpopo Tourism & Parks Board. Tel: 015 290 7355, e-mail: info@golimpopo.co.za, web: www.golimpopo.co.za

Gauteng

Groenkloof Nature Reserve, Pretoria: Tel: 012 440 8316, fax: 012 341 0483, e-mail: davidb@tshwane.gov.za (Management)/ audreyb@tshwane.gov.za (Reservations).
Rietvlei Nature Reserve: Overnight accommodation, horse riding, night drives, yacht club, camping site and party area (Lapa) for 30-200 persons. Tel: 012 345 2274.
Suikerbosrand Nature Reserve: Tel: 011 904 3930.
Tswaing Crater Nature Reserve and Museum: Tel: 012 790 2302, fax: 012 790 5034, e-mail: cultmat@iafrica.com, web: www.nfi.org.za.

North West Province

North West Eco Tourism: Rustenburg Tourism Information Centre, PO Box 4124, Rustenburg, 0300. Tel: 014 597 0904, fax: 014 597 0907, e-mail: tidcrust@mweb.co.za.
Pilanesberg Tourism Information Centre (at the Manyane Gate), PO Box 1201, Mogwase 0314. Tel: 014 555 5362, fax: 014 555 7296, e-mail: tidcpberg@mweb.co.za.

Nature Reserves administered by the province:
Barberspan Bird Sanctuary: Fully equipped dormitories with showers; bedding and cooking utensils must be brought along. Tel: 053 948 1854, fax: 053 948 0101, e-mail: barbersp@lantic.net.
Borakalalo Reserve: Moretele and Phudufudu Camps provide safari tents and facilities of varying standards. No electricity. Basic sites for caravans and tents. Tel: 012 729 1008, fax: 012 729 1009, e-mail: borak@lantic.net.
Botsalano Game Reserve: Accommodation in safari tents or Bush Camps. A camping site with basic facilities is positioned at the entrance. Tel: 018 386 2433. Reservations: Kgalagadi Safaris for overnight accommodation and hikes in the bush. Tel: 018 381 5392, e-mail: kgalagadi@lantic.net.
Kgaswane Mountain Reserve (Rustenburg): Tent and caravan sites with ablutions and basic tent sites along the hiking trails. Kgaswane Mountain Reserve, Box 20382, Protea Park 0305. Tel: 014 533 2050, fax 014 533 0397, e-mail: marcusl@mweb.co.za.
Madikwe Game Reserve: Madikwe Safaris. Tel: 011 315 6194, e-mail: madikweadmin@wol.co.za.
Molopo Game Reserve: Gerald Botha. Cell: 082 873 8780.
Pilanesberg National Park: Pilanesberg National Park, PO Box 4488, Mmabatho 2735. Tel: 014 555 5354-7, fax: 014 555 5525, e-mail: pilanesberg@nwpg.gov.za.
Tswaing Crater, Museum and Nature Reserve: Tel: 012 790 2302, fax: 012 790 5034, e-mail: cultmat@iafrica.com, web: www.nfi.org.za

Northern Cape Province

Northern Cape Tourism Authority: Private Bag X5107, Kimberley 8300. Tel: 053 833 1434/053 832 2657, fax: 053 831 2937, e-mail: northerncapetourism@telkomsa.net.
Kalahari Raptor Centre: PO Box 1386, Kathu 8446.
Goegap Nature Reserve: 15 km southeast of Springbok. Tel: 027 712 1880.
Tswalu Kalahari Nature Reserve: POBox 1081 Kuruman 8460. Tel: 053 781 9234, fax: 053 781 9238, e-mail: res@tswalu.com, web: www.tswalu.com.
Nieuwoudtville Wild Flower Reserve: Tel: 027 218 1200.

Glossary

Africans – Today this usually refers to the black people living on or descendants of the African continent.

Afrikaner – Originally denoted white people that were Dutch or German ancestry (Boers), spoke Afrikaans and who lived on farms.

Afrikaans – Language of whites of Dutch-German descent and Coloured (people of mixed races) in the Republic of South Africa. It developed from Cape Dutch and is the youngest Indo-Germanic language.

Air pollution – In South Africa this is mainly produced by the numerous old power stations using coal.

Azania – Another name for South Africa. When Arab traders reached the eastern coast of Africa centuries ago they named that part Azania, Land of the Blacks. The South African Pan-Africanist Congress started using this name for the Republic of South Africa, but it did not catch on.

Barbeque/Braai/Braaivleis – Grilled meat, usually done over an open fire.

Biodiversity – Variety of biological species; due to human influence this is dramatically diminishing, a fact that is particularly noticeable in the plant world of the Cape Floral Kingdom.

Biome – Symbiotic living of animals and plants in an environmentally similar larger geographical area, e.g. savannah, montane region.

Biotope – Habitat within an ecosystem inhabited by symbiotic species or organisms. The preservation of biotopes is an important factor for the protection of species.

Bluegum (*Eucalyptus globulus*) – was the first type of eucalyptus tree introduced to South Africa. It belongs to the Australian-Polynesian family of myrtle plants. *Saligna gum E. grandis* is grown in plantations and extensively distributed; it is mainly utilised in mine shafts and for the production of paper.

Boland (Afrikaans) – Region to the north and east of Cape Town on the slopes of mountains and extensively planted with vineyards (Winelands).

Borehole – Usually has a steel construction with a windmill built over it and is used to bring underground water to the surface. The windmill is a landmark in the dry areas.

Bushveld (Bosveld in Afrikaans) – Savannah landscape with shrubs and/or trees.

Canned hunting – Hunting of game that has been hand reared and kept on farms for this purpose, especially lions. Officially this is prohibited, but the law has many loopholes.

Characteristic species – Plants or animals that are typical of a certain area or grouping of plants.

Circumcision (abakwetha) – The traditional practice of the Xhosa tribe (removal of foreskin) aroused new attention in times of HIV/AIDS.

Culling – Controlled killing of animals to prevent over-population in game parks like the Kruger National Park.

Donga – Deep gully (up to 30 m or more) created by water erosion and human misuse of the top soil.

Ecology – Vital science concerning the relation of organisms with each other and their environment.

Ecosystem – Structural relation of living organisms interacting among themselves and with their environment.

Ecotourism – Tourism in regions that are ecologically worth protecting by avoiding putting pressure on the ecosystems in the areas to be visited, and by trying not to influence the ecological balance of the life symbioses. This is becoming more and more a factor of economic importance.

Erosion – Destructive effect of water and wind on the soil (see also Donga). In South Africa the extensive overgrazing and poor agricultural methods also result in the encroachment of bush.

Evolution – Development of living organisms from lower to higher forms of existence.

Fynbos (Afrikaans) – Vernacular name (Fynbos = fine bush) given to the vegetation in the winter rainfall region of the Western Cape that boasts a rich variety of species and forms part of the Cape Floral Kingdom.

Game Reserve – The name dates from the time of big game hunting and is really confusing when applied to wildlife sanctuaries like the Kruger National Park.

Gemsbuck (*Oryx gazella*) – Large antelope of the arid region with long pointed horns. Gemsbok (Afrikaans) from the German "Gamsbock" – wild goat of the Alpine region.

Highveld – The high plateau in the interior of South Africa is predominantly grassland (altitude 1 200-1 800 m) with escarpments to the west, south and east.

Lowveld – Low lying region with an altitude of only 200-300 m in the eastern part of the country towards the coast. It includes the greater part of the Kruger National Park.

National Parks – Usually extensive nature reserves and game parks that are controlled by the government.

Private Game Reserves – Privately owned wildlife reserves, boasting exclusivity and luxury, resulting in high to very high prices. Main features are the custom-made game drives with highly trained rangers and international cuisine on offer.

Protection of Species – The provision of protection for plants and animals living in their natural habitat. It is internationally based on the Washington Agreement that controls and prohibits trade in plants and animals of endangered species (Red Data List).

Savannah – Word of Indian origin applied to parts of the vegetation belt that cover tropical zones of varying degrees of humidity – except for the mountainous areas – that stretch between tropical rain forests and deserts. We differentiate between moist savannah, dry savannah, thorny savannah and arid savannah. They are either grasslands (some containing no trees, others with scattered trees or clumps of trees) or light woodlands.

Shark spotter – Announces sharks approaching the beaches of the peninsula by means of signalling flags and sirens.

Squatter Camps – Slums in the vicinity of the larger cities, often very spread out. In South Africa they are also known as "informal settlements" (i.e. dwellings often erected without official permission).

Transfrontier Park – Huge game parks and wildlife reserves that extend over one or more borders, like the Great Limpopo Transfrontier Park (Mozambique, South Africa, Zimbabwe) and the Kgalagadi Transfrontier Park (Botswana, South Africa).

Index

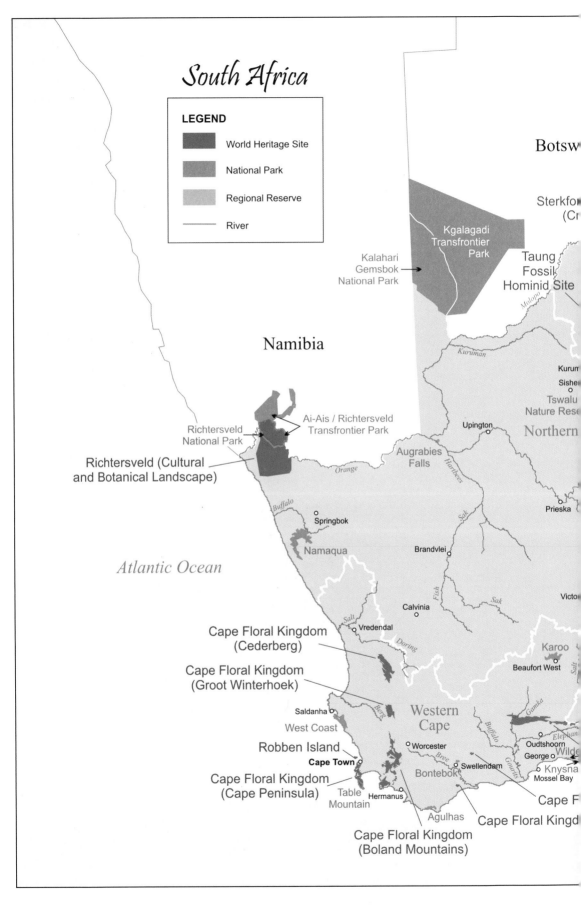